Is William Martinez Not Our Brother?

THE NEW PUBLIC SCHOLARSHIP

SERIES EDITORS

Lonnie Bunch, *Director, National Museum of African-American History and Culture*

Julie Ellison, *Professor of American Culture, University of Michigan*

Robert Weisbuch, *President, Drew University*

The New Public Scholarship encourages alliances between scholars and communities by publishing writing that emerges from publicly engaged and intellectually consequential cultural work. The series is designed to attract serious readers who are invested in both creating and thinking about public culture and public life. Under the rubric of "public scholar," we embrace campus-based artists, humanists, cultural critics, and engaged artists working in the public, nonprofit, or private sector. The editors seek useful work growing out of engaged practices in cultural and educational arenas. We are also interested in books that offer new paradigms for doing and theorizing public scholarship itself. Indeed, validating public scholarship through an evolving set of concepts and arguments is central to **The New Public Scholarship**.

The universe of potential contributors and readers is growing rapidly. We are teaching a generation of students for whom civic education and community service learning are quite normative. The civic turn in art and design has affected educational and cultural institutions of many kinds. In light of these developments, we feel that **The New Public Scholarship** offers a timely innovation in serious publishing.

DIGITALCULTUREBOOKS is an imprint of the University of Michigan Press and the Scholarly Publishing Office of the University of Michigan Library dedicated to publishing innovative and accessible work exploring new media and their impact on society, culture, and scholarly communication.

Is William Martinez Not Our Brother?

TWENTY YEARS OF THE PRISON CREATIVE ARTS PROJECT

Buzz Alexander

THE UNIVERSITY OF MICHIGAN PRESS AND
THE UNIVERSITY OF MICHIGAN LIBRARY

ANN ARBOR

Published in the United States of America by
The University of Michigan Press and
The University of Michigan Library
Manufactured in the United States of America
♾ Printed on acid-free paper
2013   2012   2011   2010   4   3   2   1

A CIP catalog record for this book is available from the British Library.

Library of Congress Cataloging-in-Publication Data

Alexander, William, 1938–
    Is William Martinez not our brother? : twenty years of the Prison
Creative Arts Project / Buzz Alexander.
        p.   cm. — (The new public scholarship series)
    Includes bibliographical references and index.
    ISBN 978-0-472-07109-8 (cloth : alk. paper) —
    ISBN 978-0-472-05109-0 (pbk. : alk. paper)
        1. Prison Creative Arts Project—History.   2. Arts in prisons—Michigan.
    3. Prisoners as artists—Michigan.   4. Community arts projects—Michigan.
    5. Prisoners—Education—Michigan.   I. Title.
    HV8883.A44   2010
    365'.66—dc22   2010014033

ISBN 978-0-472-02744-6 (e-book)

Nate Jones, wherever you are now
  you are the ground, the heart, the spirit, the struggle

Janie Paul,
you bring the haunting beauty and complexity of your art and the
multiple layers of your being everywhere, to all of us, to me

ACKNOWLEDGMENTS

To the youth and adults in the Prison Creative Arts Project workshops, exhibitions, and portfolio and linkage work, thank you. Every time you take a risk with your voice, pen, brush, and body, you reinvent and strengthen yourselves and encourage those of us who are fortunate enough to be in your presence to do the same.

To the PCAP associates, what can I say? While I cannot tell each of your stories and cannot list your 165 names, you have the final chapter of this book to yourselves, a chapter that is about all of you. At a July 2009 PCAP meeting, Evelyn Smith asked us to write down the talent we bring to PCAP. Matt Erickson wrote, "Showing up." That sticks with me. Matt shows up for everyone's readings and performances, no matter how long the drive. He drove to Ionia and Coldwater for his workshops. He drives formerly incarcerated citizens to meetings and events. He always steps up and always brings his ideas and voice to meetings whether he thinks they will be popular or not. He is always *present*. He represents the ways you all showed up, often for each other and for PCAP, but most of all for the urban youth and incarcerated youth and adults with whom you worked. Thank you.

Karen Goodyke, Laurie Hess, Pilar Horner, our early part-time administrators, and our later full- and almost full-time administrators and coordinators, Jesse Jannetta, Suzanne Gothard, Rachael Hudak, phoenix Moore, Emily Harris, Jaime Nelson, Sari Adelson, Ariella Kaufman, Jean Borger, and Mary Heinen, thank you for your ability to respond to stress, for your troubleshooting, for your willingness to sit at the table with each other and me and the members of PCAP and to work things out, for your willingness always, in spite of all, to embrace rather than condemn, and for your knowledge always at the end of the day that while this was about who you were becoming and wanted to be, it also was really not about you.

If one is to work in prisons, juvenile facilities, and urban high schools, one needs tough-minded, direct, honest guides who believe that every human being has the right to become more fully human. There are not enough such people in these places, but there are many more than most people imagine. PCAP and I could not have lasted twenty years without such people.

Gary Coakley, Sherri Gerber-Somers, Sue Keagle, Carol King, Wendy Kearney, Marlys Schutjer, and Denise Thomas, how can I thank you enough? Not only for the guidance you have given us, but for your immense energy, your long long hours far beyond what was asked of you, and your dedication to the youth most people judge and abandon and in whose possibilities you so fervently believe. Many boys and girls who pass through Adrian Training School, Boysville, the Calumet and Lincoln Centers, Maxey Boys Training School, and Vista Maria, in spite of all odds, are living whole lives now because of your belief in them and the demands you made on them. Your fiber is in my students as they go on to work in parallel fields.

Michelle Busby, Patricia Dowling, Joan Galica, Angel Glenn, Jane Grant, Roberta Herter, Andrew Kemp, Caryn Mamrack, Janice Rowley, and Charlotte Smith, your clarity about your teaching mission to high school students at Cooley, Henry Ford, and Crockett Technical high schools and Catherine Ferguson Academy, your firmness and flexibility, your demands and challenges, and your humor and love for your work in some of the most difficult teaching circumstances in this country, have been personal resources for me and taught me staying power. You have greatly influenced the University of Michigan students who have worked with you.

Wardens Luella Burke and Millie Warren and Bill Lovett, former strategic planner in the Michigan Department of Corrections, as active members on our National Advisory Board, you have told us the truth and have explained the complex purposes of the department when something comes at us out of the blue. Your direct intervention with your peers has saved our work countless times. Warden Carol Howes and Warden, then Regional Prison Administrator, Barbara Bock, your advice for us, your outspoken support, your advocacy for individuals, and your constant efforts to make programs and growth available to incarcerated men and women mean everything. Pat Caruso, when you became director of the Michigan Department of Corrections, the climate changed and everything changed for us. You are all clear- and tough-minded humanists and progressives working in painful places and are my friends.

So many others at all levels, Sherry Burt, Bruce Curtis, Fred Goff, Silva Goncalves, Mary Jo Pass, Ken Romanowski, Dennis Schrantz, Chuck Sprang, Denny Straub, and Mary King and Joe Summers (with the Michigan Prisoner Re-entry Initiative) (I could go on naming for a long time), have been forthright and supportive and have cleared the way for our programs and for individual prisoners and returned citizens. Thank you.

Christina Bates, Pete Cabell, Jody Cantwell, Pete Kerr, Phil Klintworth, Boyd Meyers, Roxanne Strouth, Beth Tuckerman, Bobbie Waldron, Cal Watson, and Kay Williams, I don't know that I could do your work. As special activities directors, you are close to the bottom of a hierarchy that is loaded on the side of security, and yet you come in each day and advocate for programs and for opportunities for prisoners and stick up for the creativity and imagination we bring into the walls. So many of your peers across the state, as we travel to select art for the annual exhibition and when we do workshops at the borders of our driving capacities, have also been accommodating, enthusiastic, and eager for our presence. Beth and Phil, you especially have understood the depths of what access to the arts means to the incarcerated, and have most fought to make it possible.

Herschell Turner, thank you thank you thank you. So many men are artists because of you. They think of you always.

Thank you, members of our National Advisory Board. One of the most important things we have ever done was find you and then listen to you. You have made all the difference, both you who have been consistent in attending yearly meetings—Gary Coakley, Julie Ellison, Suzanne Gothard, Pat Gurin, Emily Harris, Rachael Hudak, Jesse Jannetta, Michael Keck, Chiara Liberatore, Bill Lovett, Luella Burke, Andrea Scott, Marlys Schutjer, and Patsy Yaeger—and those of you who from far away have checked in and responded to our calls for advice—Harriet Barlow, Ellen Barry, Bell Chevigny, Norma Green, DeeDee Halleck, Richard Kamler, Phyllis Kornfeld, Leslie Neal, Matthew Schmitt, and Andrew Rubinson. Thank you from the bottom of our hearts.

Thank you Lester Monts, thank you John Matlock, thank you Terry Sullivan and Terry McDonald, thank you Sid Smith and Patsy Yaeger and Bryan Rogers, thank you Connie Cook, thank you Mary Sue Coleman, thank all of you at the University of Michigan, more colleagues and administrators than I can name, thank you all for the faith you had in PCAP from the start and for your financial and moral support every moment along the way.

In spring 1969, I stood in my jacket and tie sipping sherry in the Eliot House Senior Common Room before dinner. I was a young lecturer in English at Harvard, uneasy in the academic stiffness of such moments. Forty years later I can picture where I stood when Brooke Hopkins, a graduate student and house tutor, appeared at my elbow and asked me to join him teaching a full-year seminar on *Madame Bovary, In Remembrance of Things Past, Ulysses,* and the films of Bergman, Fellini, Godard, Resnais, and Truffaut that were appearing during those years. For the next two years we spent long mornings in an Eliot House basement running and rewinding the films, talking them through on the most personal and political terms. It was learning as it should be, and we brought it to the remarkable students who signed up for the seminar and for the second year when we split into two seminars to some extent because of the difference of our teaching styles, Brooke passionate, flamboyant, outspoken, I quieter, stirring the pot until it boiled. Those years changed my trajectory as a teacher and person. They also led to a lifelong friendship as letter writers, engaged talkers, hikers. Brooke, lucid, inquisitive, probing, demanding, challenging, intellectually personally and physically courageous, with a capacity for life as large as any I know, I wouldn't be where I am, where this book is, without you.

Peter Wetherbee, thank you for insisting I leave my sleeping bag that dark night on the canoe trip we took down the Connecticut River after graduation in 1960 and for figuring out how to tell me I didn't need to reach the Atlantic. That has steadied my hyperactive self all these years. Thanks for a lifetime of friendship, for the quality and character of your work, including your work with the men incarcerated at the Auburn Correctional Facility, and for believing in me, as did you too John Radner, before I believed in myself.

Peter Wood, you are the best storyteller I know, a great American historian with deep ethics and wisdom who knows the stories under the stories, analyzes the permeating continuing story of racism in this country, and constantly reminds me of the balance and justice we should be seeking.

To my great-great-grandfather Sheldon Peck, I have visited your home in Lombard, station on the Underground Railroad where my great grandfather listened to the stories of courageous fugitive slaves hidden in the potato cellar, where you painted portraits and raised twelve children, I thank you for your life and my opportunity to draw upon it. To my long-gone mother and father, your civic engagement and truth to your roots is my deepest source. To my six siblings, your wonderfully stubborn Alexander strengths, the ways each of you have found what you love, and your struggle, however troubled at times, to keep family has meant everything. You have little idea how much I draw on you. To my children Jon and Allegra, thank you always for your love and for the resilience and spirit with which you have always addressed obstacles.

My thanks once more to the people I identify in the introduction to this book, community members and community-based workers who are among my and PCAP's most powerful resources: Marta Arce, Tomas Temoche and Yawar, the theater group of Villa El Salvador, and Yuyachkani; Robert Alexander, Augusto Boal, Alan Bolt, Nidia Bustos, John Gaventa, Ross Kidd, John Malpede, Doug Paterson, Susan Perlstein, Peggy Pettit, Pregones, and Everyday Theater; Paulo Freire, Herbert Kohl, Myles Horton, and Jonathan Kozol; Miguel Ayala and Silvia Leon, Javier Mujica and Vicky Coronado, Father Jeronimo Olleros, and Rosa Maria Puma Roca and my other godchildren in Peru.

Finally, I wish to name and express my debt to four of my greatest mentors, three lifers and an ex-lifer in the prisons where I have worked. They live or have lived in the desperate condition of those who may never leave the walls, and they have taught me more than anyone what it means to be a human being. Their love for others, their courage, their laughter and resistance, their daring to create hard and true stories, their struggle to maintain the light in their souls, their great spirits are all part of who I have tried to become, and they stand behind every piece of our work. Thank you, George Norris Hall, Mary Heinen, Romando Valeroso III, and Sharleen Wabindato.

It has been a formidable and frightening task to write these acknowledgments. It shakes me that I will have forgotten someone and that I cannot include others who people me and are deep resources. You will know who you are. Please accept my apology.

This book was written in a number of peaceful places. Its seeds grew during work on another manuscript at the Blue Mountain Center, the Hambidge Center, the Headlands Center for the Arts, and the Virginia Center for the Creative Arts. The book itself rose at the Blue Mountain Center, one of my real homes (thank you Harriet Barlow and Ben Strader!), the Lillian E. Smith Center for the Creative Arts (thank you Nancy and Robert Fichter!), during two months in a cottage on a bluff over Lake Michigan (thank you

Mike Deem of Timber Bluff!), in a casita twenty minutes south of the Santa Fe Plaza (thank you Bart Herbstman and Laura Epler!), and in the Santa Fe home of Ian and Lois Alsop and the guest house of Elise and Tom Noble, whose continuing friendship has been sustaining.

Julie Ellison, thank you so much for seeking this book out for the New Public Scholarship Series and for being encouraging in every way possible — you gave me incentive to keep working. Alison MacKeen, as my first editor, your excitement about the book and your saying that you found my voice compelling gave me confidence and a sense that perhaps I really had something here. Judith Tannenbaum, dear friend, it meant everything that you were willing to read an earlier version of the manuscript and give me the thoughtful criticism I needed. Stephen Hartnett, dear friend, your careful editing of a portion of this manuscript and your constant cheering me on on every front, I always draw on that. And editors Tom Dwyer and Alexa Ducsay and director Phil Pochoda at the University of Michigan Press, thank you for hanging in there with me during rough spots and for believing in this book.

Janie, there are many reasons I've dedicated this book to you. The least is our understanding that you are PCAP's secret weapon. The most is the vibrant, warm, laughing, compassionate love you have brought into my life for seventeen years now.

Nate, I miss you always.

Buzz Alexander

looking out over the redbud tree
Ann Arbor, August 5, 2009

CONTENTS

Illustrations following page 148

INTRODUCTION

I have dedicated this book to Nate Jones and Janie Paul.

I met Janie at the Blue Mountain Center in Blue Mountain Lake, New York, in the summer of 1992. She had grown up in Concord, Massachusetts, was a New York artist, and had recently worked as an artist in communities in South Africa. So much of what has happened in the Prison Creative Arts Project and in my life is a result of our meeting. During my 1993 sabbatical, I moved to New York City to be near her, and at the end of 1994 she moved to Ann Arbor to live with me. She took a position in the University of Michigan School of Art and Design and soon started up an art workshop at the Western Wayne Correctional Facility. In November 1995 we wrote to prisons within a two-hundred-mile radius of Ann Arbor, inviting artists to submit work to an exhibition of art by Michigan prisoners. That exhibition is now in its fifteenth year, and Janie has sent as many as two hundred students to facilitate art workshops in Michigan prisons and juvenile facilities, and many of her students have joined the Prison Creative Arts Project. Behind everything in this book is her spirit, which is both gentle and fierce, her generosity, tolerance, and uncompromising insistence on what is just, and her grounding in nature and in something deep in herself. On September 9, 2007, celebrating our roots in small towns bordering Lake Michigan, we married on a bluff with the lake at our backs. I am not telling her story in this book, but I need you to know at the outset, that she is deeply a part of the story I am telling.

You will read Nate's story in chapter 7 and elsewhere. He died May 31, 2007. His family members say he passed on, which is hopeful. I think of him as having passed away. I knew him inside and outside prison, when he was very alive and while he was dying. Sometimes he was my brother.

And I could have dedicated this book to a thousand other people. Two of them are Ollie Ganz and a boy I'll call DeWayne.

On April 3, 2006, the chapel at Holy Cross Children's Services, Boysville Campus, in Clinton Michigan, was packed with incarcerated boys, some family members of the boys, and a few of us from the university. We listened to poetry readings from Basil and Paulus hall workshops. When it was DeWayne's turn, he slumped over the podium, unable to look up at his peers in the pews. Ollie, one of the student facilitators of the group, might have sat there and watched, moved and hurting for DeWayne, then later been able to tell the powerful story of how his life had kept him from coming through for himself. Instead she rose and stood by him, quietly talking to him and waiting, talking some more and waiting, and slowly—I see it now almost in slow motion—he lifted himself and read his poem.

Afterward, when the poets were celebrating over pop and cookies at the school, I took Mary Heinen, our new coordinator of the Portfolio and Linkage Projects, to meet Gary Coakley, the Boysville residential manager who had committed himself to incarcerated youth for twenty-five years and seventeen years earlier had established the Stop the Madness program there. He was moved, almost in awe, at what Ollie had done. "That's all each of these boys needs," he said, "someone to stand up there with them."

And so now I tell that story, and Ollie tells it too. It changed everything for her and set her on a path she won't leave. Possibly it changed something for DeWayne as well.

PUBLIC SCHOLARSHIP

Because the Prison Creative Arts Project is situated in a university and also in high schools, juvenile facilities, and prisons; because of the values, methods, and goals with which we work; and because we work with others as equal collaborators and peers, *Is William Martinez Not Our Brother?* is a book of public scholarship, a report from the field.

Public scholarship is a reaction against specialized academic language and against academic "overemphasis on critique" and satisfaction with mere "arenas of deliberation." It also rejects professional withdrawal from the public as well as college and university intervention in communities only as advocates, problem-solvers, and volunteers who practice "service learning."[1]

Public scholarship opposes to this an "engagement agenda" where people of diverse backgrounds and interests meet in local "enabling" or "free" spaces to complete specific tasks. When completed, these tasks constitute "public goods" that serve the common good and often link to global efforts and concerns. These spaces are not bestowed, they do not exist simply because someone puts chairs in a circle. They are spaces where people differ and may even be hostile, spaces of contention, negotiation, and struggle, of inquiry, invention, and creativity. Here power balances shift, boundaries are subverted and categories crossed, and people relearn and reorient. They are above all spaces of respect, where people *listen* to each other. Here one finds "high tolerance for complexity and fluidity . . . [and] uncertainty"; evolving, improvised problem-solving; and "relentlessly multiple" civic engagement and practice that teach lifelong democratic behavior.[2] "Throughout American history," says Harry Boyte, who is more tough-minded than many about what needs to happen in these spaces, "broad democratic movements have incubated in diverse settings which people own, that have (or in which people can achieve) a significant measure of autonomy from dominant power systems, and that also have public and political qualities."[3]

Community members, students, and faculty who do this "public work" and practice "everyday politics" grow, change identities, enlarge their perspectives, become aware of ambiguity, make "connections across lines of difference," and realize "the sense of ownership that develops through commons-building labors by groups of people." They enter into lifelong habits of engagement and strategy. They work in more diverse occupations and live in more diverse areas. Boyte reports that elementary through high school students in local Public Achievement teams, who are coached by community activists and college students, "often say their experiences in working and fighting for their projects also help them 'remove masks' and 'try out new roles' and 'give us freedom to be ourselves' . . . [E]veryday politics breaks the tyranny of technique that locks people into expert-defined roles and tightly circumscribed identities."[4]

Judith Ramaley warns that public scholarship will "remain individually defined and sporadic" unless colleges and universities commit to civic engagement on an institutional level. Thanks to the leadership of Julie Ellison and others, Imagining America rose to build "a broad movement for cultural democracy tied to . . . civic engagement efforts to change the cultures of higher education" and to "bring academic humanists back into public life through reciprocal partnerships with communities," where they might "reclaim their public soul and public muscle" and inspire other disciplines to do the same.[5]

The Prison Creative Arts Project originated in a single course at the University of Michigan in 1990. It has grown year by year, has been nourished, and now flourishes thanks to the atmosphere created by remarkable colleagues and administrators. It is impossible to exaggerate the importance of this support. In what has been variously called our Incarceration Nation or Killing State,[6] the incarcerated are considered the lowest of the low. They are stereotyped as child molesters, rapists, and murderers. They are imagined by people who have never met them as scruffy, unkempt, dangerous or depressed individuals in prison blues or stripes peering through bars, unconnected to family or other loved ones, completely devoid of aspirations, intelligence, and creativity. In the most segregated metropolitan area in the United States, many suburban parents forbid their middle and high school children to venture into Detroit. The same parents and our students' peers warn our university students against going into "dangerous" high schools, juvenile facilities, and prisons. Yet no official at the university has warned us or spoken against our projects. The university has encouraged us, provided resources, and even rewarded us for what we do.

However, I recall what may have been the first university-called gathering of faculty whose work took them into the community. This must have been in the early nineties. It was a meeting of deeply committed individuals with great projects, and yet, as my colleague Sharon Sutton pointed out at the time, the predominant mode was pipeline: we will help talented young people leave Detroit behind and come to the University of Michigan. No one advocated that they stay vitally connected with their community or return to struggle for change there. And there was little sense that our students were vital partners in the projects.[7]

The growth toward the collaborative, democratic civic engagement that is now so much more possible and prevalent at the university was slow.[8] It came from faculty members often working alone, then collaboratively, then as leaders: Bunyan Bryant and Jim Crowfoot in the School of Natural Resources, Jim Chaffers, Margi Dewar, and Kate Warner in the School of Urban Planning and Architecture, Barry Checkoway, Larry Gant, and Lorraine Gutierrez in the School of Social Work, Stella Raudenbush in Education, Mark Chesler in Sociology, Pat Gurin in Psychology and Women's Studies, Julie Ellison in English and American Culture, David Scobey in History and Urban Planning and Architecture, John Vandermeer in Ecology and Evolutionary Biology, and Barbara Israel in the School of Public Health.[9] Under their leadership and that of others, Imagining America came into being at the University of Michigan, as did Arts of Citizenship and the Ginsberg Center for Community Service and Learning, where Jeffrey Howard and Joe Galura from the beginning provided leadership.

In the early 1990s, university president James Duderstadt brought together people from across campus to write the Michigan Mandate, which committed the university to a pluralistic faculty and student body and drew from the faculty and from other institutions administrative leaders like Connie Cook, John Matlock, Paula Allen-Meares, Lester Monts, Marvin Parnes, and Evans Young.[10] It was the University of Michigan, under the leadership of Lee Bollinger that fought all the way to the Supreme Court the most out-front and courageous fight against the forces opposed to affirmative action. Although Michigan voters in 2006 eliminated affirmative action in state institutions, the university, under the leadership of Mary Sue Coleman and provost Teresa Sullivan, continues to struggle in every way to identify and recruit aspiring students from underserved and underresourced high schools and communities across the state. As a faculty member, sometimes only dimly aware of these efforts, feeling my way at my own work, I absorbed the benefits of these efforts and grew in confidence.

THE PRISON CREATIVE ARTS PROJECT

The story of the Prison Creative Arts Project (PCAP) will gradually unfold in the chapters that follow. Here is an initial idea of the scope and volume of the work.

Since 1990, incarcerated youth and adults, urban and rural high school youth, University of Michigan students, graduates, and faculty members, and some community members from the Detroit metropolitan area, working in twenty-four prisons, six juvenile facilities, and seven high schools have created 506 original plays, have created art in over one hundred workshops, and have held 179 creative writing workshop readings and produced approximately eighty-seven in-house anthologies. They have collaborated in six music and two dance workshops in prisons, at least ten dance workshops in juvenile facilities, and in workshops in all the arts in the high schools.

Since 1996 the Prison Creative Arts Project has curated fifteen annual exhibitions of art by Michigan Prisoners. In the fourteenth, 229 artists from thirty-nine prisons exhibited 390 works of art, and 4,069 people walked through the gallery. Since 1999, we have curated eleven annual exhibitions of art by incarcerated youth and since 2005 two biannual exhibitions of art by returned citizens.

Since 1996, PCAP has accompanied the annual exhibition with a total of 141 events, including speakers from around the country. Since 2001 our speakers bureau—composed of PCAP members often accompanied by the formerly incarcerated—has addressed over 130 audiences, including classes at the University of Michigan and other colleges and universities, church groups and community organizations, national conferences, and six Martin Luther King Jr. Forums at the University of Michigan.

In March 2009 we published the equivalent for writers of what the artists had had for fourteen years, our *On Words: Michigan Review of Prisoner Creative Writing*. Two hundred ninety-four writers from forty-four prisons submitted 631 pieces. We accepted thirty-seven from twenty-one prisons, with a total of forty-six pieces of poetry and prose.

Since 2001, 148 incarcerated youth, working one on one with PCAP members, have created portfolios of their art and writing. Fifty-four returned youth and adults have been paired with fifty-one community arts mentors through our Linkage Project.

FOUNDERS

My PCAP official title is Founder. Yet at the Florence Crane Women's Facility in January 1990 I met Mary Glover, plaintiff in the famous *Glover v. Johnson* case that won equal access to education for women prisoners. We consider ourselves cofounders. Although she participated in just two plays by the Sisters Within Theater Troupe, it was that lawsuit, and Mary's reputation with the warden, that made the first workshop and PCAP possible. A lifer who after twenty-six years won clemency, she now works as the coordinator of PCAP's Linkage and Portfolio projects.

As Mary would agree, however, the Prison Creative Arts Project is founded whenever youth, adults, and students step forward together in institutions where there is much pain and little trust, to risk collaboration and creativity, to begin to laugh, imagine, and play, and to take ownership of their voices. When DeWayne and Ollie stand at the podium, PCAP is founded. Every time a Gregory Taub picks up a colored pencil and decides not to copy an Elvis Presley photograph, but draw himself and his friends as hard-bitten figures indifferent to everyone, against a city landscape, and realizes, "I can take something I love to do and make something of it . . . [and be] on top of the world . . . and accomplish anything,"[11] PCAP is founded. When Jesse Jannetta, Suzanne Gothard, Rachael Hudak, Chiara Liberatore, Eric Shieh, and Emily Harris step into the PCAP office or into a workshop, when Martin Vargas, Kinnari Jivani, F. Mumford, and Wynn Satterlee pick up a brush or pencil, when George Hall, Chuck English, Toni Bunton, and Brandon Gatson write a poem, when Shar Wabindato, Bernie Mac, Henry O. Smith (Smitty), and Romando Valeroso step onto the stage, PCAP is founded.

NARRATION

On January 23, 2007, Janie gave a School of Art and Design Penny W. Stamps Distinguished Speaker lecture at the Michigan Theater. She spoke about early and continuing influences on her work as an artist and on her work with Detroit schoolchildren, her university students, and the incarcerated. Afterward she and audience members moved to the Screening Room for questions and discussion. Mark Creekmore, an activist professor in the School of Social Work, asked Janie if the Prison Creative Arts Project does narration. I had to think about that.

We have no storytelling workshops, yet we have a culture of narration. Our courses open with full-day retreats to which we bring life stories. Student journals explore how texts, field experiences, and intense class discussion illuminate students' own past and future. In the PCAP workshops we advocate ownership of one's history, one's stories, images, and words. Our annual letter to the artists asks for submissions that come from within, that are unique. And at our best we listen for each person's growth, for what happens because of the work and because we are in rooms together. During the fall and winter terms, depending on the year, PCAP has between fifty and seventy members. It is hard for us in our meetings to get back to our underlying stories, but as we meet in smaller groups during or at the end of each meeting and as we drive in pairs or trios to our sites, we find our way there.

I am the storyteller here. You will find me emphasizing theater workshops because they are my main experience. I will talk about my courses, not Janie's, though I will talk about our shared pedagogy and her virtues as a teacher. My story about the annual exhibition will be less fully aware of artistic nuance than what she would give you, though I will quote at length what she says the exhibition means. I will try to ferret out for you the elements, the simple secrets, that have made so much of our work successful, even while we falter and blunder and run into trouble and don't get it. Yet there have been thousands of stories, storytellers, founders, and creators in PCAP. I wish I could give each person the voice she deserves, the stories he needs to tell.

(RE)SOURCES

In chapter 1 I tell you how this work began for me and for PCAP. What you need to know here is that when I first came *into* the work, I found I had entered a rich, progressive cultural tradition that embraced me as I felt my way. I went to conferences of the Alliance for Cultural Democracy[12] and met Liz Lerman, Lucy Lippard, Susan Perlstein, and so many others who were generous with me. In Ann Arbor we formed our own little branch of the Alliance and sponsored a small conference where, I remember, Michael Moore showed some scenes from his work-in-progress, *Roger and Me*.

Fresh from three years of community-based video practice and my first year of guerrilla and action theater work, I went to Lima, Peru, in the fall of 1985. I met Marta Arce, Olga Bárcenas, and Milena Alva, and became an honorary member of Nosotras, traveling with them to dusty corners of shantytowns and to markets where the actors they had trained in the *pueblos jovenes* performed original plays for children that informed their parents of the national vaccination campaign and saved lives.[13] I gulped—I had so few credentials and just more than passable Spanish—and invited myself to the Eleventh Annual *Muestra* of Peruvian Theater in Cuzco. I was befriended by Yawar, a long-standing urban community-based theater group, and by members of Yuyachkani, an internationally recognized community-based theater group, and by the youth of Villa el Salvador. Their play about the founding and values of their city that had grown up out of the sand after a land seizure south of Lima took the *Muestra* by storm. They invited me to visit them and became lifelong friends. Working with my University of Lima colleagues on a video project in Huaycán, another land-seizure city built of sand and rocks, in its first year, I collaborated with the city of Lima to bring theater groups there to perform in the large woven-cane structure they had erected for public events.

Back in the States in 1986, with a year free for research thanks to a Guggenheim Fellowship, I read about the people's theater explosion of the late 1960s and 1970s, about the "Gathering" in Mankato, Minnesota, about Luis Valdez and Teatro Campesino, read all the numbers of *Theater-*

work Magazine I could get my hands on, read Ross Kidd's essays about his people's theater and theater for development work in Kenya and Bangladesh and drove to his town in Canada to learn from him.[14] Overcoming my perennial shyness, and ignoring my awkwardness as an actor, I participated in a workshop led by Robert Alexander of the Arena Theater, then watched his actors enable a group of mentally and physically challenged Detroit children to create their own characters and improvise a wonderful play set on a train. I participated in two workshops led by Augusto Boal, one on theater of the oppressed and one on theater and therapy: I risked my own stories as problems to be worked on and experienced the power of having my peers work *for* me as we improvised those stories.

Having been inspired and taught by the men and women I interviewed for *Film on the Left,* my 1981 book on 1930s American documentary film,[15] I began to travel to meet my peers who, though younger, were my elders in community-based work. I went to the Highlander Research and Education Center to meet John Gaventa, who had given video cameras to miners and textile workers for documentation and organizing. I went to Nicaragua to meet Alan Bolt at his *finca* and learned that a community's culture includes its method of planting as well as its music or theater. Nidia Bustos, director of Mecate, the nationwide peasant theater movement that based its plays in local issues and created musical instruments out of materials at hand, told me that her most important acting experience was pretending to be a hysterical pregnant woman in a truck loaded with grenade-filled pineapples in the war against Somoza.

In Omaha I had long conversations with Doug Paterson, cofounder of the Dakota Theater Caravan and professor of community-based theater at the University of Nebraska. In a Los Angeles skid row storefront law center I watched John Malpede, who turned out to be a high school classmate of my younger brother Ted, work with a homeless woman. She wrote down what made her happy ("It would be so much easier to write what hurts," she said), then acted out walking on the beach. I sat in on rehearsals and performances by John's Los Angeles Poverty Department over the next years and interviewed its homeless members. They taught me more than anyone the processes of working from scratch, building something brilliant out of chaos, and enjoying the improvisation that occurs right up through the performance.

In the Hodson Senior Center in the South Bronx, Susan Perlstein of Elders Share the Arts, three women, and I repeated over and over a sound and motion that represented our work lives—one woman placed a wig on a doll, her factory job—and later I saw their play about a hat factory strike. Susan and Peggy Pettitt brought me to their workshops at the Queens VA Hospital, where I watched World War II veterans dance in their wheelchairs and tell stories of war and recreation in the Pacific and of segregation in the South when they returned home. I watched barely wired-together inpatient men and women act out their invention of a 1940s nightclub. These men and women were recognizing and honoring their own participation in the history of their times.

In Atlanta I interviewed men and women living with AIDS and others connected to people living with AIDS and spent hours at rehearsals of Rebecca Ranson's *Higher Ground*. I then watched my interviewees perform their stories as Rebecca had shaped them, watched this keep them alive a little longer. They taught me what laughter and imagination may do when the grim reaper approaches and more about the powerful aesthetic of people who venture and perform their own lives and issues.[16]

Pregones, a Puerto Rican theater group based in the South Bronx, took me under their wing. It was my great privilege to witness in Spanish East Harlem their forum theater play, *The Embrace,* in a church, schools, and a drug rehabilitation center. Audience members came to the stage to replace the "most oppressed person" in two-scene scenarios about AIDS, trying to "change the history" and find solution to a scourge that was only minimally addressed in their community. The Pregones actors faced tense, emotional, improvisation situations. Afterward Magali Jimenez from the Boriken Health Center shared information and led charged discussions.

On May 31, 1990, in Union Temple Baptist Church in Anacostia, southeast Washington D.C., youth from a local halfway house on their way home from Oak Hill, the Receiving Home, and other juvenile facilities, completely disrupted Everyday Theater's performance of *The Lost Prize*. This play about AIDS had been underwritten by the Centers for Disease Control. Afterward I listened as Mustafaa Madyoun, one of the youth troupe directors, gave notes to the distraught performers:

Remember that what you saw tonight was this country, the effects of slavery on our people. These kids came from the shelters and halfway houses. You may have been offended and hurt by how they acted, but remember it isn't their fault. They are not in control of their situation or themselves.

What happened insults us, but remember it is their self-hatred, that they are actually doing it to themselves. It is hard for them to see someone doing something good or positive when it is not happening to them. So it is easier for them to steal the show, to get power, to upset you, to draw the attention from you—it is the only chance in their lives. . . . We must figure out how to get our point across. If we lose control, we can pause—and they'll see nothing is happening—or we can intensify what we are doing, the volume, or the action. Or we can address our monologue to them directly. You have to do something, not let it just throw you.

They haven't won—they may think so—but they lost, we all lost. They weren't really able to get what was there for them to get. They need to see a success. If they are successful in knocking us down, they just put themselves back further into their self-hatred. If we are successful, they have a chance to see what they're capable of, see hope. No one really wants to be that unresponsive.[17]

CONTEXT

The context of *Is William Martinez Not Our Brother?* is the mass incarceration of American citizens and its devastating effect on countless neighborhoods, families, and millions of American- and foreign-born children. The context is the "invisibility" of this incarceration for most Americans and the silence in our suburbs and in our schools, colleges, and universities. When millions of people were criminalized through new laws and taken from their homes and disappeared in Germany of the 1930s, when the United States continued to brutalize slaves and split slave families apart in the 1840s and 1850s, when the South through new laws and lynching imposed segregation until far into the last century, there was the same invisibility, and the same silence in safe places, including the academy. Dostoyevsky says you can tell the nature of a civilization by looking at its prisons. The context is the damage done to us all by the torment perpetrated in our name. I am writing this chapter at the Lillian E. Smith Center for the Arts in Clayton, Georgia, and reading Lillian Smith's *Killers of the Dream*. She writes,

Even its children knew that the South was in trouble. No one had to tell them; no words said aloud. To them, it was a vague thing weaving in and out of their play, like a ghost haunting an old graveyard or whispers after the household sleeps—fleeting mystery, vague menace to which each responded in his own way. Some learned to screen out all except the soft and the soothing; others denied even as they saw plainly, and heard. But all knew that under quiet words and warmth and laughter, under the slow ease and tender concern about small matters, there was a heavy burden on all of us and as heavy a refusal to confess it. The children knew this "trouble" was bigger than they, bigger than their family, bigger than their church, so big that people turned away from its size . . .

The mother who taught me what I know of tenderness and love and compassion taught me also the bleak rituals of keeping Negroes in their "place." The father who rebuked me for an air of superiority toward schoolmates from the mill and rounded out his rebuke by gravely reminding me that "all men are brothers," trained me in the steel-rigid decorums I must demand of every colored male. They who so gravely taught me to split my body from my mind and both from my "soul," taught me also to split my conscience from my acts and Christianity from southern tradition.[18]

It is visible enough, in its own way. We have in our heads what an adult told us as we drove past a prison or jail. We have our images of morose, scruffy, violent prisoners. We are bombarded with stories and images from newspaper and television inordinate focus on violent crime. The death penalty, abolished in most other countries, and recent laws that give us the longest sentences in the world imply the nature of the offender. And our complicated contemporary sex panic abolishes distinctions between dangerous repeat offenders and those who will not err again, ruins lives, and scares us all to death. *Such* visibility makes it easy for us *not to know* and makes it easy for us to condemn forever the incarcerated and formerly incarcerated. They are someone else's relatives, not ours.

When we mention our work in the prisons, it turns out that others have experiences they don't normally share. Director Nancy Fichter at the Lillian E. Smith Center writes to a man on death row. A Center resident remembers a great musician who was suddenly arrested and convicted of child molestation and is now coming home. She tracks his location on the Internet and wishes, cautiously, to help him out. And I drive down to the crossing of Routes 76 and 441: dark men in brown wearing orange City of Clayton pullovers, Georgia prisoners, are cutting a plot of grass. I have seen them on the highways of Michigan, seen them chipping ice in the city of Chelsea, cleaning the cemetery in Saline. In Santa Fe I stop in for a haircut at Super Cuts. My barber had the penitentiary contract for a year or two. A prison artist drew a portrait of her cutting hair, but the prison would not allow her to keep it. I bring her a catalog from the Tenth Annual Exhibition of Art by Michigan Prisoners. In Cordova, the drunken man who falls off his motorbike has been in and out of the penitentiary and is on parole. So Paula is wary of calling emergency services for help.

It is a deep shame in us, a wound below the surface. Sixty-two percent of the youth at Boysville are African American. Seventy-five percent of the youth sentenced to adult prisons are youth of color. Forty percent of prisoners in state prisons and jails are African American and 20 percent are Hispanic.[19] But we are told by those who do not think, or who wish desperately not to see, that we are in a postracist era. The *New York Times* exclaims in a front-page story that now for the first time one in one hundred American adults are in prison,[20] and Barack Obama, Hillary Clinton, and John McCain don't even pause. The incarcerated—2.3 million of them, 25 percent of the prisoners in the world—and their children do not appear in their speeches. Do they not know them?

Harry Boyte writes that "conventional definitions of politics, as a struggle of the forces of good against the forces of evil, offer little hope that America will see a broad revitalization of public life and democracy." He understands and is uncomfortable with the Saul Alinsky organizing model, which

> divided cities into two systems, the neighborhood and the "enemy" power structure outside. Poor, minority, and working class communities, in his analysis, were victimized by the affluent, powerful, downtown-connected interests who bestowed social services and economic largess on the already privileged areas of the city.

A few pages later, having recognized the effectiveness of citizen organizing efforts that build upon and alter the work of Alinsky, Boyte observes that "anger at injustice runs as a central thread through this organizing, which makes it disciplined, directed, and constructive." Yet "anger at economic and social injustice is insufficient to tap hidden discontents—the self-interests—of suburban, professional, and other middle class or upper middle class communities." In order for public work to take place, for engagement agenda and public scholarship to be effective, for developmental organizing to happen, participants must work past economic barriers, must not think in terms of evil, enemies, and anger. Boyte quotes Simanga Kumalo from the University of Natal in South Africa: "The movements against colonialism produced a great generation of liberation leaders. What we need now is a new generation of development leaders."[21] The great, necessary era of the Student Nonviolent Coordinating Committee and the Congress On Racial Equality, Malcolm X and Martin Luther King, and Jesse Jackson and Al Sharpton is over. We are in the era of Barack Obama, of leaders who can negotiate and unite, who understand the workings of power and bring constituencies together.

This makes so much sense, is so hopeful, optimistic, dug in, and true. It speaks to the processes and work of the Prison Creative Arts Project. At its best in the universities and colleges, such practice is tough-minded, analytic, reflective, and highly responsible. It has motivated colleagues, students, and community members across the country and is a great vision. And yet for me in most of the practice and most of the theory something is absent, something is potentially a little soft.

MORE RE(SOURCES)

As I finished *Film on the Left* and came *into* this work, I also found voices that resonated for me. Because they are in me and in most of those I engage with, the work of PCAP, *underneath,* has something a little edgier, a little more angry and combative than other forms of public scholarship.

I found Jonathan Kozol's outraged descriptions of American schools and the conditions in which so many urban school children live. I found, in *The Night Is Dark and I Am Far from Home,* his powerful analysis of the way so many of us are trained in our schools to be "good citizens," ethically indifferent to what is done to others in our name, his insistence that the reader quit reading if unprepared to take such matters seriously.[22]

I found Paulo Freire's clarity about what a member of the oppressor class who wishes to join the struggle of the oppressed must do. I found his insistence that participants in "true dialogue" will have committed to change the world, to be co-teachers and co-students, to de-code their situation, then to act and to reflect on their action.[23]

I found Myles Horton's insistence on appropriate and channeled anger, his advice against wasting words with those unprepared to act, and his recommendation to put people in places where they have to make decisions. I found his willingness to risk his life for economic and social justice, his creation of the Highlander Folk School, that profound educational space where music, dance, and storytelling play key roles, where Martin Luther King Jr.,

Rosa Parks, and so many many others would prepare to enter into or develop community organizing, passive resistance and nonviolent action.[24]

Miguel Ayala took me into peasant communities to hold posters while he taught agronomy, then talked all night and sang *huaynos* and political songs in peasant homes. Marta Arce resolved on a torture table in Brazil to commit her life to being the opposite of the torturer. Javier Mujica left his home at different hours and in different directions to thwart death squads and Shining Path because workers' rights were too important to cease struggling for. Nora came from Ireland to train paramedics, and Father Jeronimo Olleros came from Spain to practice liberation theology at Cenecape CCAIJO at a time when progressive priests were threatened. Martin Luther King Jr., wrote from Birmingham jail. With so many others he marched across Pettis Bridge. Rosa Maria Puma Roca, abused by her parents, bounded across the fields of Antapampa to greet me.

ENEMIES

In chapter 3 I tell how powerful interests chose to carry out the greatest experiment in social control through mass incarceration in the history of the world. They, the legislators who voted for and continue to vote for the laws that make this possible, the media professionals who spread fear, the special interests that block universal health care, and the economic planners who scheme out dangerous streets, rotting schools, and beleaguered teachers *act* as enemies and *are* enemies to the millions of children who will drop out, get caught up in the criminal justice system, and end up in prison. And those children *experience* in their bodies and souls that they have such enemies. And those of us who are safe and pay no attention, those of us who give handouts, and those of us who give something without rattling our worlds, if the truth were to be told, if the truth were to be admitted, we are also enemies to those children, if beneficent and well-intentioned ones. And if DeWayne and Nate have enemies, then those enemies are mine as well.

In Marcel Ophul's brilliant film *Memory of Justice,* Albert Speer—I see him standing on a hill—declares, "I didn't know [about the deportations and death camps], but I could have known and chose not to know, and therefore I am guilty."[25]

Noam Chomsky argues that those with the most access, affluence, and training to know what is happening bear the most responsibility for what happens.[26]

We must name things for what they are. But we also must not engage in public work thinking of and treating others as enemies, seeing them narrowly and denying them their full, complex humanity. We must enter the "free spaces" and other arenas with the kind of grit and determination, the kind of generosity, the kind of willingness to negotiate and move forward that Boyte speaks of so eloquently.

Elie Wiesel has helped me think about this. His "An Appointment with Hate" puzzles and troubles my students. He returns to Germany for the first time since he was a child in Auschwitz. He is to give some lectures. But he cuts his trip short and flees, having discovered that he has left his hatred for the Germans behind. Grappling with this, he comes to a new place: one must have a healthy, virile hatred for that thing *in* Germans that might allow them to act again as they once did.[27]

Myles Horton urges us to trust others in a world where human beings have not proven themselves worthy of trust.[28] If we accept this, as I do, it makes sense for us to have a similar alertness. Our country's history of violence and history of racism continue to play themselves out in individuals and in many places, certainly in our schools, juvenile facilities, and prisons. Who are the people we have put there? *Is William Martinez Not Our Brother?* is a story of limited, inadequate success.

THE AGE OF IRON

In J. M. Coetzee's novel *The Age of Iron,* Mrs. Curren, a retired white South African history teacher, has disliked but never actively opposed apartheid. As the novel begins, she has just been diagnosed with terminal cancer and begins a journal in the form of a long letter to her daughter in the United States. She has decided not to tell her about her illness: the daughter might come to South Africa to smother her mother with care, and Mrs. Curren prefers to embark on an adventure of self-examination and new risk. She writes a long, unflinching, day-by-day letter exploring her pallid self and her complicity, by inaction, in apartheid. She is flaccid alongside black South Africans like her housekeeper Florence and youth like Florence's son Bheki and his friend John, who have left school and become hardened and determined representatives of the age of iron as they combat the government. At the novel's heart is Mrs. Curren's gradual realization that in order to truly love her daughter, she must love John, who treats her with insolence, and

Vercuil, the drunk, homeless Afrikaner who appears on her property the day of her diagnosis and attaches himself to her. John, "unthinking, inarticulate, unimaginative . . . stolid," a believer in "blows and bullets," his "neck stiff as a poker," is her son. Vercuil, "an insect . . . emerging from behind the baseboards when the house is in darkness to forage for crumbs" is, in the end, her husband.[29]

WILLIAM MARTINEZ

One April morning in 1989, William Thomas Martinez left his cell and walked to the pie-shaped exercise yard 4A–4L in the Secure Housing Unit (SHU) at California State Prison at Corcoran. An armed robber from Oakland and member of the northern Nuestra Familia gang, two weeks before in the same yard he had "stood toe to toe" with Pedro Lomelli, a member of La Eme, the Mexican Mafia gang in Southern California. They had fought, Giles Whittell implies, because "feuds between the state's prison gangs are, if anything, older and more intense than between its street ones. Gang lore dictates that an inmate from La Eme . . . if thrown together with one from Nuestra Familia, has no choice but to fight. . . . Not to do so would be still more dangerous since it would shame his 'homeboys.'"[30]

Prison policy dictated that during SHU yard fights, the officers overseeing the yard from above should first shout a warning to stop. If that didn't work, they were to fire from a riot gun a round of nonlethal wooden pellets; everyone in the yard would fall to the floor. If the fight continued, the next step was the firing of a 9 mm rifle, "which came with hollow-tipped 'safety slugs,' cruelly misnamed since they were chosen for their tendency to explode in a target's body rather than go through and ricochet off the yard's high concrete walls." Martinez and Lomelli "had signed forms pledging they had no known enemies in their SHU quarters [but] everyone on the tier knew this was a lie."[31]

Taking advantage of the integrated yard policy of mixing rival gangs, intended in theory to prepare prisoners for free society, the officers of yard 4A–4L were setting up fights between rival gang members and often betting on the outcome.

One excitable officer, a Sergeant Pio Cruz, often took the role of fight announcer, turning 4A–4L into his little piece of Vegas. When a fancied combatant lived up to his reputation, he could be thanked by the guards for "making them a bit richer." When things turned bloody, they could blame it on the book.

And things did turn bloody. Corcoran was built in 1988, and in its first year prisoners were fired on 735 times, and it is estimated that 4A–4L saw "more than a thousand serious fights, not all of them reported. It was, a former head of the prison system said, 'absolutely the highest rate that I have ever seen in any institution, anywhere in the country.'" By 1995, five prisoners had been killed and many more wounded. After each of the fifty most serious shootings there between 1988 and 1995, a review board of senior officers sat round a large table on high-backed blue chairs and discussed it. Every time they managed to agree that the purpose had been "to save life or prevent great bodily injury." This made it a "good shoot," with no need to discipline the guard even if an inmate had been killed or wounded by mistake.

William Martinez, after passing through the metal detector and being subjected to a strip search, entered 4A–4L. When he saw Lomelli, he went after him and thirteen seconds later was dead. The review board after watching the video claimed that Martinez had kicked Lomelli six times in the head and was shot while preparing to kick again, endangering Lomelli's life. In fact, a careful review of the video reveals that Martinez did not kick Lomelli, that the fight had concluded, and that Martinez was shot in the back when he was walking away.[32] A tough violent kid from Oakland. Or not. When his parents, video in hand, tried to sue the prison authorities, a federal judge threw the case out.[33] Is he *not* our brother, husband, son?

CHAPTER ONE

The Beginning

PCAP began when I was a curly-haired blond boy of five with an odd name who was bullied on Chestnut Street, when I realized the bullying was unmerited since in my home I was loved and affirmed, when in response to the bullying I instinctively developed strategies—reading, modeling myself after my strong father, figuring out how to become popular—and when a seed of anger and resistance at all bullying was planted at my core. It began again when I listened to Europeans as I traveled the summer after graduation from college and settled into my studies at Cambridge and broke from my Republican family and voted for Jack Kennedy. PCAP was born in the three years in England and Italy, as I, still politically shy, thrilled at the civil rights movement back home. PCAP began in 1964 when I knew immediately that the Gulf of Tonkin incident was a lie, in 1968 when I went to New Hampshire to campaign for Eugene McCarthy and co-headed a committee for him in Ipswich, Massachusetts, in 1969 when John Maynard, Everett Mendelsohn, and I initiated Harvard Faculty Against the War, in 1970 when I participated in civil disobedience at the federal building in Boston. It was born when I moved to Michigan in 1971 and knew that what I had learned would stay with me and that I needed to integrate it into the way I practiced my career. It began later in the 1970s when I interviewed courageous men and women from the 1930s for my book *Film on the Left,* when I cofounded the Ann Arbor Committee for Human Rights in Latin America, co-organized a Teach-in on Terror in Latin America, was turned down for tenure at Michigan and watched my students organize and force a reversal of the decision. It was born most dramatically during my trips to the peasant communities near Cuzco with radical Peruvian agronomist Miguel

Ayala and when I saw an Irishwoman at the Freirean-inspired school, Cenecape CCAIJO, place a thermometer in the mouth of a *campesino* she was training to be a paramedic, and when I realized, as I walked to the outskirts of Andahuayllilas seeking *mobilidad,* that I needed to find my own way to join community struggles outside the University of Michigan.

More seeds were planted in 1981 when I created English 319, a course where my students and I produced videotapes supporting the organizing efforts of Locals Opposed to Concessions and Teamsters for a Democratic Union in Detroit, the Mon Valley Unemployed Committee in Pittsburgh, and wildcat Teamster strikers in Toledo. Those seeds grew when I realized that theater was more provocative as a political tool than video because during and after a performance, actors and audience were in the space together, not separated when the videotape ended. English 319 became an action theater and guerrilla theater course. We chose social justice causes and disrupted classrooms, libraries, dorms, and outdoor university and community spaces with our performances. We often contacted community organizations and created skits and plays that contributed to their efforts. Three homeless citizens from the Ann Arbor Shelter joined us in performing *Joey's Story,* a project with the Homeless Action Committee, and an AIDS outreach counselor from Vida Latina in Detroit helped plan and performed in our play about AIDS. A member of a local movie projectionist union educated us and performed with us in a series of skits outside theaters owned by the Kerasotes Corporation, a theater chain from Illinois that had taken over twenty-seven Michigan theaters and fired union workers and eliminated senior discounts. While we performed, we passed a sheet collecting several thousand boycott signatures, were sued by Kerasotes for half a million dollars, were defended by the National Lawyers Guild, and won the right to continue performing in front of the theaters.[1] I was drawn to the power of these collaborations across social divides.

And so in January 1990, when Liz Boner approached to ask if two lifers at the Florence Crane Women's Facility in Coldwater could take English 319, I didn't hesitate. Joyce Dixson and Mary Glover were lifers enrolled at the University of Michigan, their way smoothed by dean Eugene Nissen, my colleague Dick Meisler, and students like Liz who traveled with course materials and met with the two women. Mary would win a prestigious Hopwood writing award and graduate with honors after writing a thesis on mercy. Both women would graduate Phi Beta Kappa. I had no idea Mary had been lead plaintiff in *Glover v. Johnson,* a famous lawsuit that had gained equal educational and other rights for women in Michigan prisons. In fact, I knew next to nothing about prisons and could not in my wildest imagination have imagined that my yes would lead to PCAP and affect the lives of thousands of urban and incarcerated youth, prisoners, and University of Michigan students. I had no idea that seventeen years later Mary and I would remain close friends and be coworkers within PCAP.

Each week Liz and Julie Rancilio (both enrolled in 319), and I made the three-hour round trip to Coldwater and met with Mary and Joyce in the small muster room, just down the narrow corridor past the bubble where we were shaken down. It was an odd and resonant space for PCAP to begin: here the corrections officers gathered at shift change, here incarcerated mothers met with their children and the walls were decorated with a mural of Snow White and the Seven Dwarfs, here a black woman and a white woman, both sentenced to life in prison, met with a white professor and two white female students from the University of Michigan.

For six or seven weeks we talked theater, university, and prison, we played and improvised,[2] and we analyzed the characters and situations we improvised in terms of race, class, and power. It was an electric, lively, charged, fun space. Yet while at least equal in personal dignity and input, we were not equal in our situations. The three of us were free to come and go, while Joyce and Mary were incarcerated and under the control of others.

In 1985, not comfortable with the dominant, patronizing attitudes of my three University of Lima colleagues on a video project I had initiated in the *pueblo joven* of Huaycán, a year-old shantytown growing up in dust and rocks outside of Lima, I had asked the people who lived there to put us on camera and interview us. We set up in a space outside one of their woven cane homes, and one at a time they investigated our motives and goals. The power balance shifted. Now we asked Joyce and Mary to brainstorm in a corner of the room for twenty minutes, writing down questions for us.

As I had expected, they first asked, "What are you doing here? Are you 'interested' in prisoners?" Now we were vulnerable. We had to dig inside for the honest words that would best explain our presence. I don't remember now what we said, only that we were not pretentious. They next asked what we would do in certain prison situations. Were I new to prison and another woman stole from me, I said, I would do nothing—I certainly wouldn't report her to an officer. Mary and Joyce seemed satisfied with this, though I realize now they would have liked to hear that I would also find a way to stand up to the thief. One of my students was told to imagine herself in the shower, assaulted by a woman covered with lesions, then rescued by a male officer, who then asks for favors. What would she do? I'm sure Joyce and Mary saw that we were babes in the wood so far as incarceration was concerned and sure that they appreciated our sincerity as we groped our way. When this session ended—and twenty years later as I write this I can picture this moment, where they sat next to each other—Joyce and Mary turned to each other and said, "We have to open this to the entire population."

Warden Carol Howes approved our proposal for a theater workshop. Notices went up in all the units. One hundred twenty women signed up, some of them believing they would be coming to a performance. Sixty actually came to the large recreation room the first day, in early May. When I asked them to stand in a circle, they held hands, sensing that this was a special place where, as in religious services, they were exempted from the prison prohibition against touch. After a few words about why we were there, I gave them instructions for "Vampire," an exercise I had learned from Pregones. Everyone walks about with her eyes closed and arms folded across her chest. Then one person, eyes open, puts her hands around someone's neck; that person transforms into a vampire with a horrendous scream, stretches her arms and feels for the necks of others. Normally the space fills with chilling screams and with deep loud sighs, when hands find the neck of another vampire and turn them back into human beings. But here I soon realized that I was hearing no sounds and encountering no necks. I opened my eyes—I can picture where I stood as I write this: three of us were walking the room, thirty women had left, and another twenty-seven or so were in chairs watching us. Screaming is forbidden in prison. And for a group over 60 percent of whom had suffered domestic violence, "Vampire" may have triggered memories. I hadn't thought. I hadn't understood where I was. I was confident and excited, but had so much to learn. We gathered with those remaining, promised them we would come on a weekly basis from then on and that eventually we would create plays. When we closed, several women came up and asked, "Can we scream every time?"

Each week we brought warm-up games, exercises, and improvisations. At the end of the term, Julie left the workshop and Liz continued. I was thoroughly enjoying myself, but also very challenged. As I wrote in a June 4 letter to my friend Melissa Hagstrum,

We've been there four times, but on the fourth time, yesterday, we learned how prison politics—among the prisoners—is threatening to destroy what we are doing. The two women we worked with, strong, admirable people in for life, have been manipulating who can come . . . , and the others are resenting it and some aren't coming, and they themselves have become erratic in their commitment to the work. Neither were there yesterday, and those who were there let us know what was going on, and we've asked them to take over the responsibility for getting people there next time. We're on a six-week trial basis with the prison, and this hasn't helped. We've had powerful moments, one when Bertha was in tears [crying by herself at the side of the room; I had described an imaging exercise on family and had brought everyone to a space to begin], remembering the loss of her twin children through crib deaths. [Joyce went to her, then came and told us] she wanted to work on that loss theatrically. [Everyone was looking at me. I didn't know what to do, then suddenly remembered an exercise John Malpede had taught, so] I had her narrate, crying [her way through it], the story of what happened, while we acted out what she narrated. There are a lot of stories needing to come up and out in there, and they do come out—a substantial majority of women in prison were survivors of abuse before they committed their crime, and the "theatre of the oppressed" exercises we work from enable them to look at situations they bring up and have us work through alternative ways of handling them. It's powerful, though sometimes I feel a little out of my depth.

From my journal on June 24:

Today I am missing an O-33 workshop[3] at Coldwater, am unhappy to be away from those strong women, Mary, Joyce, Dee, Charanne, Mame, Bertha, Mary W., Ewalk, Char, and on and on. They are survivors, in very tough shape and struggling. Sharon was new last week, said she was going through a lot of bad stuff in her life, and came to the workshop because she heard that we laugh. Last week we did the costume improv and they decided to be at a family picnic.[4] Charron, who loves acting, was shot part way through and for the last 10 minutes had to lie dead on the floor!

And July 9:

How can I spend two hours in bed talking, holding, making love, talking, feeling so full, then go to the prison where these women have been cut off from anything even remotely like that, some of them—Joyce, Mary, Char—for life? How can I come into their presence like that? The feeling of help-lessness and anger Cristina [Jose-Kampfner] talks about.[5] And how almost no one knows about what it is like to be in a prison and doesn't care. . . . For me going to the prison and going to [peasant communities in] Peru are the same thing: when I come back, no one knows where they are and no one gives a shit. They don't want to hear. They don't want to ask.

When Liz left the workshop late in the year, I asked Jody Eisenstein, a former student with strong theater background, to join me. On April 28, 1991, in the recreation hall with an audience of eighty women, we performed *The Show,* a collection of monologues, dialogues, and scenes.

Jackie Wilson opened with a monologue, rushing on stage, picking up a phone, and screaming to her mother that her mother's brother had raped her. Later, she did a stand-up piece about losing her tooth while bowling. That was the range. Lupe Merino, angry that her brother got the toy guns for Christmas, climbed a tree and refused to come down until promised she could have some too. In my first performance ever, I wove an account of a recent restaurant conversation with my brother about his partner's AIDS with a memory of witnessing the death of a close friend by asphyxiation after her reaction to an anti-allergy shot. Connie Bennett, too shy to act, read from a podium a poem about a runner falling during a race, then rising and finishing. We presented comic prison scenes. In a spoof on the chow, we used a rubber chicken (still a prop seventeen years later) and wore chicken beaks and Mary pranced around in a chef's cap.

The audience gave us a standing ovation and plied us with excited questions about the scenes and process. We left very high and thought the extreme shakedown we received on the way out simply indicated a strin-gent shift command on duty that night. I was stunned when I phoned the prison the next day expecting compliments and learned from Deputy War-den Foltz that we were fired. A letter from Warden Howes a few days later said our performance had bordered on inciting to riot.

The chow scene and two other comic scenes were the culprits. In one, as a corrections officer, I told a prisoner to pack up because she was being trans-ferred to the Annex. She didn't wish to go and talked back until finally the corrections officer prevailed. In the other, three women rehearsed a dance for the upcoming performance. I, again a corrections officer, appeared, and as they noticed me one at a time, they stopped dancing until one remained dancing alone, and he cut off the radio. The audience was delighted and amused.

Dean Nissen wrote an official letter to Warden Howes, backing the project. My own letter described theater as an art form and explained that the offending scenes were simply a comic rendering of common prison occurrences that we thought would be enjoyed by all. We were not satirizing officers. As it turned out, we were lucky in our warden. Carol Howes was an advocate of programs and very supportive of the women. She was also on the advisory board of the local theater. We made an appointment with her and learned the security issues: officers who are made fun of lose authority, which can lead to disobedience and even assault. It was a useful lesson, and I vowed to follow it. She called in Assistant Deputy Warden Terry Huffman, who had been offended by the scenes, and told her the program would continue.

As I look back 243 prison plays later, I think of the moment in that office and will always be grateful to Carol Howes. It was my first experience of the difference between the creative and sometimes naive language and behavior we bring in from the outside and the equally legitimate and necessary inside language of restraint and security. Without Carol, it might have been fatal.

Word began to spread. Assistant Deputy Warden Silva Goncalves of the Western Wayne Correctional Facility in Plymouth asked me to start a theater workshop there. Then Penny Ryder of the American Friends Service Committee relayed a message from George Hall of the American Lifers Association at the Egeler Correctional Facility in Jackson: the lifers wished to create a play that would convey their real humanity to an outside audience. Soon I found myself in a meeting room at Egeler with about twenty men, all or almost all of them, I thought, connected to at least one death. They were friendly, they brought me coffee, they made me comfortable, it was like any meeting out in the world. Their agenda included voting to raise funds for the homeless in Jackson. We discussed their goals, I talked about the play-building process I had in mind, and we reached an agreement. Heartened by these contacts with Western Wayne and Egeler, I phoned the Cotton Correctional Facility in Jackson and offered a workshop, which was enthusiastically accepted.

Silva became a great collaborator, Penny, one of the great activists I know, a longtime colleague, and George a lifelong friend. When George left Egeler after our first play, we began a correspondence. Then in 2004 he turned up in the Poet's Corner, a workshop I was cofacilitating at the Southern Michigan Correctional Facility, and proved to be one of the best poets I know. Now, confined to a wheelchair at age seventy-four, he is the one prisoner the Michigan Department of Corrections policy permits me to visit.[6] With the women at Florence Crane, with these three and with many others to come, I was entering a world where people resist the humiliating, traumatic effects of incarceration. It was life-changing.

And so English 319 evolved. Winter term 1992 it was part action/guerrilla theater, part prison theater. In April the men at Western Wayne and the students produced *A Time When . . .* , a series of monologues, dialogues, and scenes reflecting their experiences inside and outside of prison. A shaken, admiring prisoner family member told me afterward, "That was totally real, that's how it is." At Egeler they presented monologues, dialogues, and scenes held together by an ongoing card-table conversation set in the prison yard. Although we didn't yet have any notion that we were the Prison Creative Arts Project, the Cotton group produced the first full-fledged PCAP play, *A Thin Line Between Life & Death.* Two hundred prisoners watched this play about AIDS from gym bleachers. During a break between scenes, a prisoner living with AIDS told the audience about the respect and understanding he and other prisoners with AIDS needed from them.[7] A year later, English 319 would be committed entirely to prison theater.

In the fall of 1989, my colleague Anne Gere called to tell me she would love to see me work with the children at the Dewey Center for Urban Education, a K-8 magnet school that serves Detroit's Jeffries Homes (housing projects). Two excellent teachers, Toby Curry and Debra Goodman[8] had established a holistic method of instruction, and two University of Michigan lecturers I admired, George Cooper and Dave Schaafsma, were already at work there. In January five students and I established three video projects at the Dewey Center, each team working with two fourth graders, two sixth graders, and two eighth graders. The children came up with the subject matter, having to do with the school neighborhood, and carried out all the interviewing and taping. The grandmother of one of the sixth graders Jeanne Gilliland and I worked with owned a soul food kitchen on Woodward Avenue. The girl's mother had baked the birthday cake for Rosa Parks's seventieth birthday, complete with the sculpted buildings and buses of downtown Montgomery. The children produced an utterly charming tape with interviews of the warm, wise, delighted grandmother, the mother, and customers. A cutaway showed the daughter, who planned to become a fashion designer, watching a fashion show. Fernando, a talented fourth grader who could dance like crazy one moment and be in tears another, whose grandmother kept her door in the projects heavily barricaded, told me the next fall that he had watched the tape every night that summer.

In the spring of 1991, after three semesters at the Dewey Center, I worked with my colleague Ralph Williams, then chair of the English Department Curriculum Committee, to put through that committee and its College of Literature, Science, and the Arts counterpart a proposal for the creation of English 310, so that the students volunteering at Dewey might receive course credit.[9] The first version started in the fall, and the course would go on to bring workshops in all the arts to area high schools and juvenile facilities.

We continued at the Dewey Center through the fall of 1992, adding photography and theater workshops. In the third year, three sixth-grade girls, Nikia, Tamesha, and Tamarra, wrote *Tell It Like It Is,* a play about girls working in a beauty parlor. One of the characters was unpopular, but when her father decided to force her to enter the military because he didn't like her boyfriend, the others rallied behind her, converted the father, and the play ended with a wedding. We brought the play to the university. I went to the back of the auditorium just before we went on and found the three girls alone, talking about how they missed their fathers: one was dead, one just plain gone, and the third incarcerated in Wisconsin.[10] The play was an unconscious response to their disrupted homes and a wish for something better with the men who were and would be in their lives. With these children, we were entering the world of the families of the incarcerated.

A new principal came to the Dewey Center and decided after a semester that we could continue only as classroom apprentices to her teachers. She was adamant. Her vision, a committed one, was different from ours, more strictly focused on academic preparation. We were unable to convince her—she wouldn't even meet with us—of the importance of our creative projects. We had to seek a new site.

Anne Gere connected me with Roberta Herter, who taught both in the day school and in the late afternoon and evening Adult Basic Education Program at Henry Ford High School. While I was away on sabbatical during all of 1993, Scott Dent, Kyle McDonald, Kendra Lutes, and others slowly began to work in the evening program, which served high school youth with children, daytime jobs, or suspensions from day school. In January 1994 in English 319 we started up two theater workshops. In the evening workshops stretched two hours, the school was not crowded, and the atmosphere was casual. I was there the night a custodian dropped into a chair, observed, and then told an actress playing a pregnant teen how to get tough with the boy she was confronting. One evening the night school principal and a hall guard paused to watch us rehearsing in the hall a situation proposed by one of the students from his own experience: a black and a white policeman pull over a black youth who is violating no laws; when he talks back to the white policeman, he is told to step out of the car. The principal and guard stopped us and explained to Dennis Guikema how to position himself at the window (Dennis had been facing the driver, not looking over the driver's shoulder) and to the boy playing the black policeman how to place himself alertly at the back of the car. This turned out to be the most powerful of a series of scenes the two workshops presented in April. When the white policeman raised his fist to strike the boy, the scene became frozen sculpture. One at a time they stepped out of the sculpture and spoke—the boy about what he was feeling at that familiar moment, the white policeman justifying his behavior by the precedent of the beatings he had received from his father, and the black policeman deciding that he couldn't permit this to happen to his community. When they then emerged from the sculpture, the black policeman blocked the white policeman's fist and calmed him down, then walked the boy to the police car.

Roberta, an established and great teacher, was also a Ph.D. candidate in the University of Michigan School of Education. She decided to write her dissertation about our collaboration. She placed a video camera in the room for one of the workshops, then wrote about what she saw. She and I had an understanding about the collaboration: neither I nor my students would come to Henry Ford as arrogant know-it-alls from the University of Michigan; the youth would determine the content and style of the plays; we would be in complete communication with her and respond to her advice and guidance. Yet the dissertation reveals that at first she feared that we would condescend to her students, fail to believe in them, and, given our class position and educational standing, be abusive in at least subtle ways. That this fear disappeared over the period of the project is a tribute to her, to the self-confidence of her students, and to the sincerity of my students and the developing work of PCAP. It is also an early lesson that of course we would not and should not be trusted anywhere until we had proven ourselves.[11]

When Governor John Engler cut off funds for much of adult education and the Adult Basic Education Program closed, we moved to the day school. Roberta found us odd empty rooms where we could work with her students who chose to be in a theater, art, or creative writing workshop once a week during class time. In 2008 the principal and all teachers were fired, and Joan Galica, our present liaison, another great teacher, chose to retire. We followed the assistant principal to Cody High School. In our fifteen years at Henry Ford, the youth created forty-six original plays and participated in another fifty workshops in other arts. In 1995 we added the Phoenix School, a Washtenaw County school for rural youth who had dropped out or been expelled from high school. By 1997 we realized that doing a workshop once a week wasn't sufficient time for us to be effective with that particular group of students, and we left reluctantly. In January 1998 we added Cooley High School, where we continue to work (forty-seven plays and many poetry and other art workshops). When PCAP member Melissa Palma became a teacher at Southeastern High School for two years, she brought us in for four theater workshops from September 1999 through April 2001; we began there again in 2007. From September 2003 through April 2006, students at Catherine Ferguson Academy (a wonderful high school for pregnant girls and girls with babies) produced four plays, a poetry reading, and a dance performance, and participated in our one-on-one portfolio project. In the fall of 2008 we added Crockett Technical High School.

⌛

In the summer of 1992, after the Western Wayne actors had completed *A Time When . . .* , I went out to meet with them. We sat in a scraggly circle in a loose group of chairs in a large, nearly empty room behind the chapel space where they had rehearsed and performed—Willie Birmingham, Ter-rance Crawford-El, Nate Jones, Harold Murphy, Todd Rash, Romando Valeroso III, and myself. They told me that while rehearsal had enabled them to "leave prison" each week, and while *A Time When* . . . had caused the audience to think, the best rewards were personal growth, learning to work together, and the way both they and the students had moved from suspicious preconceptions to friendship.

But when I said, "Well, what do you want to do next?" their faces sharpened and whipped around, their bodies straightened. It was not just pleasure and surprise. Awareness of some new connection, some unusual commitment, was suddenly in the air. It had not been some one-time project by a class at the University of Michigan. It had been a beginning. And so they took me on, brainstorming, tossing around ideas, deciding in the end to create a personal play that would speak to youth who were on the path to prison. They wanted to perform it for youth incarcerated at Maxey Boys Training School. I promised to explore that possibility.[12]

In September, Julie Nessen (lecturer in Musical Theatre at the University of Michigan), Maria Stewart, and I met with the same group minus Rash and plus David Hudson-Bey and Willie Clay-Bey. The group committed to the project and decided the play would be about situations and events in the actors' youth that had led them toward prison. Over the following months they began trying out ideas and scenes. I checked in a couple of times. Later Valerie Miller, who had worked with the first group of men, rejoined. I started to investigate the Maxey possibility. Bill Lovett of the Michigan Department of Corrections, Julie, Maria, and I first met with Western Wayne warden Luella Burke and Silva Goncalves, then with Maxey administrators and counselors. In April 1993 Lovett enthusiastically submitted our proposal to Department of Corrections director Kenneth McGinnis: for each performance, a unit of ten youth would accompany their counselors to Western Wayne; after the play they would talk in small groups with the actors, with follow-up counseling at Maxey. We had the support of Burke and of Ernie Pasteur, the new director at Maxey. In August, Maxey counselors attended a work-in-progress performance of the play now titled *Inside Out* and were "on their feet," Nessen reported to me (I was on sabbatical in New York): "They want all youth to see it." But in early October, Director McGinnis turned us down, stating that it was against department policy to allow youth into an adult correctional facility.

I had long admired John Gaventa's work in video exchange at the Highlander Research and Education Center, especially his 1974 project in which he brought a tape of messages from striking Harlan County miners to striking Welch miners and then brought back their responses. Anticipating McGinnis's response, I had already asked Fran Victor, a student of mine from the 1970s and friend, and Bill Harder of Victor/Harder Productions to film the Western Wayne Players' performance, then participate in a video dialogue between prisoners and youth. We proposed this to Maxey, but after McGinnis's decision in October, Pasteur stopped returning phone calls, then finally notified us in January 1994 that Maxey "has no time" for the project. Nor, he said, did they have time for the theater workshops his counselors had requested after seeing *Inside Out* and learning how we work.

We turned to Marlys Schutjer, director of the Adrian Training School, met with her counselors, and received approval of the video exchange. I had returned from sabbatical and joined Maria Stewart for a furious rehearsal and filming schedule, until at the beginning of May the video *Inside Out* was completed. When we filmed, the five actors who had not been transferred to other prisons were Birmingham, Jones, Valeroso, Ron Moyes, and Richard McLauchlin. On the final day of filming, they gathered in the room next to where we were filming, held hands, prayed, and spoke together, then, each taking a deep breath, stepped up into the camera and spoke directly and powerfully, two of them in tears, to their youth audience.

For all of us something profound had happened with this project. Everyone had risked so much. Perhaps even more than with the Sisters Within Theater Troupe at this stage, I realized the necessity and depth of this work at its best. And it bound the six of us for life. I was with Nate Jones until the end and in sporadic correspondence with Willie Birmingham until he succumbed to a virus at the Lakeland Correctional Facility in April 2009. Fifteen years later I correspond now and then with Moyes. Valeroso, whom the Michigan Parole Board will not release despite his acceptance by the University of Michigan MSW program, is one of my dearest friends.

On May 16 we began the interactive video project. Ten incarcerated youth who shared a cottage and spent all their time together entered the small school chapel building with their counselor, Marlis Nuzum, and sat in two rows facing the screen. Although they were highly kinetic, *Inside Out* kept them focused and tense. Fran and Bill recorded their reactions and their questions to the actors. On May 17, back at Western Wayne, we showed that material to the five actors and recorded their responses. We returned to Adrian Training School on May 19. Now the youth began to give the kind of calculated responses they thought their counselors would want them to give, so I decided to link each actor with two of them, to keep the dialogue more intimate, direct, and challenging. Valeroso, who is both a powerful and demanding presence and very honest and fatherly, we assigned to the two most resistant, most reluctant and hurt youth, and they engaged with him. We linked Ron Moyes with a newcomer who was heavily medicated and with a boy who, like Moyes, liked to draw. We returned to Western Wayne on the twenty-sixth, then went back and forth twice more, on June 1 and 10 and July 6 and 8.

The youth seized the opportunity, asking about prison food, discipline, exercise, entertainment, tattoos, danger, sex, visits, loneliness (Q: "What was it like when you got locked up?" A: "I cried the whole first night, had an emotional breakdown"); about reliving crimes (Q: "Do you have remorse for what you did? Do you have empathy? Flashbacks? Dreams at night?" A: "I have them, flashbacks and dreams"); about coping ("What keeps you going when you are depressed . . . when you get scared and lonely?"); about handling anger ("I would drink and beat up people and wake up with blood all over me. How can I control my temper?"). How were the men breaking their patterns of substance abuse? What about returning to their old neighborhoods? How could the youth avoid becoming atrocious people like their fathers, as Jones had done? The fathers among these boys wanted advice on parenting and talked about relationships with women. They shared their crimes, stories of abuse and neglect, their difficulty trusting, their need to trust. What, they wanted to know, had made the five men "start caring about others and getting away from the me-too?"[13]

The men further committed themselves, sharing increasingly personal stories and proposing techniques for taming anger and for walking away from violence and temptation. They urged the boys to think for themselves and to seek systems of support. Several of the boys were interested in McLauchlin's faith, and he shared interpretations of the Bible with them. Others exchanged poems. Marlis asked the two boys paired with Nate Jones how they felt about how easily Jones cried. One of them felt uneasy and found himself turning away; the other respected but did not want to imitate the tears. This led to a dialogue between them and Jones about vulnerability and dignity. Jones graphically described how in a prison group therapy session he risked sharing his personal past and allowed himself to cry and how he felt a tremendous weight lift from him as he did so. The boys satisfied some of their father hunger in this dialogue with these older men; the men satisfied some of their hunger to parent, to make up for the harmful parenting of their own children.

In October we showed *Inside Out* to a group of youth in the Adult Basic Education Program at Henry Ford High School. Birmingham and Valeroso participated from prison in the ensuing video dialogue. Jones, now at age forty-six a full-time University of Michigan student and English 310 theater workshop cofacilitator at Maxey, joined us at the high school. Most of the youth belonged to a local gang; nearly all were tangled in the romance and fear of street violence. At first somewhat belligerent and more sure of their invincibility than the incarcerated youth, they too began to share their lives

Nate Jones (*right*) and Richard McLauchlin. Production still from *Inside Out*. (Courtesy of Fran Victor and Bill Harder, Evolution Media.)

("It's bad as hell out here, worse"; "It is hard to do the right thing when there's nothing to fall back on"; "You can't trust nobody") and the hopes that kept them in high school. The dialogue gave Birmingham the idea for the next Western Wayne Players play, *Rico's Story*, a study in how to get out of a gang.

When Ernie Pasteur told me that they had no time for workshops at Maxey, I phoned Denise Thomas, a counselor at the Green Oak Center, Maxey's maximum security unit, who had spoken in a class of mine a few years earlier. I asked her if she had time for a theater workshop. The answer was an enthusiastic yes, and that month we began our first two workshops in a juvenile facility, one at Green Oak under Denise and the other, under Carol King, at the Huron Center, which housed youth with learning disabilities and severe damage. In April 1994 we had our first performances, a collection of scenes by the Huron Center Boys and the Green Oak Center's *Waiver Right: Right or Wrong.*

That was the beginning of PCAP workshops with incarcerated youth. Adrian Training School was next. December 1994 saw a play by one of the boys' halls and *Growing Up in the Hood* by the West Hall Drama Troupe, a girls' group. In the summer of 1997, hearing that an institutional crisis might make it impossible for Maxey to give us workshops, I phoned Gary Coakley at Boysville, and Sister Anna Joseph Wallette at Vista Maria, and we had our first plays at those facilities that fall. In the summer of 2005, the Calumet Center, a maximum security boys' juvenile facility in Highland Park (Detroit), requested workshops. We started with an English 310 poetry workshop and in December heard the group's reading: *Time to Hear It All at the Writers' Ball.* As of this writing, we have had sixty theater performances at Maxey, thirty-three at Adrian Training School (which closed in January 2009), thirty-four at Boysville, twenty-eight at Vista Maria, four at Calumet, and two at the Lincoln Center, which we added in January 2008, plus numerous art, dance, and poetry workshops.

⧗

When did we become the Prison Creative Arts Project? At first we were feeling our way. Either consciously or unconsciously we remained under the Michigan Department of Corrections' radar, working individually site by site, not wanting anything to be sent up to Lansing for a generalized negative. "We" were the students in the early courses, the students working not for credit in the schools, and those of us who continued, outside the courses, the work at Florence Crane, Cotton, and Western Wayne (where in 1994 we added a second workshop with the medicated prisoners in the Residential Treatment Unit). We were friends, hooked by the meaning of our collaboration with the youth and prisoners. We didn't have a name.

Janie Paul arrived in December 1994, began an art workshop with the men at Western Wayne in the spring of 1995, and in the fall began sending her students to lead art workshops in juvenile facilities and prisons. On October 16, 1995, I deposited some award money[14] into a bank account Pilar Anadon, my partner at two prisons and an early leader and force, and I agreed should belong to something called the Prison Theater Project. When Janie got wind of this, she objected vehemently. It was certainly not her—nor our—intention that we restrict ourselves to theater. We changed the name to the Prison Creative Arts Project.

That was our name on paper, and perhaps we referred to ourselves as such. But even as we added Henry Ford and Phoenix High Schools, Maxey and Adrian Training Schools, and four more prisons—Adrian Temporary and Gus Harrison in Adrian, Ryan in Detroit, and Scott in Plymouth, we still had no organization, no meetings, no structure, no policies. As a group we had carried off two very exciting annual exhibitions of art in the early months of 1996 and 1997 and were flushed with energy from the attention they had received and from what the artists were telling us the exhibitions meant to them. Sara Falls remembers what came next.

> Before PCAP was an esteemed and acknowledged organization, but after it was established and [had the] important classes that you taught, it was something in between: a small but regular and dedicated group of friends. I remember distinctly the summer of '97. Several of us had continued volunteering as facilitators in various prisons, but we weren't officially enrolled in your classes, and we missed the camaraderie and support of the classes. You were away (were you on sabbatical or just on summer vacation? I think the latter), and so we started meeting at Chiara's house. It was Chiara [Liberatore], Laurie [Hess], Vanessa [Mayesky], Karen Goodyke, Talya [Edlund], Michael Burke, Matt [Schmitt], and I. I must be missing some. I think Pilar [Anadon] came once or twice, maybe Charity [Claramunt], Chris Lussier. We met weekly to discuss our workshops, tell our stories, seek support around non-understanding family members or callous guards or frustrating workshops. We brought food and shared bottles of wine. We talked and laughed. We planned and put into effect guerrilla theatre during the Ann Arbor Art Fair, protesting harsher sentencing for youth. We helped each other think about how to move workshops forward. This was the start of PCAP the organization; though I don't think any of us consciously thought about it being an organization: it was just the community we had built. After you returned and fall classes started again, the meetings became more formal. For a time we met at Matt's and my house, and then we outgrew that and had to find a larger space.[15]

Once we identified ourselves as an organization with regular meetings, everything took off. In 1997 we added four more prisons—Huron Valley Men's Correctional Facility in Ypsilanti, Ionia Maximum Facility and the Michigan Reformatory in Ionia, and the Saginaw Correctional Facility in Freeland—and had twenty-nine plays. In 1998 we added the Mound Correctional Facility in Detroit and the Parnall and Southern Michigan correctional facilities in Jackson, and there were forty-three plays. In 1999, despite the temporary closing of most of our theater workshops at the prisons, we had fifty-one plays. In 1998, we added creative writing workshops in the prisons. In 1999 we had our first exhibition of art by incarcerated youth, "The Freedom of Art." Our National Advisory Board was created at the end of that year and met for the first time in the spring of 2000. And in 2000 our elected executive committee began meeting. An Access Grant from the National Endowment for the Arts in 2001 brought us our first full-time paid administrator and the beginning of our Linkage and Portfolio projects. Although we had been speaking about our work all along, 2001 saw the establishment of our speakers bureau. A 2002 Rockefeller PACT Grant enabled us to continue and develop the two new projects and to fund our annual exhibitions, and added to our prestige within the university. In 2003 we scrambled for funds and were able to hire our first coordinator of the Linkage and Portfolio projects. My Carnegie Foundation for the Advancement of Teaching and Council for the Advancement and Support of Education National Professor of the Year for Research Universities Award in 2005 gradually led to our current three years of stabilized funding from the University of Michigan. In the spring of 2006 we celebrated our first 429 plays in the high schools, juvenile facilities, and prisons and in the spring of 2009 celebrated our 500th play and brought to light the first number of *On Words: Michigan Review of Prisoner Creative Writing*. In 2006–7 we were able to hire our first program coordinator and added a course, Incarceration and Citizenship. We began to talk with other prison arts activists around the country about a national coalition, which might include a Center for Prison Arts at the University of Michigan.

CHAPTER TWO

Is William Martinez Not Our Brother?

What an interesting populace we have. Nobody seems at all worried by the fact that we have the largest prison population and that it consists preponderantly of young blacks, a whole generation in jail.

—MURRAY KEMPTON[1]

I wonder if because it is blacks getting shot down, because it is blacks who are going to jail in massive numbers, whether we—the total we, black and white—care as much? If we started to put white America in jail at the same rate that we're putting black America in jail, I wonder whether our collective feelings would be the same, or would we be putting pressure on the president and our elected officials not to lock up America, but to save America?

—FORMER ATLANTA POLICE CHIEF ELDRIN BELL[2]

At the end of our English 310 Saturday retreat, students scramble to become teams and choose sites. In September 2005 Sarah Carswell, Jeff Cravens, and Mike found each other and selected a poetry workshop at the Calumet Center in Highland Park, a new site. A few days later they learned that Calumet, unlike the other juvenile facilities, tests volunteers for drugs. Not a problem for Jeff, but Mike and Sarah told me they would fail the test. And Mike was morally and politically outraged: clearly he had a right to choose whether he would do drugs or not, and clearly it wouldn't affect his work with the boys. He told the class he would have no reservation about sharing that position with incarcerated boys. Most of Mike's classmates, including Sarah, were appalled. For Mike doing drugs was almost consequence-free, and he would have no qualms about advocating drug use with boys for whom the consequences were anything but free.

I thought we might lose Calumet, but Jennifer took on a second workshop and joined Jeff. I reassigned Mike and Sarah to a high school, where they did an excellent job, and where, as far as I know, Mike kept his position to himself.

Marc Mauer writes about Mike and about, let's say, Jamal:

Picture this scene in any middle-class suburb in the United States: students at the local high school, a "good" school with high graduation rates and college acceptances, have been getting into trouble. Nothing too serious, but some drug use, some underage drinking, and a few smashed cars here and there. Parents are cautioned by the principal to check with their kids for signs of trouble.

The parents of one 17-year-old boy had already been concerned about possible drug use, and examine their son's bedroom while he is at school. They discover what appears to be some drug residue and a substantial amount of cash hidden in a drawer. Confronting their son when he comes home, he admits he has been using cocaine and occasionally selling to some friends.

How do the parents respond? Do they call the police, demand that their son be arrested for using and selling drugs, and receive a five-year mandatory minimum for his behavior? The question is ludicrous, of course.

Instead, the parents do what any good middle-class family would do: they consult with their insurance provider and then secure the best treatment program they can find. The criminal justice system never even becomes an issue for them.

A few miles away, picture another family in a low-income section of the city. Their son, too, appears to be getting involved with drugs. Unfortunately for him, his parents have no health insurance, and there are few drug treatment programs available in the neighborhood. Finally, he is picked up one night on a street corner and charged with drug possession with the intent to sell.[3]

The "inner city youth most in need of social services," Randolph Stone, University of Chicago law professor, writing about the same contrast, "enters the resource starved adult criminal justice system."[4]

INCARCERATION IN THE UNITED STATES: A BRIEF HISTORY[5]

In the 1970s, intellectuals and policymakers began to think their way toward the greatest experiment in social control through incarceration in United States and modern world history.[6] At the outset of the 1970s, 314,000 Americans were in our prisons and jails. Policymakers so far have more than septupled that number to 2.3 million and have us spending $60 billion a year to run our correctional institutions.[7] From 645 out of 100,000 human beings in 1998, they have taken us to 750 out of 100,000[8] in what Marc Mauer insists we recognize as "cages."[9] They have brought us to a point where we have vastly longer sentences and are vastly more punitive than anyone else in the world.[10] This is, says Boston University economist Glen Loury, "a historic transformation of the character of American society. We are managing the losers by confinement."[11]

The post–World War II era of economic prosperity, optimism, and generosity, Mauer tells us, favored rehabilitation and had unusually low death penalty rates. During the 1960s, however, rehabilitation was challenged by both the Left and the Right. The Left argued that rehabilitation in a coerced system was unfair and that the current policy of indeterminate sentences gave prison officials in a racially biased institution the right to decide when prisoners would get released. The "law and order" and intellectual Right did not believe criminals could be rehabilitated and thought criminals were released too early: crime would be better controlled if they served their full sentences. Both sides favored determinate sentences. The Left was for short sentences, the Right for long. Against a backdrop of rapid urbanization and migration from the South, an economic downturn, urban unrest, riots, civil rights and antiwar demonstrations and civil disobedience, heroin and cocaine epidemics in the 1960s and 1970s (and crack cocaine in the 1980s), and rising crime rates, the "tough on crime" Right—with its simple position that incapacitated criminals can't commit crime—prevailed. The next three decades are a shameful history of massive incarceration. In 1998, when the prison and jail population had reached a mere 1.2 million, 51.4 percent of the increase had come from "the greater likelihood of a prison sentence upon arrest" and 36.6 percent from "an increase in time served in prison." Only a ninth came from higher offense rates.[12]

While this shameful history is about unrest and fear, about differing theories of crime and punishment, and about so much more, most basically it was about who would get jobs and who would not. The decision to incarcerate was a decision about a surplus workforce.

In the mid-1970s, according to Howard Croft, corporate and political leaders figured out that the United States would be able to compete in a changing world if we became a low-wage nation.[13] As Christian Parenti has demonstrated in *Lockdown America,* many factors were at play. Recovered from World War II, Germany and Japan were competitive, with lower wages, newer capital stock, and greater efficiency than the United States. Meanwhile, American companies had become poorly managed. They did not retool plants or retrain workers, and capital had "shifted increasingly toward speculation in real estate and stocks." By 1960 "American hourly manufacturing labor costs, including social security contributions, were roughly *three times as high* as in Europe, and *ten times as high* as labor costs in Japan." By the early 1970s, moreover, U.S. companies had overaccumulated commodities, consumer demand declined, and prices fell. Simultaneously the unemployment rate dropped, leaving less surplus labor to keep wages down. Wages continued to rise, "though with diminishing vigor" up through 1979. And as the Arab nations gained control over production and markets, fuel prices "began creeping up even before OPEC's 1973 price shock," raising the cost of manufacturing and transportation. Add to this the fact that "between 1964 and 1979 the federal government enacted sixty-two health and safety laws which protected workers and consumers, while thirty-two other laws were passed protecting the environment and regulating energy use. . . . The direct result of this new regime of regulation was a massive increase in the cost of business." Parenti observes:

> At one level the crisis involved a simple contest between the classes. The share of output that went to profits declined while the share going to everything else, including the social wage, increased. The working class was too powerful and, from the management point of view, needed disciplining. . . .
>
> The solution, according to New Right theorists like Milton Friedman, Lawrence Mead, and George Gilder, was to cut government. That is, cut taxes on the corporations and the wealthy, deregulate health and safety regulations, and slash state spending on education, welfare, and social programs. And to initiate this the government would have to plunge the economy into a "cold bath recession" so as to scare and discipline labor. But throughout the seventies the Keynesian consensus was too strong: monetarist austerity and a deregulatory war on labor and consumers had to wait until the accession of Ronald Reagan.[14]

Under Reagan, Federal Reserve chairman Paul Volcker (a 1979 Carter appointee) "dramatically tightened the money supply . . . until interest rates, which had been 7.9 percent in 1979, reached 16.4 percent in 1981." This induced the "most severe recession since the Great Depression," useful, Volcker said, because "the standard of living of the average American has to decline." In Ann Arbor, as in cities across the country, the streets filled with homeless people picking through garbage containers, stretching their hands. According to Barry Bluestone and Bennett Harrison, this "deep recession did precisely what it was designed to . . . it was impossible for organized labor to maintain wage standards let alone raise them. Reductions in wages rippled from one industry to the next and from the center of the country outward."[15] Industry after industry demanded concessions, wage freezes, and cuts from their workers.[16] The Reagan administration supported "the use of contingent labor" at less than union wages, legitimized homework (which led to documented child-labor-law violations and to sweatshops employing children), and, in Parenti's term, "eviscerated" social spending. High technology replaced workers, work was outsourced to offshore and other international sites where very cheap labor was available, and deindustrialization increased dramatically, to the point that "between 1980 and 1985 . . . some 2.3 million manufacturing jobs disappeared for good, taking with them attendant retail activity, the local tax base, and municipal employment." The "combination of tax cuts, welfare gutting, assaults on labor, and the deregulation of banking and finance created an estimated 2,500 to 5,000 new millionaires," while the "poorest tenth of workers saw 20 percent more of their incomes 'swallowed by taxes,'" and there was a "massive expansion of urban ghettoes." African Americans were the most severely affected.[17]

It had affected JB Baker, a prisoner at the Western Wayne Correctional Facility in Plymouth and a member of the Western Wayne Players. Since he would be going home before our next play, and since he wanted to perform, we persuaded the Narcotics Anonymous Group that met in the large East Recreation room on our rehearsal nights that it would fit their agenda to see a play. On April 21, 1997, we presented JB's autobiographical three-scene play, *LeDaryle: My Son*.

The first scene is set in JB's apartment, in 1980. JB comes home, his wife chatters about their new baby and the clothes she has bought, and he tells her that he has lost his job at Chrysler. She tells him it will be easy to find more work, but he explains that is no longer true. Upset and angry, she leaves with her son for her mother's house.

The second scene is set in JB's apartment. He and another laid-off autoworker talk about their situation. One of them knows how to break into the office of a Pontiac attorney.

The third scene is set in the house where JB's wife and son live. It is 1997.

JB is home after seventeen years in prison eager for a relationship with his son. LeDaryle punches the remote, resents his father's absence, is not interested. It is too late. JB struggles. The most he can get from LeDaryle is an agreement to go out for pizza.

JB was rehearsing for what would happen a few days after the performance. He created scene 3 as an idealized, easy reunion with LeDaryle. But Romando Valeroso played LeDaryle realistically, and it was excruciating for JB to play himself. Going home is seldom easy. After the performance, JB thanked us all, almost in tears. We have no idea what happened when he got home. Neither we nor anyone else who knew him inside heard from him.

So what happens in a recession, artificially induced or not, when the paycheck shrinks and work vanishes? The Franklin Delano Roosevelt administration created the Public Works Authority and Civilian Conservation Corps—it found jobs for people, jobs that served the nation. But if the purpose is instead to eliminate work and combat the "excess of democracy"[18] of the recent past, then there is another choice. As Mauer puts it: "in a changed economy with less demand for the labor of many unskilled workers, imprisonment begins to be seen as an appropriate, if unfortunate, outcome."[19] Parenti agrees. He cites criminologist Steven Spritzer's description of "the cast-off populations produced by capitalism as either 'social junk' or 'social dynamite.'"

"Social junk" are those whose spirits and minds are shattered; they are the deinstitutionalized mentally ill, alcoholics, drug addicts, and cast-off impoverished seniors; the lonely, beaten drifters with no expectations of a future and little will to fight . . . they rarely coalesce into an organized political threat.

The other segment of the surplus population—"social dynamite"—are those who pose an actual or potential political challenge. They are that population which threatens to explode: the impoverished low-wage working class and unemployed youth who have fallen below the statistical radar, but whose sprits are not broken and whose expectations for a decent life and social inclusion are dangerously alive and well. . . . This is the class from which the Black Panthers and the Young Lords arose in the sixties and from which sprang the gangs of the 1980s. . . .

Thus social dynamite is a threat to the class and racial hierarchies upon which the private enterprise system depends. This group cannot simply be swept aside. Controlling them requires both a defensive policy of containment and an aggressive policy of direct attack and active destabilization. They are contained and crushed, confined to the ghetto, demoralized and pilloried in warehouse public schools, demonized by a lurid media, sent to prison, and at times dispatched by lethal injection or police bullets. This is the class—or more accurately the caste, because they are increasingly people of color—which must be constantly undermined, divided, intimidated, attacked, discredited, and ultimately kept in check with what Fanon called the "language of naked force."[20]

Thus with the evisceration of social services and the denial of work, the prison building boom began. Each week between 1985 and 1995 a new federal or state prison was built. When Mauer wrote in 1998, over half the total number of prisons in the United States had been constructed in the past twenty years:

> These prisons can be expected to endure and imprison for at least fifty years, virtually guaranteeing a national commitment to a high rate of incarceration. The growth of the system itself serves to create a set of institutionalized lobbying forces that perpetuate a societal commitment to imprisonment through the expansion of vested economic interests. The more than 600,000 prison and jail guards, administrators, service workers, and other personnel represent a potentially powerful political opposition to any scaling-down of the system.[21]

The subsequent nine years bore him out. The prison and jail population just short of doubled in that time. How did this happen?

Joining the "tough on crime" agenda propagated by politicians and others was a "media frenzy" in which increasing print space and television time were devoted to violent crime without a corresponding rise in such crime.[22] The Reagan and Bush administrations developed a brilliant rhetoric of "responsibility": the poor, offenders, the mentally ill, everyone, was responsible for their own fate, no one and nothing else. In the mid-1990s I noticed a generation of young people coming into the university for whom this had become gospel.

In the early Reagan years, the crime fighting, FBI, and prison budgets were increased, and Reagan "stacked the federal bench with mean-spirited, anti-crime, anti-drug zealots, who in turn began handing down law that, as [chief of staff Ed] Meese had wished, 'empowered the prosecution.'" Meese and attorney general William French Smith began demanding changes in the criminal code.[23]

In 1984, Congress passed the Comprehensive Crime Control Act and in 1986 the Anti-Drug Abuse Act. The 1984 act created determinate, mandatory minimum sentences (which took discretionary power from judges and put it in the hands of prosecutors), established a sentencing commission "to devise strict sentencing guidelines," eliminated federal parole, and "expanded the government's ability to seize property and cash from convicted, or even accused drug dealers, in civil or criminal court." What was seized went to the police who had done the seizing, which enhanced their eagerness to "collaborate with federal agencies and try drug cases in federal court."[24] The 1986 act added twenty-nine new mandatory minimum sentences. One of these was the notorious five-year mandatory minimum for five grams of crack cocaine or 500 grams of powder cocaine, a law that targeted African Americans, the primary users of crack, and, Parenti says, "translated into apartheid sentencing."[25] Judges were given power to deny probation or suspended sentences to those convicted under the new laws.

By 1987, the sentencing commission guidelines were in place, "carrying," Mauer says, "a heavy presumption of imprisonment for most offenders and little regard for any mitigating circumstances."[26] "Thus began in earnest," Parenti remarks "the one-sided race war of the late eighties and nineties . . . open season on 'social dynamite' and 'social junk' . . . open season on urban addicts, economically discarded youth, and petty dealers . . . the beginning of a nationwide wave of raids and ghettos sweeps," like New York City's Operation Pressure Point and the "notorious Operation Hammer in which 14,000 people—mostly young Black men—were arrested and booked in mobile command centers during a massive paramilitary occupation of south LA's deindustrialized ghettos."[27]

Perhaps one might have hoped for changes under the Clinton Democrats despite their move to the center. The early months of 1993, Mauer says, "represented a time of cautious optimism for criminal justice reform" thanks to a growing awareness of racial disparities in the criminal justice system and numerous well-articulated proposals of alternatives to prison. In less than a year, however, "this optimistic scenario had been transformed into a repressive criminal justice climate rivaling that of any time during the preceding twenty years," created by "a vicious cycle of reaction composed of political grand-standing, media sensationalism, and organized advocacy by 'law and order' proponents." The shift was dramatic and tragic. Mauer:

> One recent series of events is quite telling. Early in President Clinton's first term in office, following the Los Angeles riots, he called attention to the nation's urban crisis. Many experts were recommending a $60 billion economic package to stimulate job creation and economic development. Assuming that the political climate at the time would not support such an expenditure, the administration instead proposed a $30 billion package. Caught up in deficit reduction fever, though, the House passed only a $16 billion bill, which was promptly killed by the Senate in favor of a $5 billion allocation for unemployment insurance and some other domestic programs. The rationale for the cuts was essentially that the federal government could no longer "throw money at problems."
>
> Who would have benefited the most from such a stimulus package? Clearly, those people who are both most victimized by crime and by limited economic opportunities—primarily low-income African American and Latino communities. Just a year later, though, members of Congress apparently had second thoughts about such spending and determined that they could in fact allocate $30 billion to these communities. This time, though, the appropriation took the form of a massive crime bill loaded with 60 new death penalty offenses, $8 billion in prison construction, "three strikes" sentencing, and other provisions certain to escalate the prison population. Amidst these punitive allocations were modest funds for programs to prevent crime and to reduce violence against women.
>
> The members of Congress did not state, of course, that the result of the legislation would be to incarcerate impoverished young black and Latino men. At current rates, though, we can expect that about two thirds of the prison cells constructed through this act will be filled by minorities. This is not exactly what neighborhood leaders had in mind when they called for targeted investments to help rebuild their beleaguered communities.[28]

The White House, "trying to take 'the crime issue' away from Republicans," had joined forces with them. They went so far as to suppress a report by a Justice Department working group formed by Janet Reno that questioned the impact of mandatory minimum policy on low-level drug offenders. Former deputy attorney general Philip Heymann described the Clinton approach as "the most careful political calculation, with absolutely sublime indifference to the real nature of the problem."[29]

"THE MEMBERS OF CONGRESS DID NOT STATE . . ."

Let me repeat Mauer's words: "*The members of Congress did not state, of course, that the result of the legislation would be to incarcerate impoverished young black and Latino men.*" In 2005 Michigan black youth were 88 percent more likely to be arrested than whites, 50 percent more likely than whites to be referred to juvenile court, 97 percent less likely to get placed into a diversion program than whites, 2.6 times more likely than whites to be placed in secure detention, 65 percent more likely than whites to have a petition filed by the prosecuting attorney, 38 percent more likely than whites to be found guilty of a delinquent offense in the Family Division of the circuit court, 54 percent less likely to get placed on probation than whites, and 4.2 times more likely than whites to be incarcerated in a secure correctional facility.[30]

In 1997, according to the Census of Juveniles in Residential Placement (CJRP), African American youth had a custody rate of over five times that of Caucasians. And while only 23 percent of youth in Michigan were minorities that year, minorities made up 61 percent of youth in detention.[31] The proportions haven't changed. The current figure at Boysville, where PCAP works with incarcerated youth, is 61.7 percent African American and 3.3 percent Hispanic.[32]

Minority youth and adults are more likely to be stopped while driving. Minority youth and adults selling drugs are easier to find on street corner drug markets than white youth and adults selling and using drugs behind closed doors in attractive suburban homes. More likely to be arrested, minority youth and adults are also more likely to come before a judge and jury dressed in jail clothing, disheveled and tired from a noisy night in the jail, than a white youth whose family meets bail and who arrives in a nice jacket and tie. And so the minority youth or adult is more likely to receive a sentence, or a longer sentence. When Suzanne Gothard and I went to Wayne County Court to support Jerry Moore, the young white and Asian American prosecuting attorneys were sharply dressed. They, the judge, the police who came into court to testify, the bailiff, and the stenographer were all very comfortable and casual, even affable, in their interactions with each other. The defense attorneys were mostly African American, in tired clothing. They did not rub shoulders with the court folk. Jerry and most others came into court fatigued and bedraggled in green Wayne Country Jail scrubs. When Jerry made one of the most powerful pleas I've ever heard—about his growth in prison during his earlier incarceration, about his struggles to find employment as a former felon, about his participation in the Annual Exhibition of Art by Michigan Prisoners, about his poetry, about the essays he published while inside, about his job, about the mother of his baby and the down payment he and she had just put on a mortgage, about his mistake driving away from the police when stopped, because he had no car insurance, about his *life*—we watched everyone from the stenographer up to the prosecuting attorneys and judge instinctively freeze and turn aside, turn off. It was written all over them. A few of them shuffled papers. Perhaps they had come to do justice, but we sensed and saw that they *understood* their real goal was to put away everyone who came before them. Because we and others had written strong letters, the judge "generously" gave him concurrent, instead of consecutive, sentences of three to seven years. In the hall afterward, his lawyer, a woman who had experienced a stroke recently and who had fought hard for Jerry, was in tears.[33]

At midyear 2006, 41 percent of males incarcerated in federal and state prisons and local jails were African American. Relative to their numbers in the general population, about 4.8 percent of all African American men were in custody at that moment, compared to 1.9 percent of Hispanic men, and .7 percent of white men. African American men were incarcerated at 6.5 times the rate of white men.[34] On February 2, 2008, the Pew Center reported that "for the first time in history more than one in every 100 adults in America are in jail or prison": one in thirty men between twenty and twenty-four, but one in nine black men in that age group.[35] The figures go on and on. Most readers of this book will have seen them, many readers will be both infuriated and tired of hearing year after year that there are more black males in prison than in college and on and on and on.

What does this mean? It means destroyed, challenged communities, where those citizens who are committed to those communities, who build lives and fight for their neighborhoods and children, who resist, are up against terrible odds. It means a disproportionate ratio of women to men in affected neighborhoods, means men who play the field, children raised by single mothers, children whose mothers are incarcerated being raised by others, children who themselves have a better than 50 percent chance of themselves entering the criminal justice system. It means youth who see prison as a ritual, a coming of age. It means the spread of AIDS and hepatitis C and mental illness both inside and outside the prisons, it means the deadening of creativity, spirit, and nurturing qualities, the breeding of distrust. It means illiteracy, unemployability, humiliation and trauma, loss of status, shame for children and families, displacement from home to home. It goes hand in hand with underfunded schools and denial of health care and loss of communities' formal mechanisms of control through family, church, and school. It goes hand in hand with substance abuse, prostitution, and physical danger, with youth looking over their shoulders as they walk home from school or cruise the streets as high-school dropouts. Detroit youth have the lowest urban graduation rate in America: 24.9 percent. Half of them will go to jail and prison. Black urban youth exemplify the way mass incarceration means the "systematic imprisonment of whole groups of the population." They are a new "social group" that Bruce Western calls the "mass imprisonment generation—black men without college education born since 1965" and that, with others in their economic bracket, Nell Bernstein says have become a "criminal caste." Almost all prisoners, and in many states the formerly incarcerated as well, are disenfranchised. They have no vote, no political power.[36] The effects of all of this are, in Mauer's words, "shattering" and "catastrophic."[37]

And the effects are economic. Poor rural youth and adults can remain in their towns because poor incarcerated minorities from the cities bring jobs, higher federal and state funding, and sometimes more representation in Congress or the state legislature, since prisoners are counted as local residents.[38] It means a cheap workforce. In Michigan, which has the nation's slowest economy, prisoners who are paid cents an hour replace municipal workers, cleaning litter, or ice, or weeds from highways, streets, and cemeteries. Elsewhere prisoners answer phone calls for state tourist bureaus or airlines, package Christmas gifts, and sew buttons on expensive designer jackets. Health maintenance organizations spring up to provide what is often poor care to people who were without insurance prior to incarceration, phone companies make huge profits off long-distance, raised-rate calls from prisoners to families strapped for funds, and companies get exclusive contracts for prisoner clothing. You and I pay for construction and maintenance of prisons, for supplies, for goods, for health care, for the salaries of an expanding prison workforce: in Michigan in 1983, one in eleven state employees worked in the correctional system; it is now one in three. Money is siphoned off from education, firefighting, safety, environmental protection, and other social services.[39]

The effects are economic. Because it is about cheap labor and denial of work, our policymakers overwhelmingly choose prison over alternative educational, treatment, and job-training solutions. With their urge to incarcerate, they remove JB Baker and hundreds of thousands more from the economy, including "socially integrated offenders," people with educational backgrounds and jobs who are unlikely to reoffend, and they keep people long past the peak years in which they are inclined to commit crime, at a cost of $25,000 to $35,000 a year per prisoner.[40] Nils Christie compares this to social control through incarceration in other times and places:

> Gulags, Western type will not exterminate, but they have the possibility of removing from ordinary social life a major segment of potential trouble-makers for most of those persons' lives. They have the potentiality of transforming what otherwise would have been those persons' most active life-span into an existence very close to the German expression of a life not worth living.[41]

A more fully accurate comparison, closer to home, is to the post-Reconstruction criminalization (through laws about loitering and debt) and incarceration of former slaves and their use as free labor, building roads and working the land, sometimes on the very plantation grounds they once worked as slaves.[42]

INTENTION

Mauer's eleventh chapter is named "Unintended Consequences." The book of essays he published three years later with Meda Chesney-Lind is instead titled *Invisible Punishment: The Collateral Consequences of Mass Imprisonment.* That is preferable, because of course he knows that at a certain point politicians and policymakers realize what they are doing and choose to do it. It becomes intentional. He clearly implies this when he writes that "the members of Congress did not state, of course, that the result of the legislation would be to incarcerate impoverished young black and Latino men." And in chapter 12 he puts it squarely:

The toll that this has taken on the African American community, and increasingly the Latino community, is now truly staggering. Women of color are increasingly experiencing the combined impact of social and economic trends, as the confluence of poverty, substance abuse, prostitution, and incarceration envelopes larger numbers each year. One would think that such a state of affairs should give pause to those who smugly contend that prison "works." But thirty years of politically inspired rhetoric, *willful* ignorance of research and programmatic developments, and constrained policy options have conspired to make the United States choose the most punitive of responses.[43]

If it is willful and if the consequences are so catastrophic—so many stunted lives, so much state violence, so many physical and spiritual deaths—then we are talking about crime, perhaps crime against humanity, and the tragedy is that it will not be brought to court.[44]

Mauer also refers to the "current malaise." Jonathan Kozol argues that our schooling has taught most of us to be "ethically indifferent." Nils Christie refers to Zygmunt Bauman's study of the "production of moral indifference in modern societies."[45] Others talk about consent and about the phenomenon of normalcy. The catastrophe becomes invisible. We live with it, accept it, and except at rare moments, regard it as normal. I go to the annual Convention of the American Correctional Association and listen to interesting talks, I give one myself, I walk around the city-block-wide floor of booths and learn about the latest in concertina wire quality and about mobile prison cells. Everyone is friendly ("You're from Michigan! What do you do? Do you know so-and-so?") and proud of the products he or she is selling. They are professional and do good work. It is like any conference. Massive incarceration is the law of the land. We don't know, or we forget, the agony, the deprivation, the desperate children who cut themselves, the disease. We easily stand by while specific groups of fellow citizens are taken from their homes and sent to camps and prisons. Some of us volunteer in the urban and rural schools and communities they are taken from, some of us in their places of containment. Simon Wiesenthal and Elie Wiesel, writing about the Holocaust, say it was the bystanders who hurt them most.[46]

"Those of us on the outside," says Jessica Mitford,

do not like to think of wardens and guards as our surrogates. Yet they are, and they are intimately locked in a deadly embrace with their human captives behind the prison walls. By extension so are we.

A terrible double meaning is thus imparted to the original question of human ethics: Am I my brother's keeper?[47]

Some of my students and I attend a talk by Robert Moses in the early fall of 2006 and hear him identify as the central problem of our country that "we do not think of others' children as our own." My students make this a theme in English 310 and English 411, my film course on United States prisons. When in 411 we watch *Maximum Security University* (1999), a film edited by California Prison Focus that analyzes the official prison tapes of corrections officers killing prisoners in the wedge-shaped recreation yard at Corcoran Prison, we focus on the killing of William Martinez and ask ourselves, Is William Martinez our brother?

William Martinez, child growing up in Oakland, inducted into Nuestra Familia, armed robber, murdered in prison. Mauer pauses at the end of a chapter where he has compared the cost-effectiveness of incarceration to the cost-effectiveness of alternatives. Such analysis, he says, "can lose sight of the human factors involved."

When one of our loved ones is ill or in trouble, most of us rarely hesitate to employ whatever financial and human resources we can muster to deal with the problem. This might involve specialized medical care, tutors for learning-disabled children, or a nursing home for an ageing relative. Deciding how to use taxpayer funds wisely is a contentious issue, of course. One is led to wonder, however, to what extent the zeal with which efforts are made to demonstrate the value of imprisonment is a reflection of the "otherness" of those being imprisoned.[48]

Is William Martinez other? Is he, with his poverty and his violence, not our brother?

Was "William Martinez"[49] not our child when he was born into a crowded tenement, dangerous streets and a disruptive and disrupted family, when he shared his primary school classroom with rats, tattered old textbooks, and a leaky roof? Was he not our child when he watched his father beat his mother, when he was sexually assaulted by his cousin, sister, brother, mother, or father, whipped mercilessly with an extension cord, when a bullet or cop took his father, or his mother, or his older brother away? When corporate leaders and politicians and policymakers decide that "William Martinez" is trash and must spend twenty years in prison on a mandatory minimum drug conviction that is longer than any sentence for such an offense anywhere else in the world, is he not our brother?

It is a very difficult question. It has all kinds of implications, however we answer it, for who we are and will be in the world.

Is it the wrong question? Possibly. It may be too harsh, unrealistic. Asking it may be a failure to see the world as it is and to accept and embrace our place in it and either do or not do our piece of kindness somewhere. Still, it is one of the oldest questions in the world, and it seems intellectually, academically, and morally responsible to go to places where the question is in our face and to see how we come out.

It is such questions and others that my students begin to confront as they enter the places inhabited by those on the other side of the coin that came up heads for us.

In English 310 on September 26, 2006, we discuss Peter Sacks's *Standardized Minds*. We go around the room in a loose talk circle, sharing our personal experiences. It becomes clear that Sacks is right in his observation that many women and minority people find the tests difficult because their more holistic approach to experience makes them see many possible answers to a question. Yet everyone in 310 did well enough to reach one of the country's best public universities. It is also clear that we represent Sacks's statistic that for every additional $10,000 of parental income, SAT test scores go up thirty points.[50] We tell stories of expensive preparatory courses and personal tutors. The talk is anecdotal and amused, avoids the obvious. But finally it is before us. We who have come, most of us, from such affluence, we who have made it to an elite institution, we who have done so well on the tests, are going to Cooley High School, to the Calumet Center, to Boysville, to Vista Maria, where so few of the youth had or have any chance to do well on the tests. What is it about, that *we* get to go to such places and have the experience—however powerfully motivated we are—of working with *them*? We didn't choose our place of birth, but this is the reality. What is it about? Do responsibilities come with doing a lively theater workshop at Cooley High School? Or not? If so, what are they?

The *First Year Student Survey 2006* gives a partial picture of University of Michigan students.[51] While many students change dramatically in their opinions and beliefs over their four years, and while English 310 and 319 students generally, but not necessarily, have more progressive values than most, their backgrounds sharply accent their differences from the youth and adults in the high school, juvenile facility, and prison workshops.

Students who entered the university in 2006 have affluent parents: 57.8 percent of their parents have an annual income of over $100,000, 34.5 percent over $150,000, 23.1 percent over $200,000, and 15 percent over $250,000. The student body is disproportionately white and has lived in disproportionately white areas: 85.3 percent of students whose parents attended the University of Michigan and 79.1 percent of those whose parents did not, come from mostly white or completely white neighborhoods; 71.9 percent are white/Caucasian, 15.6 percent Asian American/Asian, 4.9 percent Mexican American / Chicano, Puerto Rican, and other Latino, 4.4 percent African American / black, and 1.7 percent American Indian / Alaska Native and Native Hawaiian / Pacific Islander. They come from two-parent households: 82.6 percent of their parents are living together, and only 2.1 percent of them have a parent who has died. They have sterling high school records: 90 percent had average grades of A⁻ or above. All but 11.2 percent took advance placement courses in high school, and all but 15.5 percent took advance placement exams. Their four top career choices are engineering, medicine, business, and law.

Just over 10.2 percent of incoming women and 18.2 percent of incoming men agree that "racial discrimination is no longer a problem in America"; 57.6 percent of the women and 62 percent of the men agree that "affirmative action in college admissions should be abolished," although a survey of all university students showed that approximately 75 percent opposed a proposition that year which swept away affirmative action in the state. Almost half, 43.8 percent of women and 48.4 percent of men, agree that "there is too much concern in the courts for the rights of criminals," whereas 52.4 percent of women and 47.2 percent of men would have the death penalty abolished. A strong majority, 71.5 percent, believe that "only volunteers should serve in the armed forces," and 34.4 percent of women and 43.5 percent of men believe that "undocumented immigrants should be denied access to public education." Three-quarters (73.6 percent) believe that "through hard work everybody can succeed." Only 5.1 percent of men and 8.2 percent of women expect to participate in student protest and demonstrations, while 23.3 percent of men and 48 percent of women expect to participate in volunteer or community service work. A very small percent consider themselves far left (2.7) or far right (.6), while 39.3 percent call themselves liberal, 37.4 middle of the road, and 19.4 conservative.

On the whole an entering class will reflect the values of the homes they come from, and for some of them much will change. But what we see are comfortable and privileged students, protective of their class position, empathetic and proactive in limited ways, the women more progressive than the men.

Those are statistics. University of Michigan students also have a deserved and long-standing reputation for outspoken, often radical, involvement in the issues of their day, and the university over the past years has increasingly committed itself to community service and social justice work and to making it possible for students from challenged backgrounds to attend and find support. We have many students with great heart and courage and whose engagement with the world makes me blush for my own inactivity in the years of the silent generation. Students who interview for English 310 and 319 are a blend: curious, aware that something is wrong and wanting to go and find out, relatively naive (with exceptions), privileged (with exceptions), white women (with exceptions), risk takers, and almost to a person from very different worlds than those of most of the high school students, incarcerated youth, and prisoners they will encounter.

One thing that Myles Horton and Paulo Freire stand for in common is their refusal, in theory and practice, to be elitist outsiders in their work with exploited and oppressed communities. They advocate and practice dialogues that are dominated by no one and held between people committed to change. They have a profound respect for the opinions, ideas, creativity, courage, and possibilities of every person. They are models for the work of PCAP. In English 310 and 319 we read Horton's *The Long Haul* and Freire's *Pedagogy of the Oppressed,* and each term I give a quiz on the latter. If I don't, the language is so difficult that some students don't complete the reading and we are doomed to a discussion either of banking education or of who is oppressor and who is oppressed, issues broached in the first chapters. This is a disservice to Freire, to those classmates who have completed the book and are eager to talk about it, and to the people in our workshops. Each time I include the following question:

3a (Ten minutes) You are a student in English 319 at the University of Michigan, a university in the state of Michigan, one of the states of the United States of America. It is February 21, 2006. You and your classmates are working in teams in Michigan prisons and juvenile facilities and in

Detroit high schools. Draw a picture that represents the coded existential situation of the members of this class.

3b (Three minutes) List one to three generative themes that you imagine would come from the decodification of the picture.

The question is based on Freire's discussion of the process by which an investigative team works in a community where it has been invited to assist in a project of resistance and change. The team, collaborating with community members, observes and asks questions. At the conclusion of the investigation, they present drawings or photographs of specific community images. These representations generate discussion and analysis and provoke questions. And out of the analysis come crucial themes that lead to further analysis as the community moves toward whatever well-considered action it is willing to risk. The photo or picture is the coded existential situation: the discussion, analysis, and question asking are the process of decodification.[52]

Sometimes at the end of the quiz I ask two students to take all the quiz pictures into another room, then to return and draw on the board a composite picture. We then engage in a process of decodification, sometimes going to the board and adding to the drawing. In so doing we arrive at some of our own generative themes. We become clearer about our conflicts and about our choices.

I have in mind a very simple composite picture drawn a number of years ago. On the left an imposing prison structure with inhabited cells. On the right the University of Michigan, an array of buildings with stick figures possibly—I don't remember exactly—at desks, walking the streets, entering fancy shops. And a road between the two, and on the road, headed toward the university, a little car with four stick figure students returning from facilitating workshops at the prison. I don't remember the discussion now, except that it was engaged and lively. I imagine little added drawings of dollar signs, question marks, sketches and arrows that indicated power dynamics.[53]

I think now of the car. Depending on compatibility, most of the drives we take are intense. On the way out they are full of our personal lives, preparation for the workshop, anticipation, worry. On the way back they hold the sense, the agony, of leaving. We analyze what happened, talk about the participants and dynamics, and we laugh, celebrate, worry. And at the heart of it all is a rich tension over the two places we inhabit and the one the prisoners inhabit at this moment in time and over the fact that they will never inhabit the university. And at the heart of it all is a stirring rising from a first experience of solidarity and shared work in the face of national hostility to the incarcerated and national injustice, a stirring that can lead to many new places.

Were the prisoners to draw, it is possible that they would make the same picture. Possibly the car would be headed the other direction. And the decodification would have other aspects, another tone, but the same tension would be there and the same stirring.

While the prison population continues to surge.

CHAPTER THREE

The University Courses

At the end of a long quiet corridor is 3275 Angell Hall. When the Department of English moved from Haven Hall years ago and the lottery brought me second pick among senior faculty, I chose this office for its windows, distance from the department office, and small open space outside where we could crunch down for small group meetings. Around Thanksgiving each year I tack a handwritten sheet to the bulletin board on the door, listing interview times for English 319. If more than one student turns up for an interview, I'll talk with as many of four of them together. They glance around the impossibly cluttered office and squeeze in.

I ask them first what interests them about the course and get responses ranging from "It sounds good" to "I like helping people" to "I like acting" to "This gives me a chance to get out of the classroom and have a hands-on experience" to stories of previous commitments to community action or personal connections with incarceration or with the communities from which the incarcerated come. I probe a little to allow them to tell me more, and then I talk for ten to fifteen minutes. They need to know what they are getting into, what I will ask of them, and the ways the experience might be both hard and painful.

I take them through the course: the strenuous first weeks—reading, evening workshops, a full-day retreat, extra classroom hours, and travel to sites for orientations; the weekly workshop at a high school, juvenile facility, or prison and weekly team meetings; and the final performances at the sites—the programs, flowers, and high that everyone experiences. I tell them about the texts, the weekly journals, and the final analytic essay, and I try to give them a feeling for what will happen in our classroom. Then I tell them what I expect of them.

I ask them to respect the youth and adults they will work with. Almost none of them will get to the University of Michigan, which immediately differentiates them from my interviewees, no matter what their own race or background. Most of those in my office come from at least relative affluence: the schools and prisons serve and hold people from relative or deep poverty. By far the majority of those we create plays with are African American. And so the neighborhoods, the experiences, the stories, the vocabulary, the issues, the styles are significantly different. My interviewees have experienced pain, but the odds are that those in the workshops will have experienced more, sometimes very much more. Respecting them means embracing everything they walk in with and being up front about what we bring. Everyone in the room has energy, spirit, and content for the plays.

I ask them to respect everyone at the facility, even staff who behave in a way that doesn't seem to merit respect, shouting at, humiliating, insulting, and arbitrarily penalizing the youth or adults. There are no easy jobs in these schools or prisons, which are largely hierarchical, often disrupted, sometimes dangerous places that have little real public support and are full of people who mostly don't want to be there. Many teachers, correctional officers, and other staff take the stress home with them. So greet everyone, make small talk, thank them. If they block you from something you need for the work, don't get in their face. If you can't negotiate it, back off, go home, call me: we'll figure it out. Remember: they work there, and there are several levels on which you don't belong there. If you are impolite or dismissive, they can make it difficult for you to get to the workshop, and being in the workshop and working well there is our priority.

I ask them to believe in the youth and prisoners, believe that they will pull up their talent, work together, and have a performance. This may turn out to be the hardest thing I ask. They may see no evidence that it is working, only see people arguing, closed down, acting out, too affected by their environment, by family issues, by illness, to focus. The youth or prisoners may enter the room two weeks before the performance and announce they don't want to do the play anymore. And they will watch my interviewees like hawks: University of Michigan students are outsiders and likely, like so many others, to give up on them. And yet they so much, underneath, want the students to be the right people, the people who believe in them. So they know when believing in them has stopped, and when it stops, everything changes. It resembles a relationship: if two people believe in each other, everything blossoms; if they don't, the relationship continues, but nothing grows. There will be a performance, but it will be so much less than it might have been.

I ask them to practice a process of discovery. We do not bring texts to be memorized or lesson plans. We are not teachers. What is created depends upon who is in the room and on what the processes of improvisation and listening make possible. Ideas, stories, characters, themes, and messages emerge from any or all of us, and everyone patches them into a play. Control freaks or students who think of themselves as future teachers, actors, and directors will have to shake old habits and procedures.

I tell them English 319 is hard and can be painful. It is not hard because of the workload, nor because it will consume their thinking and feeling time like no other course. It is hard because the youth and adults shouldn't and often don't trust university students, who are likely there to add a "community service" or "outreach activity" component to their resume, or who have come for an easy A or to study "urban youth" or the "criminal mind" or be cool and to regale their friends with stories about ghetto kids and criminals. Such attitudes and behavior are abusive. My interviewees *will* get a grade, may very well want this on their resume, will write analytically about their experience, and will share it with those close to them and do so without abuse. But the youth and adults will find out for themselves which kind of students the interviewees are. They will ask hard questions: "So what grade did you get for today?" "So you get to leave here and I have to stay, what's that about?" "My mind is like a black box, you are pampered and comfortable, you have no idea what is in it." And they will shut down or act out, then watch what the students say and do. They will see 319 students come back each week, writhing, struggling, trying things out, confronting, asking for help, and the youth and prisoners will know who they are. It is hard not to be trusted, hard to be tested.

I tell them about Asia Orlando. Because she had a one-year-old son, Asia was enrolled in night school at Henry Ford High School in the fall of 1995. When Roberta Herter offered her English students the option of participating in English 310 workshops, Asia chose both photography and theater. After we brought her and her classmates to Ann Arbor to see a play by Oyamo, she told her grandmother that she wanted to go to college. Two weeks later, when two gangs stepped outside a skating rink to fight and the crowd followed, Asia's sister advised leaving, but Asia wanted to see what would happen. A stray AK-47 bullet pierced her head. I might tell them of the shaken voice of Nate Jones on my answering machine, Tony Jenkins arriving at my door unable to talk, the gathering at my house to watch the perfunctory news clip, to cry, and to relate phone calls to mothers, who explained to their 319 daughters that "it is different" in the ghetto or whose sympathy dimmed when they learned of Asia's baby. I might tell them about Asia's photo of her son in the photography album, about testifying by Henry Ford and university students at the end of the play they decided to complete in her honor. I don't tell them about how Asia, and Hasham on the Adrian Training School phone with me after his uncle had unloaded five bullets into Hasham's body and Moyes showing me where his mother broke his arm twice when he was five and telling me of his fourteen suicide attempts and Ben, wrongly convicted, trying to kill himself in prison, haunt me. I don't tell them about my therapy for secondary trauma.

I do tell them about the high schoolers wounded by guns, about a boy now in prison for sleeping with a sixteen-year-old schoolmate, about those evicted for fighting and drugs, the odds they'll end in prison. These are not simply "odds" now, but youth the interviewees will know who will disappear onto the streets, without e-mail or phones or trust. I tell them about incarcerated youth on suicide watch, the girl screaming in her room, the girl slamming her head against the wall again and again, the girl sent to the psychiatric hospital for slashing herself, the girls' play about slashing, the girl's poem about what she would do with a broken bottle to the man who killed her mother. I tell them about boys in orange uniforms, runaways or potential runaways, desperate because nothing is working for them or because someone back home is with their girl or because they are being physically or sexually abused by boys in their unit. I tell them about restraint methods that prevent youth from hurting themselves or others, about Maxey Boys Training School with its fence, its wrist monitors, the new policy of body cavity searches at the end of family visits. I tell them I know men in prison who wore ear necklaces in Vietnam, men and women who have been inside too long, who are cut off from their children, who live in humiliating and traumatizing conditions. And I tell them of another kind of pain: in the schools and prisons they will see close up the economic injustice of their country. I tell them that once they see or hear such pain, it will be theirs, to respond to in their own way. I tell them we talk these things out in class.

Then I tell them about the excitement and pleasure of working with kinetic talented youth and engaged, highly talented adults. I tell them how much they will know by the end of the class, about the exhilaration of the performances. And I tell them about their classmates, people sharing a common risk, struggling with each other, backing each other, and forming lasting bonds. If they still wish to take the course, I ask them to think it over and let me know for sure in an e-mail message, giving me their reasons including any new ones in case I have to decide among them. I hear from almost all and post a list around December 12.

⧗

In early January we gather for our first two-hour class, thirty-six of us. I go over the syllabus, talk in some depth about the high school, juvenile facility, and prison sites and about our liaisons, about requirements and grading. After a break, we stand in a circle and imagine characters for ourselves. I then dump several bags of costumes and props on the floor so they can choose what will help them define their character. They leave the room (I stay, creating myself a character with what remains) and silently get into character, reenter the room, and interact. Next, as ourselves, we meet one on one. I do a high five with Natalie and we say our names. We touch fingers and say where we are from. We shake hands and name our favorite food.[1] The final exercise is a snake. We line up, half-circled through the room. Greg, at one end, turns to Alison and says his name accompanied by a sound and motion that indicates how he is feeling in the class. He moves on to Melissa then to Andy and on along the snake, repeating the name, sound, and motion. Alison turns to Melissa and follows him. And so on. To end our first class, we each repeat our name, sound, and motion and explain what we meant by them.[2] Thus begins a demanding week.

Our assignment for Thursday is Jonathan Kozol's *The Night Is Dark and I Am Far from Home,* which is an analysis of the strategies by which our schooling prepares us to be "good citizens," ethically indifferent to the oppression of others. I pair students off with partners they don't know and scatter them to the hall or empty rooms nearby. They take twenty minutes of equal speaking to share personal stories the book has called up. They analyze their stories and discuss the book. When they return, they may write a question or statement on the board. We start from the board or stories or issues that they volunteer. We see what is in the room and dig in. Often, but not always, they revert to habits from other classes, becoming theoretical, distant, and even competitive.

That night we clear a very large classroom of its chairs and for three and one-half hours, in pairs, small groups, and one large group, engage in games, exercises, and improvisations that are full of energy and fun. After two hours three former 319 students, PCAP members, arrive. The group numbers off into pairs and takes three minutes to establish a relationship in which one is prisoner, the other visitor. I then position them on opposite sides of a row of eighteen facing chairs. The PCAP members introduce themselves as belligerent, impatient correctional officers, the prisoners and visitors put on blindfolds, and the officers shake them down and lead them to their seats. Prisoner and visitor, constantly and arbitrarily harassed by the officers, talk for ten minutes, then each for eight minutes listens to the other speak an internal monologue, then they speak together another eight minutes, then during the final five minutes the visitor must inform the prisoner that he or she will not return. They are escorted back to the wall. I turn out the lights, and, blindfolds off, they sit or lie and unwind. The pairs then join and compose quick poems, visitor to prisoner and vice versa. All the visitors read their poems aloud simultaneously, and the prisoners do the same. It has been an intense, harrowing experience, not a replication of a real visiting room, but a replication of some of the worst of the experience of incarceration. We finish the evening by circling up and debriefing.[3]

A few students come begrudgingly to the full-day retreat at the Wesley Foundation Lounge, located in the First Methodist Church on State Street, a greater problem for the English 310 fall retreat if there is a home football game. One or two oversleep and arrive late, and sometimes someone is absent because of a wedding or funeral (we pass a tape recorder, they listen, then introduce themselves later, in class). We have access to a stove and refrigerator and take small breaks and break for a lunch composed of the food they have brought to share. We move chairs and couches into a large circle in the large brown-paneled room. I take one of the few stiff chairs, to stay alert. Coffee waits at two stations, traffic noises push against the windows. Someone begins. She tells the origin of her names and what she would like us to know about her. She tells us her schedule, whether she has a car, whether she wishes to work with boys or girls or men or women, and whether she wishes to work in a high school, a juvenile facility, or a prison. She tells us what it is in her life that has her willing or eager to work with people who most people she knows believe to be dangerous, or scum, or at best not worth her time. Some instinct may have told her she needed to do this. She may have worked at a summer camp for children with AIDS or interned in Washington with the ACLU and gone each day into Southeast DC to talk with indigent seniors. Her sister or brother might have cerebral palsy or be addicted to a substance and in and out of treatment. She herself might be fighting physical or mental impairment, have abusive parents, have spent time in a country jail or juvenile facility, have a father who spent ten years in prison when she was a child. She might have activist parents who inspire her, might have interned with the American Friends Service Committee and read hundreds of letters from prisoners about indecent health care, might be a member of a very effective campus antisweatshop organization. She will have stories for us. We will ask her questions. As she speaks, she might be shy or scared, she might become impassioned, might cry, might make a commitment to the space and those of us in it that will send us into a long, vulnerable, open, high-stakes day.

The week has given the students extensive, varied, focused, often one-on-one interactions with each other, and now they are ready to scramble and find partners. We go around one last time, saying names, schedules, where they wish to work, and whether they have a car. Then they are on their feet, finding each other, bunching up and talking, negotiating, remembering that I've asked them to be patient with this process, and finally coming to me in pairs and claiming sites. Everyone waits until the process is complete, then participates in the adjustments we have to make. Every site needs at least one workshop, everyone needs a partner, each team needs a car. We rearrange the chairs and some stay to clean up and dump the big green bags in the dumpsters out back. Everyone is exhausted and exhilarated. They will write about this day in their journals, come back to it in their final papers. They have realized that they are in a class of amazing people. We have told personal stories and made commitments to each other and to the work we will do. I know this doesn't insure that we'll be a great class. It only means that we have given ourselves a chance.

The following week, we have a second evening workshop. Students learn more exercises, games, and improvisations to bring to their workshops and in the final exercise get their first whiff of our working method. They spread out through the darkened room and out loud hold a ten-minute conversation with someone in their life they have been unable to talk with and need to confront. They speak and imagine the responses. Since everyone is speaking, no one overhears: the conversations are private. I leave the room or walk rapidly back and forth so that I also hear nothing, or only snatches. Some conversations are intensely personal and difficult, so when we sit on the floor in a circle afterward, I only ask for volunteers to share their conversations. I take notes as they do, alert for stories where third persons are implied. I choose such a story and ask the storyteller, if she is willing to put her story up, to choose two others to play herself and her antagonist. Ann chooses two women to play herself and a roommate she is confronting about stealing her boyfriend. She gives them details about the characters and situation, and they begin the confrontation. After a while I scoot around the circle and whisper to Billy to walk in on the scene as the boyfriend. He does, and then I whisper to Gig to come in as his buddy, who may be attracted to either Ann or the antagonist. Later I stop the action and ask if others wish to replace any of the actors and take the situation to a new place, or if they wish to add a character.[4] This is how the students and youth and adults will create plays, building on stories and characters offered by the participants. We debrief, ask Ann what happened as she watched her conversation played out.

Team meetings are crucial. I meet an hour each week with two or three teams, grouped according to the kind of facility they work at. Like the weekly journals,[5] these sessions keep me informed and enable me to be helpful. They report, I listen, I ask, they converse, they brainstorm. I encourage and strategize with them after a disastrous session, celebrate and strategize with them after a strong session, trying to move the group and play forward. I often detect what they have not detected: problems within the group, between the team members, or between a team member and a participant at the site. I am able to warn and help them respond. The first two team meetings are preparation: no team can go to their site until they have met twice with me and been oriented by their liaison.

In the first meeting I ask for questions, concerns, and anxieties. They may wish to know more about the prison or school. They may ask: How does this actually work? Will the kids like me? Will I be respected by the men? What do we do the first time? I have never acted; will I be able to do this? What kind of space will we be in? What should I wear? What if some- one asks for a relationship? I answer their questions and am reassuring. If their site is a prison or juvenile facility, they are nervous: their reading for the week is a PCAP handbook excerpt full of "warning stories," accounts of all the mistakes 310, 319, and PCAP members have made over the years, some of them leading to elimination of a facilitator, some to elimination of a workshop, all of them putting the work at risk. I reemphasize the importance of obeying rules and regulations[6] and tell them that if they do make a mistake, they must tell me immediately, so I can troubleshoot and do damage control. From me they will get no blaming, only support: this is not easy work, I myself am one of the warning stories, we are colleagues, and they are in the process of learning.

In this session I explain that we do not ask the incarcerated about their crimes. After all, they do not ask us about the private things we are ashamed of, just as we do not ask each other. Also, as Chiara Liberatore once articulated in a 319 discussion, we may be the only people in their lives who do not know, and they deserve to have such people. Furthermore, if they do tell us, we may shift our attitude toward them and thus begin to participate in their punishment. That is contrary to our goal, which is to engage with them in our mutual efforts to grow. An incarcerated youth or prisoner may confide his crime, either because he likes and trusts the facilitator and wishes to go to that level or because he is testing him, to see if he is for real and the kind of person the incarcerated so much needs him to be. If someone tells us something brutal that has been done to her or that she has done, then we simply have to draw on our own resources for responding. My advice is to register the pain—they know it is painful and will not respect you pretending it is nothing—then thank them and let them know you understand it must be hard to have that in their life, then talk about the play and your admiration of their contributions.

I conclude the meeting by addressing teams where one or both members are working in a facility where the workshop participants are of the opposite gender. I mention that it could also be a same-sex issue. Someone may ask for a "special friendship" or slip a note into the student's notebook or pocket or slip it into their hand at the end of a session. They may create a role that allows them to play the student's spouse or lover, or always sit next to them, casually touch, then gradually escalate unless stopped. High school workshops are coeducational, but high school youth can ask, and have asked, for a date. At the first indication, the student should begin to respond, sharing it with their partner, letting me know immediately, bringing it to team meeting. If the student is given a note by an incarcerated youth, report it immediately to the counselor, who will deal with it as a treatment issue.[7] If approached or given a note at a prison, explain your professional reasons for being there and indicate that he or she is risking the future of workshops at the prison. If that doesn't work or the behavior is more subtle, circle the group up and talk about what it means as a woman, for instance, to come into a men's facility, and the respect you require. The group almost always responds supportively and the problem ends. PCAP women are available to help you figure out what to do.

In the second team meeting, we prepare for the first workshop. In their overcrowded classrooms at Cooley High School, Angel Glenn or Janice Rowley will say a few words to the forty students and then the team will be on its own. At Henry Ford High School Joan Galica will have the team describe the workshop to the class; those who choose to participate will stay in the room while she takes the others to the library. Prisoners who have signed up will straggle into the room for ten minutes. The incarcerated youth at Adrian Training School, Boysville, Calumet, Lincoln, Maxey, and Vista Maria have been assigned as a unit to the workshop. They might be sitting there, arms folded, slumped, looking to the side, staring blankly or defiantly. How will you begin? How will you have a lively, engaged group by the end of the session?

The teams share what they have imagined, and we brainstorm effective warm-ups and games and what to say. I advise them not to sit together: that isolates them and gives them a power they don't want. I suggest that they greet everyone, then immediately get them on their feet for one or more movement exercises. Afterward, sitting in a circle, each person might introduce herself and say what has brought her to the workshop (if it was voluntary) and tell about her experience, talents, interests, and ideas for a play. The team members should do no more than that, avoiding presenting themselves as accomplished actors or directors and avoiding talking too much. While some workshop members will pass and others will have poor reasons ("My buddy told me to check it out," or "I heard there would be women"), others will jump to their feet and sing, recite a poem, do an imitation, talk about a play they have written, talk about working on lighting or scenery. At the outset one team member has explained that she is taking notes[8] and now the note-taker can exclaim, "Wow, look what is in this room" and list the talents, interests, and ideas. The messages are that you have come not to "teach them," but to listen, that you are very impressed with what you've heard, and that the play will come from what and who is in the room, that it is theirs. Afterward, take some time to articulate what is ahead and conclude with a high-energy activity, Freeze, Kitty Want a Corner, Apples, Oranges, and Bananas, Bear and Woodcutters.[9]

I finish by telling a story. Years ago Nancy and Charlotte, facilitating a lively workshop at the Egeler Correctional Facility, began as great friends. Charlotte set Nancy up with a friend, they double-dated. In those days I met an hour a week with each team, and meetings with the two of them were engaged and fun. But by the end of term they hated each other. Charlotte was a take-charge person, doing everything; Nancy was fine with that; Charlotte had become resentful that Nancy wasn't carrying her weight and was scornful; Nancy became hurt. In team meetings they stared away from each other and wouldn't interact. I had let it go: they were having an experience from which they would learn. Later I realized that I had allowed them to deny the men in their workshop what would have been gained from the spirit and energy of their friendship. At the end their dislike was so strong that neither would make arrangements for the play to be taped and made available to prisoner family members. Several years later, because I now told that story, Jaime and Lee Ann, one strong woman dominating another in the workshop, confronted their growing alienation and solved it in favor of the boys they were working with. All new teams, I explain, have goodwill but potentially conflicting styles. Some people talk readily and too much, others are shy; some interrupt, some withdraw; some don't notice when they are gaining all the attention. So check in with each other: it isn't about being bad, it is about the workshop and its possibilities, about the incarcerated, not about us. If it is insuperable, if you are afraid of your partner's response, let me know, we'll figure it out. Also, if you have had a bad night, are ill, have broken up with someone, let your partner know when you enter the car: they will step it up in the workshop. And enjoy the car ride home, but debrief about your collaboration and about where the play is going.

That's it. That is all the preparation they get. I have not given them texts or lectures on crime, criminal lives, prison culture, the streets, the culture of poor urban neighborhoods. It is only fair: I have not given the urban youth or the incarcerated texts or lectures about the lives and cultures of elite university students. A majority of the students will enter the spaces self-conscious about their limited, even pampered backgrounds and their lack of street smarts. They will worry that the prisoners and youth will see them as rich, pretentious, naive brats. Sometimes they are right. While on the whole the high school youth don't worry much about how they will be perceived, incarcerated youth and adults will enter the workshops expecting students to have prejudged them as hardened criminals and to patronize them while instructing them in the arts. Sometimes they are right. The students are mostly white, mostly female, mostly affluent, the prisoners African American, Hispanic, Native, poor white, usually male, poor.

I know they will work together and have a play. And my knowing it enables them to know it. PCAP is built on such trust. Nothing is more central to our work. As Jesse Jannetta, who became PCAP's first full-time administrator, wrote in a booklet of tribute and analysis:

> From my 319 journal: "At the potluck, after Buzz left, Leslie Neal said something that really struck me. She said that she couldn't understand why the work that we're doing works. The results show that it does, but the weight of her experience tells her that it shouldn't. She thinks it's a little dicey that a bunch of college kids are sent into the prisons to do the workshops with only two or three weeks of training behind us." When you're up close to the prison workshops, and PCAP, it can be easy to forget how amazing, how unlikely it is. Re-reading my journals from that class brings me back to that time, when nothing seemed less likely than that I would be driving out to a prison every week, working too with a group that was a new thing to each other, creating a play that was also a new thing. Why did I think I could do it? Because Buzz thought I could do it, trusted me to do it. So I did.[10]

At the outset, workshop members may experience some suspicion and awkwardness and even raise challenges based on what is true in the stereotypes they have of each other. Yet the negotiation of the social and political divides actually is not difficult. Normally the fears disappear by the end of the first or second session. Entertaining, wacky, low-risk acting exercises (and drawing and writing exercises in other workshops) in which everyone participates lead gradually to a space of vitality, risk, and respect where everyone deepens their participation and struggles to bring forth their own stories, images, and ideas. The collective task of creating, week by week, a quality public performance further draws everyone together across superficial and real barriers.

A central theme in Leslie Marmon Silko's *Ceremony* has influenced my perspective: there are stories told by the destroyers and stories told by those who heal and unite, and the larger story of the fate of our planet depends on which storytellers prevail, those who mine uranium and make massive bombs, torture others, and pollute our minds and land, or those who maintain community, preserve air and water, and modify deep traditions to accommodate the present. While we are complicated, uninformed, confused beings, in the end what each of us becomes, does, and speaks are stories, as Elie Wiesel puts it, on the side of angels or on the side of demons.[11]

I think of my courses as stories or plays in the process of creation. If we listen well to each other, if we think beyond our individual alienation and narrow goals, if we manage to share what we believe is at stake in our lives and this work, if we bring the risks we are taking in our workshops to class, and if we have heard the voices of the incarcerated and the high school youth, if they have become a piece of how we talk and what we say, then the outcome is positive and collective, and it leads somewhere. If we remain alienated and competitive, if we don't figure out and oppose the destructive forces among us, the outcome is negative and leads nowhere good.

Our personalities and chemistry, the evening workshops and retreat, the team meetings and workshops, the journals and texts are elements. We come together week by week in the classroom and attempt to build something. What then is the classroom like? When I describe it to the interviewees, I tell them that I do not lecture, that I expect them to step up and participate, just as they will expect the same of everyone in their workshops. I tell them that if they are silent, I will be silent with them, that if they are exploring, vital, and responsive to each other, I will be there with them, questioning, provoking, seeking. My telling them this does not mean that they will be able to overcome animosities, old alienated classroom habits, their own diffidence or shyness.

⧗

We sit in a large circle, the twenty-five of us in English 310, the thirty-six of us in English 319. Before class there is laughter, chatter, running back and forth, a charged atmosphere rising from small-group meetings, sites, a sense of potential. After announcements, discussion can take a variety of directions. If we've had a text to read, students will pair off and talk about it, then write questions and challenges on the board. I might have an exercise intended to disrupt, to provoke, to unify: I introduce it, and we dig in. I give the quiz on Paulo Freire's *Pedagogy of the Oppressed*. Most classes are "open sessions," where we don't know until it happens how we will begin. Someone may have come in burning with a question or issue, and we go with that. We gradually develop themes that become important, and we return to those. We may need to confront our own process. At a weekly team meeting, students may have brainstormed how to take the class forward and come in with a plan to make that happen.

What is my role? When I am *present,* at my best? I wait, I listen, I let the conversation stir, I refuse to dominate. It is key that I *really* am interested in what individuals say or try to say, that I affirm that their anger and compassion matter, that I know that any one of them can give me a story, an insight, a trigger, can frighten me or make me question myself, that I know that they, dug in, can take themselves and me to places we hadn't thought of before. It is essential that I am not outside the story, telling it, outside the play writing it, that I am one of the characters, that I am *in* the discussion and that I believe something is at stake in being there, whatever it turns out to be—our souls, the lives of the urban youth and the incarcerated, a struggle for justice, our futures, an emerging community—and that I'm there to work together on it. I never begin with questions to which I know the answer and to which my students must make their way. We start from student brainstorming and from what they write on the board, from their questions, issues, challenges. The class would be different if I were only a teacher sending them out to have an experience and helping them analyze it, coming once to their workshop and then to the performance, if I were only the contact with the liaison, reader of their journals and papers. Instead they see me committed to doing the work and know that I founded PCAP and am a member of theater and poetry workshops in two different prisons, that I speak publicly and bear witness to the voices inside and to the economic practices that have selected certain groups out and isolated them from the rest of us, that I participate in guerrilla theater, lobby, devote hours and hours to the annual prison art exhibition, and go to bat for my students and for the incarcerated.

I believe in chaos. A classroom confrontation in my large 1976 film course on the War in Vietnam opened me as a teacher. Gary was a tall, forceful Vietnam veteran who had not been home all that long and who (we learned at the end of the course) had spent a year in the Phoenix Program interrogating villagers while a Vietnamese assistant screwed a coat hanger into their ears. Charlie was a very intelligent, hard-thinking, articulate sophomore from New Jersey. Gary believed something Charlie said was naive, and the two of them went at it aggressively. From my podium—we were in a room of nailed-down seats facing the front—I stepped in and smoothed things over, explaining to each of them what the other had meant to say. They subsided, and probably most of the class breathed a sigh of relief. The tension was gone. But afterward Gary and Charlie came to me separately and explained that they could take care of themselves. I thought hard about that. I didn't need to bring to the classroom my own childhood experience of being the kid on the block who was bullied. I didn't need to protect people. I could allow the classroom to be a place of chaos and ferment, where mature beings could learn from and deal with what turned out to be in the room. From then on I let things stew and boil.

I may provoke the chaos. In one session I review what we have learned about the neighborhoods and situations from which most of the incarcerated come and the hard stories coming out of our workshops, then read a troubling passage from Jonathan Kozol's *The Night Is Dark and I Am Far from Home*.[12] I then ask the students to think without speaking for two minutes and to decide honestly whether hearing these stories angers them. Next I ask those who are angry to find another room and talk for twenty minutes. I remain with those who stay, usually a sizable majority. I tell them that there are many possible emotional reactions to the stories, and each student in turn describes his or her own authentic response: sadness, being overwhelmed, recognition of the way things are, hopelessness, and so on. Then the angry students return. The first time two of them wrote on the board, "We are angry at those who are not angry." That time and always, the discussion is fierce and conflicted, sometimes opening our differences like a raw wound. The journals continue the discussion.

I may provoke community. I ask students to bring an object that means a lot to them and that they are willing to pass around. They number off into groups of seven or ten and go into separate rooms. Each group sits on the floor and speaks in turn without interruption. First each tells the story of the object, with no time limit. Then in silence they pass the objects from right to left, each holding each object for a minute, feeling its texture, leafing its pages, examining details of a photo, and thinking of the story that comes with it. Next, again in silence, they pass the objects around, but this time deciding which object most represents their small group and its stories; each member can, when the object is in her hands, discard it by placing it in the center. The final object becomes the group's power object, and each member, holding it, has two minutes to speak, sing, or act, as he is moved. The group prepares a skit or other form of presentation to convey to the other groups what happened in their room.[13]

And I listen for the energy, passion, and need that one or more of them bring into the room on a given day. I know that if it is honored, something important will happen.[14] I follow Myles Horton's two-eye theory: I have one eye on where each individual and the class are and another eye on where they might get. I listen for their potential to move forward.[15] I understand that listening implies a commitment and is different from merely hearing. I once showed *Inside Out*[16] to the women in the Sisters Within Theater Troupe and remember Jackie Whitmore's response. The play tells its target audience of high-risk youth to let out what is inside, to "tell someone, whether it is your mother or father or brother or friend," because if you don't, it "will burn and you'll end up doing terrible things like we all did, and you'll end up where we are, and this is a terrible place to learn what it is to be a man." Jackie, in tears and anger, told us that she had told what was inside her to counselors both at her juvenile facility and in the prison. But they had their own agenda and thus their own way of hearing what she said and didn't listen. While I don't always have energy and time to give back fully, or solutions to give,[17] in my head are their journal explorations and our weekly dialogue, and so I listen for the questions inside myself and others that may help them move forward. I owe them all. What is he or she, what are we all really saying, trying out, trying to get at, avoiding, not seeing, risking, and what can I give back with a few words, a question, or a story that touches that risk or avoidance or gap, that jogs or opens a little light or troubles the mind, that gives someone else an opening to join in and move us all forward?

I listen in order to speak when the time is right and my speaking can be authentic, grounded in the discussion, the people in the room, and myself,[18] so that I might ask about what puzzles me in what we have said, about what we may really be saying or avoiding, so that I might, if it feels right, lunge in with my own passion, with my memory of Asia Orlando's death, the brutal courtroom sentencing of Jerry, the brutal public hearing suffered by Sharleen, the agony and spirit of Nate Jones, Jason's monologue "Will the Punishment Never Stop?" and the way his words echo in every returned prisoner I know, and the peasant community of Yutto and the shantytown of Huaycán and the Jeffries Homes in my voice and words. I listen in order to speak so that others can speak. If the class falls silent and treats my words as the final word, because of the power accrued to me as an older white male professor with a reputation, then they have disrespected me, and I tell them so. But I also avoid speaking in a manner that allows that to happen.

Herbert Kohl's classroom, as he describes it in *36 Children,* has a very fluid structure. It responds to the moods, needs, and intellectual interests of the sixth-grade children. It responds also to the hard and beautiful stories they have in them and is cognizant of their lives and issues beyond the classroom. Some 310 and 319 students find this kind of structure both hard to imagine and intolerable. They argue for "more classroom structure" for children and youth, and probably for themselves, imagining something akin to the conventional classroom with its rows facing the front, its lesson plans and planned goals. In the middle of such an argument in 310 in the fall of 2006 Noelle Williams suddenly observed that there is a further structure in Kohl's classroom: the structure of the space between Kohl and each child. I thought this brilliant. Between Kohl and the individual child a hard-earned dynamic space charged with Kohl's respect for the child and the child's world; charged with his belief in what the child, if listened to, would be able to invent, say, write; and charged with the response of the child.[19]

The following January, Janie, Emily Harris, and I talked over a quiet meal in Janie's and my home. Janie was up for promotion to tenure, and her materials had been sent for comment to her former students and to her peers in the fields of Art and Design and community action. Emily had visited Mary Paul, one of the students, in Chicago, and Mary had told her that Janie's spark and commitment differed from what she had found in other community outreach courses and had set her on her career path. Thinking this over, we found two factors that made Janie similar to Kohl. The first was her own deep commitment to the fourth graders she worked with in two Detroit schools, to incarcerated youth and adults, and to people in the community. What was happening to them mattered, their ability to resist mattered, their lives mattered, *and* it mattered to her that those lives also mattered to her students. The second was her commitment in the same degree to each of her students. Her passion for working with each one created a structure akin to the one Noelle found in Kohl. As we talked on, I realized that for the two of us it was more: we wanted our students to figure out how to establish similarly committed structures with each other and to figure out, whenever possible, that such structures could grow between them and individual youth and adults in the high schools, juvenile facilities, and prisons. We wanted our students to discover the kind of trust, patience, and belief in each other that would allow community to emerge from chaos. While the two of us stumble, doubt, mess up, complain, and become diverted by the demands now made on us by fast-pacing, intrusive technology, sometimes something of the sort happens. Laurie Hess remembers that "[Buzz and Janie] keep pushing, struggling and hoping for the real men and women in their workshops. They have faith in people both inside and outside of prison who have often lost faith in themselves. They help us to find the beauty and the passion in ourselves, to dare to risk living a life that matters."[20]

⧗

I have said these classes are stories or plays that may end well or end badly, allies of alienation and destruction or of community and justice. English 310 in the fall of 2005 is an example of one that ended well. In the October 25 Freire quiz, they had seven minutes to answer the following question:

> Give Freire's likely analysis of the following story: A man walks along the beach and sees that thousands of starfish have been washed up on the shore. He comes to another man who is throwing fish back into the ocean one at a time. He says, "You are wasting your time: there are thousands of dying fish, and throwing back a few does nothing useful." The second man replies: "You are wrong: even if I save only a few fish, those fish are alive."

Those who thought Freire would praise the story did poorly. Those who understood that he would recognize it as a deceptive individualist myth whose function is to stifle collective action did well. This familiar, celebrated story actually restricts what one should do. The second man does not ask the first to join him, nor does he ask him to run to town (or pick up his cell phone and call) to summon others to join the effort. It is a story on the side of the demons disguised as a story on the side of the angels.

Over the next month, intrigued, the students spontaneously elaborated on the story. The story, one of them argued, should have the two men (and the other men and women who join them) investigate the stranding of the starfish and find out who is responsible. Others argued that they should also look into the effect on the local fishing industry. Jeff Cravens insisted the man should plunge into the water and join the starfish and become a part of their effort to resist. This in turn led to a discussion about whether members of the class, knowing all they now knew from the reading and from their workshop experiences, should take a plunge and devote their lives, skills, and careers to struggling together with people in the economic situations of those in their workshops. A troubling, highly conflicted, and potentially alienating dialogue ensued. Say someone in the class has chosen only to lead a strong, wonderful workshop with incarcerated girls, then leave such work behind forever: will they have merely dabbled? Will they have done something wrong? Should they be disdained by and perhaps in turn disdain those who make a radical plunge? These questions were in the air and it grew tense. Struggling through this, the class in the end decided that they valued each other and were allies. All of them had crossed a border, all had been challenged by what they met, and all had engaged creatively with the urban and incarcerated youth and with the prisoners. Those who moved on to other parts of their lives would stay in touch and lend support—advocating, making connections, fund-raising—and those who plunged would feel the connection, keep in touch also, and recognize the breadth of the work that needs to be done. That they had successfully crossed the divide between university and school and prison was a key factor in their ability to cross their own divide.

A week later Karen Soell announced that she needed to talk about an article and some letters that had appeared that week in the *Michigan Daily*. Every February, university and community women perform Eve Ensler's *Vagina Monologues* and donate the profits to Safe House, a county shelter for battered women and their children. The directors for 2006 had decided to have the play performed entirely by women of color, so that voices representing the special issues of battered minority women might more fully emerge. In response to angry letters in the *Daily*, Karen wished to defend the directors' decision. Julia Taylor, herself an actor and director struggling brilliantly with a workshop of very desperate girls at Vista Maria, disagreed: if the auditions were not open, it would be reverse discrimination. It was a fierce discussion among allies. Julia listened carefully, including to what Cuban American Valerie Haddad and Korean American Jennifer Oh had to say, and changed her mind. The class decided they would organize a meeting in support of the directors, with Karen, Alissa Talley, Sarah Carswell, and a few others taking the lead.[21] It is an anti-starfish, anti-destroyer story, and the planet gained.[22]

That class deserved the gift that Noelle's equally successful 310 received in the fall of 2006. We were fortunate to have present throughout the term a reader of the story we were creating. In our final session we decided on a talk circle. One at a time, without interruption, we spoke what was on our minds, reflecting, offering each other words, thinking about what the youth we worked with might have needed from us.[23] Alison Stroud, who cofacilitated a poetry workshop at Boysville, is profoundly deaf and had been supported in class by a stenographer, Kate Miller, typing out our words so that Alison, an excellent lip reader, could see in detail what we had said. Now, after speaking to us, Alison turned to Kate and said, "Now you talk!" Kate replied, "I'm sorry, but it is policy that I'm not supposed to speak in classes." But she paused, and then: "But the children . . ." She hesitated again, and then: "I have two children, and I want them to grow up to be like all of you." The class was visibly moved. Several students, when it was their turn to speak, thanked her. She had taken in our story. She had seen who the students had become, she had heard their struggles with each other, their outbursts and tears, their arguments over the value of their work, the hard personal questions they asked about false and true generosity, what was in their voices as they talked about the youth and the workshops, and their growing commitments to each other and to those who had been granted so much less. She was able to tell them that they had become powerful together and that children's lives would be different because of them.[24]

CHAPTER FOUR

The Workshops

I

"In the yard, I am like this!"
Hollis-El shows a clenched fist.
"In here like this . . ." he opens a tiny space
between forefinger and thumb.
"Then I return to the yard,"
and he clenches again.

II

"In California I loved to walk the beaches
and redwood forests." Native American lifer,
adopted and beaten by his Polish family,
runaway, now forever resident in a Michigan prison.
"The theater workshop is like that."

III

At the university
a circle of stiff classroom chairs
which we unbend with our minds
"The men at Ryan and I
come to the workshop," Chris says,
"for the same reason:
something is missing in our lives,
and we come there to find it."

—FROM "FOR MIKE, BECAUSE YOU ASKED," BY BUZZ ALEXANDER

I don't need to cater to any of you, I don't need to cater to you. My brother is in the hospital paralyzed from the neck down, my niece was in a coma, and my wife was buried today, my daughter is out there with no parent, and I need this workshop, I need its focus, I need to keep my mind off these other things.

—WILSON-BEY AFTER LEAVING AND THEN RETURNING TO A THEATER
WORKSHOP AT SOUTHERN MICHIGAN CORRECTIONAL FACILITY

Children and youth, incarcerated youth, and prisoners, working with English 310 and 319 students, with Art and Design 310 students, and with PCAP members, have presented their plays, poetry, art, and other work in primary schools, in rural high schools, in urban day and night high schools, in girls' and boys' juvenile facilities, and in men's and women's prisons. The youth have been in special education and standard classrooms, in sex offender halls or pods, in cottages or halls of severely damaged youth, in geographically organized units or units organized according to crime or problem. The adults come from the general population in low- and medium-to-high security prisons, from the prison mental hospital, from residential treatment units, and from prisons or parts of prisons assigned to youth sentenced as adults.

Sometimes their audiences have been limited to peers, with no outsiders allowed. Now and then, the audiences have been limited to outsiders, which defeats one of our principal purposes, of having the performers become models for their peers. The audiences are usually open to both peers and outsiders. In some prisons, the prisoners and outsiders are segregated from each other; in others we can freely mingle and converse. Family members are invited to the youth performances, as they were in the early days in the prisons.[1] For a while we could videotape performances and readings and make copies at cost for family members, but this was outlawed in the late 1990s.[2] Our audiences have been as small as four members and as large as 270, perched on bleacher seats in a prison gymnasium.

The performers have presented in classrooms so crowded with desks they could hardly move, on high school stages much too vast for their ability to project, and in a variety of smaller high school spaces, in juvenile facility and prison chapels and recreation rooms, on stages with and stages without curtains, in rooms full of echoes, in gymnasiums where their voices sank at their feet, in gymnasiums using fifteen microphones, in a tiny space just off the living quarters in the women's prison mental health unit, in the patio of a women's prison as the sun went down and our voices carried to the actress who had provoked a fight in the yard the night before and ended up in segregation. At the Western Wayne Correctional Facility, the men built a five-piece stage that was stored in a corner of East Recreation. When the men left, the women who replaced them added a green carpet to the stage and our voices stopped rebounding. We have brought urban and incarcerated youth to the University of Michigan for second performances and presented in small and large classrooms, in auditoriums, in theaters.

Our shortest play was five minutes. It was created in desperation in the hour before the performance: the youth talked about the source of a ring, earring, necklace or bracelet they wore, and they imagined a story about a stolen ring. Our longest plays, rehearsed for months, last an hour and three-quarters, or until the facility closes down for the night and sends us home.

Some of the plays are silly, some poorly done, some rich in character and meaning, complicated, sophisticated. All of the plays are successes.

Only 5 of 506 plays have been scripted. Before we decided against scripted plays, the Sisters Within Theater Troupe performed *Junkie* by Martha Boesing (1992) and *17* by Fritz Hale (1995). The other three, *Y2K and the Wicked Stepmother* (2000), *Street Life* (2002), and *To Kill the Mockingbirds; a monologue play* (2002) were strategic responses to efforts by prison administrators to prevent the plays.[3]

Process and product are equally crucial. PCAP workshops always lead to a reading or performance. When 310 and 319 students object—"We have great rapport, great communication and community, it makes no sense to shift everything into a deadline and product"—I remind them what it has meant to them to stand before an audience and ask them to imagine what it will mean to someone who has never been celebrated or applauded even once in his life. Our performances are celebrations, with programs, with refreshments and flowers in the youth facilities. Sometimes performers and audience testify. The performers gain reputations among their peers as actors, poets, dancers.

In this chapter I am going to talk largely about the theater workshops.

The first two meetings of a new workshop we play and talk. The goal is to have fun, loosen up, get comfortable, learn what brought each of us there, test out the waters, play games, do exercises, learn light improvisations. In the third meeting, we are likely to introduce some kind of conflict exercise. We number off into pairs, and each pair has five minutes to come up with a one-minute conflict that will not be resolved and that is based on observation or direct experience. The first time we used this exercise, an English 319 student and a Maxey boy became two men clearing their lawns of leaves, one with a rake, the other with a blower that kept sending leaves onto the lawn of the first. Participants learn that stories can come from their everyday lives and personal histories (we discourage borrowing from television or the movies), that two people with conflict makes for drama, and that conflict is not easily resolved. If we have time, we choose one of the conflicts and either (1) have the two actors create new scenes, one preceding and one following the original scene, choosing others to join them if the new scenes require other characters, (2) replace the actors with two others who take the scene in new directions, or (3) have other actors enter the scene and add complications as they see fit. The participants see their plots thicken and stories deepen and learn how they will eventually create their play, mounting scene upon scene, adding and developing characters as we go, always working through improvisation. At the end of this session, we ask them to come next time with ideas for a play.

In the fourth meeting, after some exercises, we go around the circle and listen to ideas. If no one has ideas, we ask everyone to be silent an entire five minutes and think of stories from their experience they would like to see performed. We choose first the two or three most thoughtful and developed ideas and ask those who have proposed them to choose as many actors as they need, then go into a corner and come up with the scene they have in mind, which need not be the opening scene of a play. After five or so minutes, they show the scenes, we all discuss and decide upon one or more. Often several ideas merge into a single plot or into plot and subplots, since characters can live in the same building or neighborhood, go to the same school, or be confined in the same prison.

Ongoing workshops need not follow the same process. Often members already have ideas for the next play. In a single brainstorming session, the men at Western Wayne decided upon a play that would warn youth away from the paths that had taken the men to prison. Shar Wabindato and Jackie Wilson of the Sisters Within had enjoyed playing the owners of a clothes cleaning establishment in a brief scene in *Dream Stage* (1995) and requested to play similar roles three plays later. We immediately put them up front and sent in a series of improvised characters who disrupted their cleaning operation. This became the first scene of *Puddin's Place* (1997), an hour-and-forty-five-minute play full of rich complications. More recently, Naomi Fitchett announced that she wished to play a young person dying of cancer in order to explore the death experience of her twenty-one-year-old brother. This became *What's in the Water Cooler? The Lost Room . . . What!!!?* (2007). A play can develop also from something less direct. *Inside and Personal* (1994) rose from two sources: an improvisation in which mothers in prison phoned their daughters at home and the intense discussion that followed; and a discussion that took up an entire workshop, about what the Florence Crane Women's Facility water was doing to prisoners' skin and prison health conditions in general. Pilar Anadon and I listened without interruption except to ask questions. At the end I asked what the discussion had to do with our next play. The women responded that the next play needed to be serious and be drawn from some of the harsh realities of their lives.

Once the workshop group makes its choice, the rest is a matter of patient week-by-week exploration of plot, character, story, and meaning. English 310 and 319 groups must have a play in ten weeks of hour-and-a-half sessions, sometimes with extra rehearsals if permitted. PCAP groups generally have unlimited time.

It is seldom easy—and I can't emphasize this enough—because we work in constantly disrupted environments. Attendance is often spotty in the high schools, especially in early morning classes. Holidays, teacher conferences, school closings because of inclement weather, crowded classrooms, a week of standardized testing, fifty-minute sessions rather than the hour and a half at our other sites, and normal adolescent inattention and chaos wreak havoc. The last two factors are compounded in the juvenile facilities by painfully unresolved experiences and issues of individual youth and frequent tensions in groups that are together twenty-four hours a day. Sometimes a session is canceled, and sometimes we lose half an hour when the youth circle up with a counselor to address an immediate problem. Youth act out, youth close down. While the counseling staff is usually very helpful, some counselors or night staff carry on loud conversations with each other, make phone calls, or divert individual youth with conversations or random critiques of their behavior. Sometimes at the two girls' facilities, the staff has forgotten we are coming,[4] and the girls have been sent off to some other activity; at best, it takes extra time to gather them and get started. An emergency count, a monthly simulated mobilization that closes the prison down, heavy fog or other extreme weather that makes yard movement hazardous for prisoners and officers, disciplinary measures like segregation, top lock (confinement to one's cell), and loss of privileges, or a prisoner sent back because of an unbuttoned shirt or for arriving a minute late, one of us forgetting our driver's license, corrections officers randomly sitting in on a session,[5] participants transferred to other prisons,[6] family visits, illness, and general environmental stress are constant challenges to continuity in the prisons. Participants in any youth or adult workshop may decide two weeks before a performance that they don't want to do the play anymore or decide they need major revisions. Individual participants might choose to fade back into the prison, where we have no opportunity to talk with them, find out what is happening, and encourage them to return.[7]

I admire prison theater based on texts, including the remarkable work facilitated and directed by my colleagues Jonathan Shailor, Kurt Tofteland, Jean Trounstine, and Agnes Wilcox.[8] We have chosen another route, building plays by improvisation. We value actors' inventiveness, imagination, and personal histories, stories, and issues, and we love the process of figuring out the plot, characters, and meanings together. Each improvised scene is rehearsed again and again. We avoid memorization: usually we have only a short time to create a play, our workshops are open to all levels of ability and literacy, and attempted memorization could cause onstage agony. Also, especially at the prisons, frequent transfers and disciplinary sanctions may bring last-minute losses that give no time for new actors to memorize the text. With improvisation, we can scramble at the last moment. Actors— who know what is to happen in each scene—can take on second roles.[9]

Each participant chooses or invents a character when ready to do so. Some choices are obvious at the outset, and some actors are eager to jump in. Others wait to see how the land lies. I could not figure out who I wished to be in the Sisters Within's *Reflections* (1998), a play about four generations of a family. I gradually realized that each major second-generation character had suffered a significant death: a medic in Vietnam had watched a buddy die; one, watching television, had seen her husband, a prominent civil rights activist, assassinated while making a speech; another had aborted her fetus; and a fourth was attempting to kill off her blackness and become white.[10] Their mother, an old woman now, was an impervious matriarch seemingly without flaws, who had lived her life out in a successful lesbian relationship. I decided to play a dead baby boy, the result of an abortion the mother had kept secret throughout her life. When she appeared, a black sheet in the corner of the room would stir slightly when she spoke, and as she revealed her secret on her deathbed, the sheet rose and exited through the door at the rear of the stage.

A key moment is the character interview. The character stands before the other characters/actors and tells what she knows of herself, then answers questions that probe her history, her memories, her darkest or happiest moments, her faith, her relationships with other characters or with others in her past or present, her needs, her feelings about issues in the play, and so on. Her answers give other characters material for their scenes with her, reveal new dimensions to and suggest new characters for the plot, a father, a missing sister, a doctor who has moved to a small town to escape the corruption of the big city and who refuses to help someone with a sex change. The characters rise not only from our imaginations, but also from our own experiences and needs. Bernard Arnold, a new member of the Western Wayne Players, was interviewed during the formation of *Brothers* (1999). Someone asked his character to talk about his relation to his father. Bernard began to answer, then paused, stunned, and declared, "This is real!" The others laughed and said, "Welcome to the Western Wayne Players!" When an actor becomes aware of this dimension, the play takes on increased urgency.

After several weeks, we begin to bring a list of the scenes developed so far. We describe each scene, sometimes with a few pieces of dialogue we wish to remember. This is as much text as we have, and the scenes continue to be improvised as we rehearse them. The actors review the scene before they go on stage and are generally true to it, but improvisation continues into the performance itself, sometimes bringing new comedy, new emotion and power.[11]

And the plays, at their best, lead, like most plays, from disrupted communities and individual conflicts to adjustments, resolutions, and a sophisticated reestablishment of balance. The plot of *The Genie and the Hood* (June 1999) has the thousand-year-old Dr. Krasenknopf and his somewhat younger genie, Hasan, opening a ghetto pawnshop. Their even younger accomplice is fine as long as she is kept in alcohol. When three men see the magic lamp in the window, they enter and touch the lamp. A gong sounds and Hasan appears (speaking in rhyme) and offers them three wishes. He and Dr. Krasenknopf then use their wishes to divide and destroy the ghetto. Eventually some women, including the accomplice (the evil pair have mistakenly let the community go dry), figure out what is happening and they realize that they can defeat Dr. Krasenknopf and Hasan with the power of women's laughter. They teach it to others and march on the pawnshop. Krasenknopf and Hasan, defiant and nearly victorious at first, melt to nothing. The community has resisted, come together, learned and asserted new values. However, while this is at least a temporary victory for the community, the final scene shows Krasenknopf and Hasan standing in their new pawnshop in Kansas City, Missouri, as townspeople peer in at the lamp. The struggle continues elsewhere and always.

THE ROLES OF THE UNIVERSITY FACILITATORS

Although we usually come from some degree of affluence and academic success, although most of us are white and female, although at the end of every session we return to the comfort of our Ann Arbor apartments and homes, and although it is because of us that these creative spaces have opened, in a very crucial sense we are no different than the other workshop participants: we are there to play games, take risks, be vulnerable, brainstorm, discover, co-create, act, and co-direct. We bring our backgrounds, personalities, talents, and skills and throw them into the mix. This cannot be sufficiently emphasized: we *all* get down to the task. It is not about talk, not about theory, not about instructing, it is about collaboration and praxis. In a way, it is magic. The differences remain *and* evaporate.

In the courses we insist that the play (or poetry or art or dance) is "theirs"—we don't bring in texts or lesson plans—and that the product will rise from the workshop dynamic. Some students understand this to mean we are passive: "they" will make it all happen. These students do not recognize that the participants have not done this before, that they are uncertain and likely to flounder in the open-ended discovery process of the workshops, that they may think of us as "teachers" even though we refuse the role, and that they need the kind of guidance we, with our training in the courses, can provide. We must be willing to call the group to focus (a great challenge in the youth facilities), provide games, exercises, and improvisations, move the process along, make sure the character interviews are challenging, engage the whole group in feedback on the scenes, and contribute our own ideas and feelings about both story and process. In most workshops either immediately or very quickly, others join us in all these roles.

When students or PCAP members feel younger and inexperienced or white or lacking in street experience or in experiences of abuse and pain and hold back, they fail the members of their workshop. A moment everyone in the fall 2006 310 will remember is when Grace Pan, suddenly in tears, urged her classmates to make demands on the youth they were working with: that would offer them the respect they deserve. When PCAP members Emi Kaneko and Katie Craig, feeling their experience to be elite and their poetry amateur, did not take risks and step forth boldly as writers, they were disrespecting the men at the Parnall Correctional Facility and holding back the workshop. When we identified this in a group meeting, everything changed.

Because we have access the others do not, we have certain responsibilities. We bring in notepads, pens, and paper, costumes and props, scene lists, programs, flowers for the high school and youth facility curtain calls, refreshments when the facility lacks the budget to provide them. We stay in touch with the liaison, we phone ahead to make sure everything is in order, we enter the facility with positive spirit and respect, we adhere to the facility rules and regulations. We do all we can, from our vantage point as volunteers from the university, to make everything go smoothly and to protect the workshop.

Protecting the workshop can mean struggling for significant meaning. Although the plays move toward resolution, the resolution can be problematic. In a Maxey play, a boy about to hit another boy is taken into the future and shown two outcomes: to end up in a mental institution or to live in a luxurious house with his wife and children enjoying his success as a corporate giant. He chooses the latter and does not strike the other boy. But the boys did not imagine other ideals—becoming a social worker, a teacher, a public health worker, a member of Doctors Without Borders. The team did not offer such possibilities for discussion. Whatever the boys decided, the discussion would have been valuable. If they chose the same outcome, they might have added new dimensions.

A member of the Western Wayne Players proposed a play in which former students arrive at their high school reunion, discover the community has deteriorated, and fix it up with their wealth. It felt unreal and magical to me, and so when we put up the reunion scene to start things off, I leaned over to Romando Valeroso and another actor and said, "Go on in and mug them." They rushed the stage, forced everyone up against the wall, took their wallets, and left. Suddenly things became more challenging. The high school principal (a member of the reunion class) recognized the two "thugs" as students and thought they could be persuaded to change. However, when he called them in and when the alumni offered jobs and an elite academy for the neighborhood, the youth rebuffed them. Increasingly frustrated, the actors playing the rich characters decided the two should be arrested and incarcerated (one wounded and in a wheelchair). At this point, Pilar Anadon, Maria Stewart, and I objected. We wondered why they would advocate as the solution for urban youth the incarceration they themselves had suffered. When we suggested that the alumni listen to the boys, the same actors were aghast: what could the thugs possibly say? Other actors supported our suggestion. So Froggy, the classmate who had stayed in town and become an auto repair mechanic, who was still snubbed by his classmates, and who knew the youth, arranged a meeting. Valeroso and the actor now playing the second "thug" stunned the alumni with their detailed analysis and criticism of the high school and community environment. They argued that they could organize the community. The alumni acquiesced and offered backing. The play ended with a community celebration of a successful fund-raiser organized by the boys. The prison band contributed an original song.

Protecting the workshop can also mean struggling together for its very existence. Toward the end of the Sisters Within Theater Troupe's residence at the Florence Crane Women's Facility,[12] the women, Pilar, and I were faced with increasing hostility from the warden and the regional prison administrator. Perhaps they had come to identify us with Mary Glover and Tracy Neal, lead litigants against the Michigan Department of Corrections and former Sisters members, though we had always known better than to discuss the lawsuits or to get involved in any way. In the fall of 1999, the warden notified us that our next play would have to be from a written text. She gave us half an hour in the muster room to discuss this with the women. There we quickly recalled a title we used to joke about, *Y2K and the Wicked Stepmother,* and immediately imagined a basic plot and characters. The next day the women met in the yard, elaborated the plot and sent us what they had. We developed it into a full-length story, submitted it to the warden and regional prison administrator, who then told us it had to be a line-by-line text. Instead of quitting, we agreed that we would submit such a text. Then each week we created the play in our usual improvisational manner, but with Pilar writing down the lines we came up with. The text was approved. Although the hostility continued—we were denied outside guests, limited in terms of props and costumes, received glares from prison officers, were told after the performance that the promised refreshments were locked up and couldn't be accessed, and were harassed on the way out[13]—we gave two spirited performances of that wonderful play. Our celebration after the second performance had the solidarity and depth of having fought for the play and refusing to yield in the face of so much opposition.

INSIDE THE WALLS

An exercise we frequently use is "Magician."[14] Someone stands on a chair and hollers, "I am a magician, and I turn you all into angry red rabbits" (or "into your father" or "into bees on my left and people afraid of bees on my right" or "dancing mummies"). When that person has finished several transformations of the group, he or she cries out, "I am a magician, and I turn Pedro into a magician." Pedro then ascends to the chair. In a variation on this exercise, each boy in Lauren Rubinfeld and Mryna Vaca's workshop at Maxey (2001) would shout, "I am the magician and I give my power to ____." Terry gave the power to De'Aries, then De'Aries gave it to Ricardo. When Ricardo was ready, he shouted, "I am the magician and I give my power to these walls." Lauren was "speechless." She wrote about it in her final paper:

> Ricardo recognizes that his power is being replaced by the power of the walls and the fences that surround him. When I drive away from Maxey, I can't just snap right back into the outside world. After hearing the voices of my boys, their screams, their ideas, their cartwheels, their imaginations yelling, it is so difficult to drive out of the gates of Maxey, where even with my windows rolled down, I cannot hear even one sound escape from the fences. They are being silenced. And their silence screams to me louder than the loudest shriek Ronnie has placed in my eardrum. They are my shriek. They are the shriek that sustains my anger—my anger that propels me. My anger at the neighborhood (that we are all a part of) that surrounds Maxey and is comforted by the silence of boys' voices. They are comforted by the silence of my boys' futures.[15]

THE WALLS

The incarcerating walls are constructed from many materials. Tormented, alienated, overcrowded homes, dangerous streets, ragged rotting schools and overworked, demoralized teachers, lack of medical access, hunger, illiteracy, physical and sexual assault, environmental pollution, the helpless rage of those around one. Low expectations, degradations, accumulated insults to the spirit. Everyday violence. The rat in the corner, the rat in the crib. Gangs, the color of one's skin, the color of one's class. Guns and drugs. In one's head the moment that led toward the police car, the jail garb, the shackles, the voices of others in the courtroom. Rotating poorly paid counselors, inadequate psychiatric attention, haunted minds, chaos, cuttings, suicide attempts, screams, running, state uniforms. The humiliations of count time, of arbitrary orders, of lost control in almost every aspect of one's life, of health care that neglects and kills, of food that bloats, of constant noise, constant boredom, of stabbings and rape, of having to watch one's back, of having no choice as to one's company, of parole board denials, of knowing the public hates you, of being imagined as a person without loved ones or aspirations or creativity, of attending funerals under guard, of missing a child's graduation, a child's marriage, a chance to care for a dying parent.

The walls close in on one's soul. Jimmy Santiago Baca talks about crossing the invisible line into numbness and never coming back, about the light inside that is extinguished. It happens when the insults accumulate, when one is silenced, when one is given a disciplinary ticket for singing or bursting into dance, when one is treated like trash. Tait Sye reports in his journal:

> Denise also told us about one youth in particular. When he first came to Green Oak Center, everyone thought he was hopeless. But he turned out to be an exceptional person. He did everything that was asked of him, received his GED and now everyone thought that he would be released last June. The judge denied his release, and told him he would review his case in 6 months. Just last week he went back to the judge expecting to be released, but to the surprise of everyone, he was sent back to Maxey. We were later introduced to him, but he was very quiet. Denise asked a group leader how he was doing, and the group leader responded that he could cope better if the judge had said why. If there was a reason, something he had to work on. But there was not. . . . The judge essentially took one year from his life without offering a reason.[16]

Why?

THE WALLS

In *The Night Is Dark and I Am Far from Home,* Jonathan Kozol demonstrates how the high schools most of us attend train us to be "good citizens," smart, imaginative, intelligent, well-intentioned adults who, while we may volunteer and donate to charity, are ethically indifferent to the sufferings and struggles of others, unconscious of the everyday violence that surrounds us, or, if conscious, not inclined to do much or anything about it. Through fragmentation of our learning, through group recitations of the Pledge to the Flag, through elimination of "I" from our essays, through emasculation and taming of major rebellious figures we study, through obscuring the fact that great figures were once children like us, through softening, diminishing, and managing our inclinations to righteous anger or action, through celebrating individual achievements, the schools divert our force into safe channels.[17] In fifth grade, my son brought to show-and-tell a story of human rights abuses in Chile. His teacher was moved and asked the children to write "world wishes." They all wished for a better world, and it was taken care of. In seventh grade his art teacher asked the students to draw a picture of freedom. My son had lived with us in the mountains of Peru and visited peasant communities, he had listened to our talk. He drew a man with a black beret at a podium, speaking, and below him were men with their rifles raised in response. Che Guevara. His art teacher refused the drawing—he had, according to my son, accepted a drawing of a man in a white sheet— and asked my son to think of something in America he liked to do. Totally unsure now, my son said he liked to camp, and that was approved. He drew a picture of a tent in a campground.

This is all natural enough. It is the role of the schools to reproduce the social order. Some do so in a way that allows for individuality, self-criticism, intelligence, imagination, creativity, and other characteristics that allow some of us to be vital citizens who can advance science, develop markets, cure patients, write important books, and so on. At the same time we learn language—"it has always been this way; there have always been rich and poor; one person can't change the world"—to consent to the absence of such schooling for others or to be compassionate and activist in limited ways. My students, so many of them lively, deeply intelligent, wonderfully creative individuals, are at risk of crossing an invisible line into numbness, of having the light of passion for justice that is taught in some American history texts, some churches and synagogues, some families, go out. When I was growing up on the North Shore of Chicago, no one in my family, no one in my schools, no one in the Sunday school at the Wilmette Methodist Church even hinted that there was anything problematic about the world as it was, and no one needed to tell the kids from Chicago that they weren't welcome on our beach. I was endangered, being primed for numbness.

THE WORKSHOPS

Chris says something is missing for all of us and we come to the workshops to find it. Hollis-El opens a tiny space between thumb and forefinger, Dell Konieczko remembers the beaches in California, Wilson-Bey needs the workshop, Robin's daughter is killed and she needs the workshop, Susan is reliving her abuse, her crime, she needs the workshop, Romando vowed he would never become close to someone again after Vietnam and after he watched his buddy blow his brains out in the VA hospital, and he becomes close to Pilar, Maria, Janie and me, Nate says he found his first real friend through the workshop, Samarrah writes that if they close her workshop they'll take away the only place in the prison where one of the men says he feels human. In the Poet's Corner in 2001, Mike Modeste challenges me to write a poem about what the workshops mean to me. In "For Mike, Because you Asked," I begin with the first epigraph to this chapter, then add,

IV

Antonio comes to extend what he knows of love
  and anger
Gucci comes seeking new families through finding
  his old,
Chi comes to find the stories and voice that will let him
  pass wisdom on
Co-Pilot comes to tame his whirling thoughts into
  powerful renderings of his time
Mike, you come to find rhymes for your hard past
  and for the discipline and insight that motivate you now
Sarah comes for the composite person and comes to delight and surprise us
  with her lyrical twists, her quick laugh
Phil comes out of a commitment to us and to himself

And I come, like you all, to find justice

V

I find it in our unusual laughter
I find it in our challenges and risks
I find it in the gasps I hear when someone reads a powerful poem
  or finds a right line
I find it in the safety of our space and in our liking for each other
I find it in our generosity
  in our forgiveness for what we have not done well
  in the voices we discover as they lift up out of us,
    like smoke and fire,
    singing
I find it in our attempts to understand why we are here,
  in our anger when it rises
I find it in Co-Pilot's desire to write poetry like cutting quick right

> *for a jump-shot and passing off, spontaneous,*
> *I find it in Chi's assignment not to revise*
> > *in Gucci's photographs*
> > *in Phil's mantra*
> > *in Sarah's many names*
> > *in Antonio's family and Co-Pilot's cohesiveness*
> > *in the insistence of the podium*
> *And Mike, I find it in your direct, penetrating questions*
> > *and in our answers*

VI

> *Prisons are about no, the workshops are yes*
> *Prisons are limits, blocks, barriers,*
> > > *workshops*
> > *are openings, doors, dances, breakings through*

> *Prisons are about poverty and poor opportunity,*
> > *boarded houses and rotting schools,*
> > *a system that leaves so many children out,*
> *Workshops are a piece of the reply,*
> > *they are about the strength of our stories,*
> > *about our voices, our songs, our laughter, our resistance,*
> > *about our families,*
> > > *our neighborhoods,*
> > > > *our communities,*
> > > > > *ourselves,*
> > *about what might and may be.*

I think this is it. Most of us entering the workshops, youth, prisoners, students, are having fun, are happy, or not necessarily happy, to be there, are scrambling to write a poem or create a character or draw something that isn't in the room, and one of us will have a beef with the person across the table or at the podium, or we'll feel chaotic and like we are getting nowhere, and we may feel that what is being created—and we are often right—is shallow, undeveloped, not fully formed or articulated, and many of us are preoccupied with other facets of our lives. And yet I think for most of us, underneath, there is always a sense of the potential for something being found between us, among us.

In an English 310 exercise, I number my students off into groups of three, then have them decide which two will play incarcerated youth and who will be the new earnest student facilitator from English 310 who comes to work with them. I send the facilitators from the room and tell the incarcerated youth to make everything extremely difficult for the facilitator. What happens is sometimes even agonizing to watch: the facilitator faces inattention, chaos, individual acting out or closing down, youth storming out, and hard hard challenges and questions. Afterward we debrief. One year, Jessica Anthony, who had played a Maxey youth, told us she had kept pushing the facilitator because she so much needed him to be the right person, to say the right things, to be the person she, from an abusive, negligent background, needed more than anything. And he hadn't been able to give her what she wanted, he wasn't ready, attuned, authentic. He couldn't focus on *her,* his words were nice, conventional. I'm sure he also desperately wanted her to understand who he was, what brought him there, his needs, his wishes for the relation, what was authentic in him.

What I am missing when I seek the workshop may be different from what Chris seeks or Shar or Wilson-Bey or Ricardo. But all of us have been cut off from each other. All of us have been malnourished. All of us are full of experience, talent, and history and are rich, problematic personalities, but we have all been deprived by the walls which have been built between us. At some inarticulate or not well articulated level we want connection between us, and community. What is so exciting about the workshops is that this is in the air, in our process. What is so exciting is that the creative tasks challenge us to find within ourselves what we have to give to ourselves and others and that something happens in the room when we succeed. Whether we know it or not, the workshops are charged with this possibility. Most of the time we probably fail—none of us get the words right—but it is in the air, and when it flares, for a moment or completely, we find what we are seeking. That it has been in the air is evidenced in the frequent refrain among us when a workshop ends, that "we have been a family."

Often as a workshop ends—especially in the juvenile facilities where we are not allowed to have contact afterward—my students are upset that they will not see their workshop members again, and the workshop members are aware, we're all aware, that the walls are still there, that mostly—not always—our lives will continue on separate tracks. Yet those for whom the experience has been profound will seek each other in other people. Once someone has been respected, one seeks respect. Once someone has broken through to connect, one will know how to do that and seek it. Once some-one has engaged across the social chasm in a task-oriented, democratic way, one will seek to do that again, and to find circumstances and careers where it might be sustained, deepen, and be effective.

Our plays move toward reestablishment of community because plays do. But in incarceration places, it is more. So much has been broken. So much has been denied. So much, in a nation of mass incarceration, is clearly wrong. And many in the room have been terribly wronged and many may have done terrible wrong. The deep, hurting, painful need to fix it all is pro-found. The aura of understanding, generosity, and forgiveness and the spir-ited reaching across the room and across boundaries is such a gift here, as it is whenever it happens in any of the hard places on this earth.

BUTTERFLIES

When I visit workshops in the youth facilities, I am exhilarated by the energy, eagerness, excitement, and imagination of so many of the youth. But I always come away deeply saddened by the hurt reflected in their eyes, their bodies, their allusions, their relations with each other, their stories, their poems.

Sometimes when I see the unnecessary cruelty of their lives and of the incarceration places where they and adult prisoners are confined—the con-stant "no," the gratuitous restraints and limits that have nothing to do with security or safety, the deliberate humiliations and targeting by those staff and officers who have burned out or are wrong for the job—a large boot grinding a beautifully colored butterfly into the ground rises in me. Snoop sings loudly in the shower, Sheila sings on her way to her unit: each gets three days of top lock. Cathy may not take with her to a new prison the silk flower we presented at the end of *Junkie*. When Nate Jones enters the cell of an old prisoner who has become physically helpless, in order to assist him, he is given two days top lock. Our workshops are places of growth and con-nection. They are blossoms. For our thirtieth and final play at the Western Wayne Correctional Facility, built long ago on a toxic waste site and now shutting down, Assistant Deputy Warden Pat Rodger arbitrarily decides we may not have costumes and props—even though we have had them for a hundred plays before that—and makes us remove them all before we per-form. Why would she do that? Another assistant deputy warden hates pro-grams, lies to me on the phone, offers obscure time slots for the workshop, limits the number of women who can participate, limits the number of women who can attend the performances, limits the outside audience. At one facility, a special activities director formed a prisoner arts committee and wrote a proposal to the Michigan Department of Corrections for an arts program at the facility, a collaboration with the Prison Creative Arts Project. They turned him down.

CRISIS

From 1990 to 1999 PCAP worked prison by prison. We offered workshops or were invited to offer them and then provided the best-quality work we could. If anything needed to go higher in the Department of Corrections — and almost nothing did—we relied on the special activities staff or assistant deputy wardens for programs to recognize that and take care of it. We didn't call attention to ourselves. Although by 1999 we had held three annual exhibitions of art by Michigan prisoners, the workshops were generally under the radar. I knew that a moment would come when that would change.

In January 1999 MDOC deputy director Dan Bolden summoned me to Lansing. In the past, two friendly wardens and a department insider had helped me understand him and his decisions and on a few occasions they had spoken with him on our behalf, so I knew him to be a peremptory man with great power and not friendly toward programs. As I drove north on January 25, I knew the workshops were at risk.

Bolden is a tall, imposing man with a slight limp from an old basketball injury. He had started his career many years earlier as an officer at Jackson prison, a very tough place. After initial pleasantries, he told me, "I like the art exhibition; I've even gone to the legislature to defend it. But I don't think I like these theater workshops."[18] I leaned forward: "I'd like to tell you about the theater workshops." I warmed to my explanation of our working with prisoners' stories, the improvisation, the respect we bring to everyone at the prisons, our careful, adamant training of our volunteers, the communal themes of the plays in which families and neighborhoods reunite and pull together, the skills gained, the way the workshops helped with prison security.

"What about the gun at Lakeland?" he asked. An actor at the Lakeland Correctional Facility two years earlier had fashioned a gun as a prop without the collusion or knowledge of our team, and a fake gun is of course a potential danger in the prison. The play was canceled. I answered that we had not known, that now no props are made without our permission, that any questions about props go to prison staff, and that there had been no such incident since that time.

"What about those women who wrote to the prisoners?" Charity, one of our most committed members, a School of Social Work student, had sent postcards to the men in the theater workshop at the Saginaw Correctional Facility during her 1998 summer trip. She signed them with a heart, as she does all her correspondence. Cathy had worked on a documentary about the group's last play, then wrote a letter to one of the men and talked about personal matters. It wasn't a love letter. Someone tipped someone off, and officers searched the prisoner rooms and turned the evidence over to the warden. Volunteers are forbidden to correspond with prisoners at the prison where they volunteer, and Warden Burke, a great supporter of our programs, had no choice but to ban the two women from the prison. At the time I wrote to both Warden Burke and Dan Bolden and now repeated what I said then: that we were in the wrong. I told him that our strict training had become stricter and that no such incident had happened since. We learn and we tighten up.

My responses were disarming and acceptable, but he wanted changes: we must send him our scripts for approval, and he needed a mission statement. Knowing that this meant potential censorship and also knowing that if I disagreed, our work in the prisons was over, I assented and promised him the mission statement within a week. We shook hands and parted on friendly terms.

Early the next week, English 319 teams about to start their theater workshops were turned away at the door. Over the next ten days one by one they and PCAP theater teams fell, with a few exceptions. At one facility the special activities director kept things going until finally receiving an order to "cease and desist." On the other hand, the Florence Crane warden decided that *all* workshops should be closed down, not only the Sisters Within Theater Troupe, but also our dance workshop, our creative writing workshop, and a debate club that we had helped another University of Michigan campus get started.

I immediately completed the mission statement and sent it off, then phoned Bolden's office. I was told he would get back to me when he was ready. I phoned again. No response. No communication. I was cut off. Although he and I were both well-paid public servants, he treated me as he would treat a prisoner. I was owed no explanation.

I gradually pieced together what had happened. Sara Falls and Matt Schmitt, two dedicated veteran PCAP members, were working on a play in the Residential Treatment Program Unit at Western Wayne. In the play, a man planning to quit the drug trade agrees to one final street deal; during the deal, he wounds a policeman. Neither the Department of Mental Health counselor nor the officer who sat in had objected to the plot, and Sara and Matt hadn't seen the problem. The warden for some reason had requested a copy of the scenario, and when she saw it she erupted: corrections officers are referred to as "police" by prisoners, and the wounding of a policeman might be suggestive. It was clearly a mistake on our part. She called at least one other warden and told him we were killing police in our plays. I assume she called Bolden and told him the same. I believe this was his excuse to close us down.[19]

My students were puzzled, angry, and hurt, and wished to fight back. On February 12, Samarrah Fine wrote,

I just got back from a reading of prisoners' poetry. It was beautiful, and moving, and real. Just like the first time I saw prisoners' artwork I was surprised by the talent. I imagine that most of these artists entered prison without realizing the talent inside of them, never having the opportunity to express it. Again I am reminded of the importance of our work, helping people express their inner voice, allowing them an outlet, respect that they are not given in their daily situation. Life inside a prison must be hell, a hell that is too painful to imagine. One of the prisoners explained, in his poem, how it is only through workshops (like the creative writing, art, and theater ones) that he is treated as a human. When I heard these words I had to bite my lip and hold back the tears. My normally calm hands became clenched and the muscles in my back stiffened. If these workshops are the only way that prisoners can feel human, why are they being canceled? Obviously, rehabilitation is not the goal of the correctional system and neither is justice. I am not quite sure what the goal of the system is. Right now it seems like the correctional system is simply a pawn in a complex game of political chess. I hate chess and I hate it even more to know that what seems like a harmless game is hurting real people. It is killing real people.[20]

On the fourteenth, another student, whose team had actually gotten in once before this all broke and had a great, lively beginning, reported on what happened next:

We drove up to Parnall and went to the front desk. The guard at the desk was an unfamiliar face. It took him a while to make the phone calls to tell them that we were here. For some reason, I had this feeling that we, our group, was going to go through with the workshop. I had confidence that Parnall was going to choose to ignore the memo. Silly, I know. But I was hopeful. Then we got the news. News that really pissed me off. The moment the guard told us that the workshop was cancelled until further notice, my heart sank. I soon felt the frustration and anger that everyone else (in our class) has been experiencing. Last week at our group meeting, when Shira and Colleen's workshop was officially closed, I couldn't really understand how they were feeling. Now I do. Sure I'm pissed off that we can't continue this great work with the men at Parnall, but I also wonder what exactly these men were told. Did the guards tell them that there was a memo going around to many of the prisons that put a hold on all of the theater workshops? For some reason, I doubt they did. Maybe this is unfair, but I imagine that some guards (or anyone) believe that the prisoners do not need to know the truth—they're only *prisoners*. My worry is that the men in our workshop were told that we (Zach, Steve, and myself) decided to stop the workshop. They wouldn't be told that, right? . . . I felt like I was actually making a difference, however small, when Jimmy told us that we were helping the people from staying away from the invisible line. And now that our workshops are all cancelled, I hope to do my best in keeping people across that invisible line. I really don't understand why we are being held from doing our workshops. How can one person have so much power? Can't they see that the workshops mean something to us and the prisoners? I guess I'm being naive—there's so much more that I just don't know.

On the twentieth, Brian Goodman tried to puzzle it out:

I guess on the bright side, all of these problems really go to show what powerful, important work is being done in these programs. If the prisons are so cautious and people are so vehemently against these programs, then they must have a fairly profound effect. It's just that where I, and I'm suspecting the rest in this class, would see this effect as very positive, others see it as very negative. I can see the point of trying to control the power a prisoner has in prison. But I think that is being confused with the power a prisoner finds within him or herself. Let me *in*!

Also on the twentieth, Liz Grubb, writing about her PCAP workshop at Southern Michigan Correctional Facility, talked about the first workshop session after their first play. The men, aware of the threat, had spoken about the need for everyone to be responsible in every way and had spoken about what the workshop meant to them.

> They know that there are HIGH STAKES on this workshop, that we could all lose it with the drop of a hat, and they gave Co-Pilot a hard time for getting in *trouble,* with guards, drugs, "drinking"—we talked about avoiding problems *for* the sake of the workshop and out of respect for group members. Obviously, it wasn't Liz, Josh, or I who brought ANY of this up, it was Michael, Potsel, Jones-El, Co-Pilot . . . they set up ground rules of attendance, respect, focus, commitment because they know *it's vital for them* and *vital for the outside,* my dad, etc. It's workshops like last night that remind me of what I'm doing here, I talk about what this all means to me, to them, but the men told *me* why they do this—and I will die if this ends, too. We have to fight for this.

Lee Shainis had already written about fighting: "I would still like to know what the true driving force behind the shut down was. I think we should start writing letters to whoever was responsible for the shut down." In the middle of Liz's journal writing, I phoned her about the "cease and desist" at the one prison.

> It wasn't a surprise to me at all. But I'm racking my brain to think of what we can DO now, we aren't powerless, we have to be creative and organize and pull together now ESPECIALLY. We need letters and testimonies from prisoners, their families, our friends, those who have seen the work, those who have heard it, people who don't want to release more damaged human beings out onto the streets, people who want to hear from the millions behind bars. It has to be massive, creative, complete. Not because we have built much of our lives on this work, but because a very vital and sacred part of these men and women's lives is being violated, and because the rest of the world should be able to communicate with *All* people.

I had to scramble. I transferred prison teams to juvenile facilities. I transformed theater workshops into poetry workshops. I asked Phil Klintworth if he would like a poetry workshop, then sent Shawn Durrett and

Melissa Spengler, who had been assigned to Huron Valley Men's, to Southern Michigan Correctional Facility. This was the beginning of the Poet's Corner, which I would join in 2001. At another facility, we shifted to poetry, but at the insistence of the prisoners we placed those wishing to do theater in the next room. They were actually able to perform in April. Three prisons didn't read, or ignored, Bolden's directive, and so we continued. I had received no communication from Bolden or anyone else, and so it wasn't up to me to tell the staff what to do.

In the meantime, total silence. I had nightmares. In one, a solid heavy black blob grew larger and larger until it obscured everything: I was looking at the boot from the butterfly's point of view. Over the years I had achieved nearly complete autonomy in my academic life; I was respected, had been awarded, could teach the courses I wished. Now, I realized, I had very little autonomy: I could be disregarded or cut off at any moment. I recalled how hurt and permanently affected I had been the two times my generally very loving father had responded to my behavior with the silent treatment. Dan Bolden was tapping that hurt and tapping it more deeply, because what PCAP had created had become beautiful to so many people.

And I was figuring out what to do. I knew how to organize in the way Lee, Liz, and others were advocating—and as a last resort would have done so—but I also knew that such an effort would alienate not only Bolden, but others in the system, and would most likely fail. I had waited nearly a month to hear from him, so on February 19, Laurie Hess, Jesse Jannetta, and I drove to Lansing to share our situation with state senator Alma Wheeler Smith and her administrative assistant Simone Strong. I also met with Cynthia Wilbanks, University of Michigan vice president for government relations. Smith and Wilbanks conferred, then on February 23 sent Bolden memos requesting a meeting. That day he wrote me a letter reinstating the workshops. Regional prison administrators were to review and approve the plays before they could be performed. And performances and readings were forbidden to "use controversial topics. This includes those that may incite prisoners that could lead to their acting out, topics which are immoral, sexually explicit, exploit women, or have overt racial tones." While "controversial topics" was open to interpretation and could lead to censorship, we clearly knew better than to "incite" prisoners and of course had no interest in plays that were exploitative or racist or that advocated violence.

Our regional prison administrator, Denise Quarles, in a March 12 letter asked us to submit the scenario to a prison staff person, who would ensure "that the content of the script is appropriate for a prisoner audience." It would then come through the warden to her, and she would make the final decision. The first play we submitted, later that month, *Choices in Life,* came from a PCAP team at the Ryan Correctional Facility.[21] The plot included three separate endings—in two a man is wounded and in the other killed. The result in the first was incarceration, in the second his accomplice checked into drug rehabilitation, and in the third, where the man dies, community members met to seek solutions to community violence. It was against violence. RPA Quarles told us to eliminate the three violent scenes. I wrote an elaborate letter describing the antiviolence purpose and requested that she revise her decision. A brief return memo indicated she had the backing of Bolden and would not reconsider. The team was discouraged and decided not to revise, although I pointed out that they could take the violence offstage but refer to it and still present the three outcomes. As it turned out on later occasions, RPA Quarles accepted such revisions, and no other play was stopped.[22] By June 8, seven workshops had submitted scenarios that had been approved, and the plays had been performed. We were back in business and the plays were as honest as ever.

In 1998 we had added a dance workshop at the Florence Crane Women's Facility, and the women had performed twice, on April 28 (no title) and on September 6 (*Ineffable Women*). Under the guidance of School of Dance student and then BFA graduate Amy Martin and her partners Emily Konzen and Karen Goodyke, the women improvised and choreographed original pieces and utilized the Evergreen Gymnasium floor and stage spaces for their performances. It was as beautiful and important as anything we have ever done. Bolden's February 23 letter to me announced, "Dance Workshops—After review of this program, we have decided to discontinue it completely."

Again we gathered forces. Amy wrote to Bolden, explaining the workshop and telling him that "it is done tastefully, with no physical contact, and no sexual connotations."[23] Judy Rice, assistant professor and director of ballet at the School of Dance, also wrote, praising Amy as "consistent, responsible, reliable, and trustworthy . . . one of the top students in her class . . . so competent that I often asked her to substitute teach for me."[24] Bolden's administrative assistant Julie Southwick had informed me in a phone conversation that his "decision was based on the assumption and understandable fear that dance would include physical contact of the kind that is not permitted in the prisons." In my cover letter to Bolden, I explained that Amy's work did not involve that kind of contact, told him Assistant Deputy Warden Dan Hawkins, who had attended rehearsals, was willing to characterize the workshop for him, and asked to continue the dance workshops with "a guarantee that the dances will not include physical contact of the kind forbidden by Department regulations, understanding that if we do not follow the guarantee the workshops will be ended."[25] The response from Bolden, through Julie Southwick, did not engage with our letters. She wrote that Bolden would allow us to teach a dance theory class: "however, the dance workshops, as explained in your letter of March 23, 1999, is [sic] not authorized by Deputy Director Bolden."[26] In other words, "I told you no!"

I thought about this. Since we had guaranteed no touch and were still denied, I took the liberty of assuming the issue wasn't touch. So why would dance be denied and art, poetry, and theater allowed? We had already had dance workshops in the boys' and girls' juvenile facilities. In Florida Leslie Neal was in the early stages of developing a dance program in the prisons that would become fully supported. What troubled someone like Bolden? Any of the arts can appear dangerous to someone intent on oppressing growth and the human spirit. So why dance in particular?

It may be what the antagonist sees. Writers and artists sit quietly at tables, and when they stand and share their work, they seldom engage in movement. Theater involves movement, and mostly more than one person before an audience at any moment, and because of theater we had been closed down and now were under the threat of censure. Prison dancers move through space in a place of human confinement. Because dancers usually do not speak, the body is accented, the body evokes sensuality, and the accompanying music is often emotional. And more than the other arts, dance reminds warders of the humanity of those they keep. Many, perhaps most, warders are not afraid of that humanity and support its expression and growth. Others are afraid. Or it may be they understand that in order to circumscribe and confine human beings, they need to suppress all that might touch and move them.

Another 319 student had been taking a course on Primo Levi from my colleague Ralph Williams. She had learned "how when every liberty is taken away the need to feel human is overwhelming. I think these drama workshops allow prisoners, juveniles and students to regain their humanity. Auschwitz was a very extreme form of imprisonment in which innocent people were denied basic human rights. But I think some of the same issues might come into mind when someone lives in prison."[27]

Sometime in 1991, Sharleen Wabindato walks into the TV Production Room, where the Sisters Within Theater Troupe rehearses. She has long straight dark hair, sharp alert glowering features, personal force. She is a lifer in her fourteenth year in prison. She gives only what she wishes to give. She watches. She decides what she will trust, and she trusts very little. But she is there. But that, she tells us, is all. We'll get no risks from her, nothing of what is buried within. I ask if she'll do a brief improvisation with one other person whom she can choose, an improvisation in which she makes exactly the same point. Sitting near the door, she agrees, and remains in her chair as Dora does the scene with her. She makes her point fiercely, closed, sure. And we thank her. She has acted, and on her terms. She has her reasons and we trust that, trust that she is there.

In *Junkie* Sharleen has entered fully into the role of a whimsical light-headed addict. Worried about her lines, she has me sit in the front row so she can see me and be encouraged. When we begin to work on *Inside and Personal,* she says, "We have to dance." And she doesn't take a role. She dances. Prison overcrowding has eliminated our recreation room performance space, but on May 21, 1994, on a beautiful warm evening, we perform outside on a patio that Mary Glover, no longer in the troupe, rose early in the morning to sweep out for us. Drusila Blackman, Jackie Wilson, and others act out Drusila's story of a prisoner with AIDS. Dru alone on stage announces that her baby has died, another statistic in the onslaught of AIDS. The music comes up, and Shar and Sunny Nienhuis dance to "Gone Too Soon," moving apart and together, something in the evening light that haunts us forever with its beauty and haunts everyone to whom I ever show the video. Shar dances in every play thereafter and becomes one of our most powerful, risk-taking, vital actors. After dance is forbidden, we perform *Open Arms,* a play in which many of the women risk stories about themselves and their children. Shar joins Susie Boyd, Suzie Dewitt, Kalah Gunn, and Sunny Nienhuis in shaping a series of shifting sculptures as Shree Murrell Ford sings the title song to open the play. It is as moving as anything we have done.

In the workshops we seek what is missing, we undertake the task of collaborative creation and find each other, we resist the walls built into us and built between us. We are sloppy and chaotic and contentious and sometimes superficial and unconnected and slow. We become vulnerable and we blossom. We dance. It is what we have come to do, and we will do it.

CHAPTER FIVE

A Matter of Language

On April 5, 2006, I received an e-mail message from Maureen McGraw, Library director and our liaison at the Thumb Correctional Facility:

> It is imperative that you meet with Connie Carriveau (Manager of Programs and Education), Deputy Will Riley and myself before the next theatre/creative writing class session.
>
> The U of M students will not be allowed back into the facility until we have had an opportunity to discuss some issues of concern.
>
> Please get back to me as promptly as possible. The next class session is Sunday.

I immediately messaged Paul Feigenbaum and Kristen Lindquist (the PCAP poetry workshop) and Mihal Ansik and Anna Paris (the 319 theater workshop), asking what it might be about. Their answers stumbled in: maybe it was this, maybe that, but really they had no idea. I thought of requesting a phone conversation: Lapeer is eighty minutes away and the trip would consume more than a half day of my overwhelming schedule. But the e-mail message was peremptory, I didn't know Deputy Riley personally, and my instincts told me to keep quiet and get out there.

The previous year the Michigan Department of Corrections had closed Michigan's one private prison, the Wackenhut facility in Baldwin, located in Michigan's poorest county, Lake County. Governor Engler had established what he called this "punk prison" for youth sentenced as adults, "young violent offenders." The nonunionized, mostly white rural officers were afraid of the prisoners and would remain at a distance and write major disciplinary tickets, contributing to the tension in a very charged prison.[1] When the Baldwin prison closed, the youth were sent to a unit at the Thumb Facility. We had worked with this population at the Michigan Reformatory in 1997 and 1998, and in the fall of 2005 I asked Thumb's warden Millie Warren if she would like PCAP workshops for the youth. Committed to programs, and especially solicitous for these boys, she seized the opportunity.

I call them boys and youth. Yet I had visited the 319 workshop and had immediately felt the difference from the boys at Boysville, Calumet, and Maxey. The Thumb boys had some of the same energy and laughter, but were also older in some subtle sense. There was more tension in them and between them. They were both incarcerated youth and adult prisoners.

Two mornings later Maureen, Connie, and I sat at one end of a long conference table facing Will Riley. Riley, cordial, exuding power, firm, in his fifties, affirmed his liking for PCAP programs, which he had observed at other prisons. He wanted to describe the problems he was seeing so that we could continue at Thumb. He laid out the issues, and the issues were real. I told him we would adjust. Back home I messaged the facilitators to meet me on Saturday, letting them know "not to worry, we just need to get very clear and then go ahead with the really great work all of you are doing."

They had in fact done nothing wrong. Kristen and Paul's writers had told them that having an officer in their small room limited the risks they could take with content. Kristen and Paul requested of Maureen that the officer sit outside in the hall. This made complete sense. Anna and Mihal, lively, spirited, bold women, coeval with the youth, led vigorous warm-ups, took friendly interest in each actor, and complimented them as they stepped up to take roles, invent plot, and move the play forward. They had split into subgroups, and although Mihal's group stifled itself and was often silly as it developed a plot related to Hurricane Katrina, this had not altered Mihal's posture.

But they had done wrong. The two youth who wished the officer away, Riley pointed out, wished to write poems with sexual language to provoke Kristen or poems that hinted their attraction to her. They would sit next to her, risk an "accidental" touch. It could escalate. The young men enjoyed watching Anna and Mihal jump about during the warm-ups. One altered his hairstyle, probably to get attention, and was pleased when Anna complimented him. The others noticed. In the unit, of course, they talked about the two women and argued over who was liked by whom. They might end up fighting each other. It might play out, too, in the workshop and escalate, even with Maureen in the room and an officer not far away. Recently some of their peers, not from our workshops, had jumped a dividing fence and beaten badly two older prisoners from the general population.

It was difficult to explain how both sides were right, but the students accepted it and moved forward, adjusting their behavior. Anna addressed the issue at length in her final paper for 319, and I responded:

> Right, it is very complex, very complicated, the fact that you *and* the prison are right about the guys. They are happy, they are enjoying the workshop, they are enjoying the chance to work with two energetic committed women coming in from outside. It may be giving them some tools and skills, something to work for. They are good guys, full of fun, wit, seriousness, potential. At the same time, they have committed violent crimes and whatever is behind those crimes hasn't suddenly disappeared from their make-up, they haven't necessarily gotten rid of the triggers that lead to that kind of behavior. They are not always like they are in the workshop. The prison officials observe what happens. They are with them twenty-four hours, they are trained, they understand what is going on sometimes better than we do, they know what can happen. They get nuances we don't get. And, yes, the prison is oppressive, limiting, traumatizing, and the guys are hindered by that, hurt by it. And on and on and on. And, right, doing this work, you have to live with it, all sides of it. I like it that you are figuring this out and tough and wanting to continue.[2]

PRISON LANGUAGE

Prison is a *place*. Each of us has imagined it and been encouraged in our imagining by media representations. And it is real. Architecturally, it takes many shapes, although the prison building boom of the 1980s and 1990s brought many replications. Everywhere concertina wire, almost everywhere guard towers, everywhere a parking area with spaces designated according to the mostly military hierarchy of the prison and warnings: no alcohol, no photographs, no cell phones. In English 411, my film course on U.S. prisons, I require my students to go to the parking lot and lobby of a local prison or camp (there are twelve within forty-five minutes)[3] and write reflections in their journals. Some have my first experience: in the lot I felt watched and guilty, as if I had done something wrong or would make a mistake and be apprehended; I imagined and romanticized the women I saw yard-walking beyond the concertina wire.

Typically lobbies have a long front desk attended by an officer, a sign-in book, stapled pages of visiting rules, free lockers or lockers that swallow your quarters, ganged plastic chairs where you wait, family member or volunteer, until they are ready for you. Once there were prisoner-written newspapers, no more. It is a drab space. Photo portraits of the governor and the director of the Department of Corrections hang over the desk. Sometimes a prison artist, for pennies an hour, has painted a mural, usually a landscape. Sometimes along the wall, a glass case with prisoner crafts or drawings for sale. Sometimes T-shirts with slogans intended to be funny. Postings of union information, announcements of a facility picnic. Occasionally officers escort shackled prisoners in or out. In the early morning you may see released prisoners accompanied to waiting cars by apprehensive, excited and happy, or neutral family members.

You enter the security zone ("the bubble") through a door from the lobby, which opens, then closes behind you. You empty the few permitted items from your pockets and pass through the metal detector, which is sometimes very sensitive, sometimes not at all. A male or female officer, depending on your gender, shakes you down, passing their hands over your body, sometimes quickly and perfunctorily, sometimes thoroughly, rarely violating boundaries. It takes getting used to. If you have left something in your pocket, you return to your locker. If you have failed to remove some aspirin, it will be photographed and you will be ejected, perhaps forbidden to return; if it turns out to be a drug, you are likely to be prosecuted. You remove shoes and socks. The officer shakes them out. You show the bottom of your feet, stick out your tongue, lift your hair. The officer marks your hand with invisible ink, and you show it under ultraviolet light: no prisoner will take your clothes and get away with impersonating you. You receive your personal protection device (PPD — pull the pin and officers come running) and hook it on your belt. The officer skims through your notebook or pad, makes sure you have a see-through pen, shakes down your props and costumes. She returns your state ID. The door into the prison opens, then closes behind you. No two bubble doors may be open at the same time.

You pass the command center, pull the pin on your PPD (it registers on a monitor), the sergeant or lieutenant nods, enter the yard with your escort, an officer or special activities director, and head toward the education building. If no escort is available, a yard officer "eyes" you ("does a visual") to assure you are safe. Perhaps the yard is empty—it is count time or a higher-security prison where yard hours are few. Or it is full. Prisoners, in our first years dressed in their own clothes, now dressed in blue with an orange stripe, their number stenciled on the back shoulders, are on their way to chow, to work, to programs, they are on the phones, in the weight pit, playing basketball, throwing horseshoes, clustered, walking, curious about you, sometimes casting out a greeting or catcall. Officers stand alone or in pairs, greet each other, sometimes exchange greetings with prisoners or hurry them on, have a firm bearing that is not quite military.

Whether the authorities are casual and friendly, even happy to see you, or rigid and peremptory, they are in charge. They may greet you, accommodate you, smooth your way, chat with you, laugh with you. But they can choose to be cold and hostile, treat you with suspicion as a naive outsider who doesn't understand prison and prisoners and who might mess things up, and you have no recourse. If there is a problem with the call-out for your workshop, if you have forgotten your ID, if you are wearing clothes you've worn many times before and suddenly there is a problem with them, they can call back to shift command or to the units and work it out or they can refuse to do so. They can enjoy your props and costumes or they can shake them down and eliminate one after another.[4] When they escort you through the yard, they can enjoy learning about your workshop and praise what you are doing, or they can tell you the prisoners will manipulate you, that everyone in your workshop is a sex offender or violent, that the prisoners are scum, that you should not stand too close to them. It is their choice.

We watch the power dynamic between officers and prisoners. We see officers who are relaxed and good-natured, who josh with the prisoners, and who are liked, and this pleases us. We see the opposite, a nervous or hostile or distanced officer who sends a poet back because he is missing a button or has his shirt untucked or is thirty seconds late. And, whether friendly or not, it can always turn: it is at the officer's pleasure. We see that something is always under negotiation, that relations are charged, that there is in fact danger, there is humiliation, a walking on eggshells, challenges and provocations, disciplinary tickets and reprisals in the air. Then we realize: although we are not incarcerated, it is not so different with us. Our presence and options depend on the benevolence or neutrality or hostility, on the mood of the officers, on what they imagine or choose to perceive: overfriendliness with prisoners, a touch, a note passed.

This is the language conveyed by the institution to free-world people who enter, and to the incarcerated.[5] Prisons are complex worlds with rich and varied dimensions, yet the predominant communication is one of power, constraint, limitation, containment, an impulse to deny, take away, restrict. The predominant communication is not about creativity, enlarging personal capacity, growth.

To a great extent this communication is not only justified but justifiable. Prisons are volatile and need to be safe for everyone. Prisoners vastly out-number officers on duty. Prisoners experience what for many is the trauma of having little control over their lives, the constant humiliation of being under the thumb of others. Most carry inside themselves the neglected, crowded, abusive, frustrated, destructive and self-destructive environments they were born into that by one path or another brought them to prison; the violence of their neighborhoods, the gang rivalries, the gunfights, the hurt bystanders and children; whatever triggers them; what has been done to them; what they have done to others; the children they miss even though they might have hurt them; the tensions and dangers of prison, hierarchies, power struggles; their malnourishment; and, for so many of them, their illit-eracy. Romando Valeroso explains to my students over video[6] that when he leaves his cell in the morning, he says good-bye to the photographs of his loved ones. He doesn't know if he'll see them again. In "I Remember . . ." George Hall writes about

the years of isolation . . .

F-Block in Marquette,
where once doors were literally
welded shut . . .

and watching a man die
over three packs of cigarettes.

He writes in "Taking,"

I will myself not to hate
into bitter oblivion
as little by little my keepers take

more and more from me,
my self respect, my clothing,
all the small things of comfort,
and next my word processor, they say,
we are taking everything.

I wonder if they can see
what smolders darkly
inside my mind,
what force it takes
to will into myself docility,
not to react violently
to their intrusions.

I will myself not to hate
into bitter oblivion
not to strike blindly out
in helpless frustration
and thus to destroy
what little is left of me . . .
trying to hold onto
what little dignity
is left in me.[7]

The Corrections Union newsletters I read on the wall inside the Huron Valley Women's Facility as we wait for our escort detail the latest fight between inmates, the latest stabbing of an officer, the latest hospitalization. Officers—who work in a military hierarchy; who, even with the best intentions, wear away in the face of provocations, in the face of having to deny and order and give pain;[8] who often harden, become numb, and retaliate; who often have to put loyalty to fellow officers above fairness to a prisoner with a grievance; whose home lives are so often damaged by what happens at their workplace; who participate in the tension and latent and real violence of the prison—know that if they allow a prisoner to overstep a boundary, it can lead anywhere. Containment and constraint are necessary.

As we walk out of the parking lot into the lobby and come up to the desk, pass through the bubble and into the yard,[9] what do the officers see?

We are very young and therefore unseasoned, susceptible.

Although at the beginning we may have some fear, we are also, as a rule, spirited and flamboyant. We laugh, often loudly. We chatter among ourselves, and it is usually obvious that we like each other. We have a rather intense, young energy. We walk with confidence. On the whole we come from privilege, unlike nearly every prisoner, unlike most officers. Most of us attended excellent high schools, had parents with high incomes who read to us as children and tutors, classes, and coaches to help us pass standardized tests, all factors in our test success.[10] We may have held summer jobs, even working-class jobs, we might have part-time jobs now, but our need to work comes from our attending the nation's most expensive public university. Most of us have traveled abroad. In our bodies, our words, our heads, a feeling of entitlement. One or another of us might talk about "my place" at the university as something due to us. For many of us it is a new and hard idea to think of William Martinez as our brother. Only recently have some of us realized that a commitment to social justice means radical reorientation.

We dress down, in willing compliance with prison and juvenile facility policy. We wear baggy clothes and avoid extravagant jewelry and makeup. We understand why this is important. Yet even dressing down we dress well. It is clear in our bearing that we are accustomed to dress well.

We touch. Many of us come from families and all of us come from a university youth culture that is physical: we hug, kiss, shake hands, place a hand on an arm or a shoulder for emphasis.

We are compassionate, altruistic. Most of us are women, too few are men. We may still be mired in problematic notions like "helping" and "reaching out." We are optimistic, might be naive, might romanticize the boys and girls, the men and women, in our workshops. It is likely we won't always be alert.

We have a political bent, are very aware of social injustice, of poverty, of the broad disparities in the United States and what groups are most affected. Most of us, some with ambivalence, find ourselves on the side of the incarcerated and their families, victims of a cruel deliberate policy of mass incarceration. We might be too ready to take in prisoner stories and respond by doing what we have been told not to do. We may scorn the custodians as keepers and oppressors of prisoners. It is all too possible that we hold economically and culturally induced stereotypes of the human beings who have found jobs in prisons. We may see them as enemies.

We are creative. We have been to plays, concerts, galleries, and poetry slams. We are artists, actors, poets, dancers, or are in the process of becoming so. We believe in freedom of expression and in self-expression. Whatever our individual fears and constraints, we believe in improvisation, risk, vulnerability, the telling of our personal stories, in honesty and authenticity.

We believe in growth.

THERE YOU HAVE IT

On the whole PCAP believes in creativity and growth. On the whole the prison believes in containment and security, though those who either pay lip service to growth or genuinely believe in it make it possible for us to be there. And PCAP and the prison are both right: unless they are stifled, human beings have a propensity and a right to become more fully human, and prison is volatile and needs discipline, clear policies, strict demarcations. The question is how to accommodate the two languages.

TROUBLE

Like all volunteers and all correctional staff who enter prisons, we make mistakes and find ourselves in trouble. Although it is *very* rare that these things happen—and most of them have happened only once—English 310 and 319 students, Art and Design 310 students, and PCAP members have dressed inappropriately; carried out cards or notes or gifts from the incarcerated; been out of place; accepted love poems from the incarcerated; written to the incarcerated at their prison where they volunteer;[11] spoken back to facility personnel; been consistently late for workshops; failed to respond to signs of sexual aggression; overseen (in a juvenile facility) the publication of an anthology with inappropriate material; forgotten where they are. Because 99.9 percent of the time we prevent such behavior, even when provoked or tempted, we have a great reputation and continue working in prisons and juvenile facilities after twenty years.

Still, now and then goodwill, goodness of heart, thinking the best, not wanting to tell, unseasoned instinct, bravado, rashness, stereotyping, admiring, loving, not wanting to be racist or classist, not wanting to leave one's politics at the door,[12] failure to fully assimilate the complexity of the place and the complexity of the lives of those who work and who are incarcerated there—sometimes these things prevail.

Youth is not a matter of years. I have been out of place. When the women were moved from the Florence Crane Women's to the Western Wayne Correctional Facility in 2000, lifers were sent to the Scott Correctional Facility and we lost Shar Wabindato, one of the Sisters Within Theater Troupe's most influential members, initiator of dance, creator of deeply moral roles, a person of courage. Four plays later, in late 2002, I learned she had been transferred to Western Wayne, then saw her pass by the recreation room on her way to a visit. In my ninth year at Western Wayne, I was at ease and sure of myself. I went down the corridor, up the stairs, and greeted her as she passed from the prisoner waiting area into the visiting room. An officer standing by asked, "Who are you? What are you doing here?" When I tried to explain, she sent me back to the recreation room, then later came by, asked more questions, and wrote a violation report. It was helpful that we were in good standing at Western Wayne. I explained the circumstances to Assistant Deputy Warden Chapman and acknowledged that I had violated volunteer rules and apologized. He wrote me a gentle and supportive letter of reprimand. In another facility I might have been risking the workshop.

PREVENTION

Training

Our training is more thorough than that of any other university group and is often more tough-minded and detailed than the orientations given by prison staff. Everything is at stake: safety, our reputation, our ability to continue in the facilities and thus opportunities for incarcerated youth and adults to have creative spaces where they can invent, find themselves, work together, and grow.

We worry that students from other programs, less trained and motivated by pass/fail grades and course requirements, will do something that will eliminate us all. Years ago, a Project Community student entered the bubble at Western Wayne with marijuana that (I assume) he had neglected to remove from his jacket. He was ejected and threatened with prosecution. In the following weeks prisoners leaving PCAP workshops received full-body searches, and performers in our Residential Treatment Program theater troupe were not permitted to shake hands or stand close to outside guests. During the reception, at least ten officers (normally there would be at most two), arms folded, watched every interaction. I felt as if I had been transferred to some repressive foreign country.[13]

In our training we *stress* that facility rules and regulations be obeyed, no matter where our impulses, instincts, judgment, and compassion are leading us. We may be right in seeing particular regulations as oppressive, but we are not experts on security, not necessarily keen observers of behavior. We don't know what might happen when we or an incarcerated person takes a first step in the wrong direction. We are clear that when a youth sneaks a note into a facilitator's notebook, the facilitator must inform both me and the facility liaison immediately. We go carefully through procedures for handling any kind of inappropriate approach by an incarcerated youth or adult.[14] We require everyone to read our in-house manual, which details our mistakes and their consequences, as well as instances when someone averted a mistake. The mistakes are heralded as "Warning Stories":

WARNING STORY: A 319 team with a great prison theater workshop felt uncomfortable with the behavior of one of the men—he always sat by them, sat close, the vibes were off—but he never did anything overt. *So they didn't say anything in their journals or team meetings.* The night of the performance he brushed his hand slowly over the butt of one of the students. She reported it to Buzz the next day, but not that night to the special activities person. An investigation revealed that the prisoner was there for criminal sexual conduct, and he was sent north to another prison, losing some of his good time. The student was asked if she wanted to press charges for sexual assault, and she decided not to do so. If the team had mentioned their discomfort to Buzz, he would have told them what to do, and the incident would not have occurred. Staff at the prison were going to end our workshops there for a while (this is one of our best sites), but luckily the supervisor of the special activities director said he wanted to continue the programs. *We almost lost that one.* REMEMBER ALWAYS TALK IN GROUP AND TEAM MEETINGS ABOUT WHAT MAKES YOU UNCOMFORTABLE. YOU'LL GET EXCELLENT ADVICE AND BE SPARED SOMETHING LIKE THIS. *And if there is an incident, report it immediately that night at the facility. We can be in trouble if we don't do so.*

That some students go to their first several workshops super anxious—

because of the warnings—that they will make a wrong move, is not a problem. It is better than the opposite. We have told them that we consider them colleagues working in trying and confusing circumstances, that we know there are pitfalls, and that if something happens, there is no blame, only troubleshooting and problem-solving. We assure them that most of the incarcerated and most officers, counselors and staff, as long as we are honest, are also committed to solving and moving on.

Communication with the Facility

I usually make the first contact with the facility, with a counselor, teacher, program director, special activities director, assistant deputy warden for programs, deputy warden, or warden. My status is useful to PCAP. A professor at the University of Michigan, I am also known as the founder of PCAP, which has an excellent reputation. I listen to their program needs and make clear that our purpose is to serve facility goals, that we follow rules and regulations and compliment their tough-minded orientation with one of our own, that we provide weekly or biweekly supervision of our "volunteers,"[15] and that we stay in very close touch with the liaison. While they don't have the same status and authority, sophisticated and experienced PCAP members can easily make the contact as well. After the initial contact, I turn over relations with the new liaison to those who will actually be at the facility and am in reserve—again as a useful, experienced, professional figure— for any moments when a call from me might move things forward or solve problems. Sometimes the contact will want something written, as Christina Bates at the Gus Harrison Correctional Facility did for a poetry and a theater workshop in January 2006. In my reply, I cited our past years of workshops in the prisons, let her know about our strict training and adherence to facility regulations, and described the procedures we would follow and the skills the participants would gain. The poetry workshop "will meet for an hour or more once a week."

> The team will first ask the participants to talk about their experiences with poetry, what they wish to work on, the kind of content and form they are interested in, and their aspirations as writers. From then on the team will encourage individual growth in writing skills and handling of content. Within the workshop each week, the team will bring individual and group writing exercises, with sharing and discussion of each written work. They will also assign poems to be written during the week to be brought in and

read each week. We stress clear oral presentations, constructive feedback, and an atmosphere in which participants can write honestly. When the participants are ready, we hold a reading at the facility. This will probably take place at the end of April. Often we also put together an anthology of each poet's best writing and make a copy for the facility library and two copies for the participants, so that they may send one home.

By participating in the workshop, participants gain skills in working together, in listening carefully and offering constructive feedback, in trusting their own stories and histories and imagination, in taking responsibility for their own work, and in speaking articulately before an audience. The attention and praise of the audience, as well as the week by week growth in their ability to write and share, add to each participant's sense of his own possibilities.[16]

This professional, reassuring, listening beginning is followed by regular checking-in, seeking advice, and coming through. The liaison appreciates the respect and usually enjoys the energy and spirit of the PCAP people who come in. Thanks to this communication, he or she is comfortable dealing with difficulties, ready to communicate, and amenable to negotiation and healing when problems arise.

Supervision

The 310 and 319 students write about their workshops in weekly journals, which get long responses, and talk about their workshop in team meetings where their peers respond and advise. I am alert to the nuances and am able to detect developing problems. Every two weeks, at PCAP general meetings, consistent small groups—each with a mix of new members and experienced members—meet and provide the same service to each other. When something problematic does occur at a facility, I take the occasion to send out a reminder to everyone. And before a performance, knowing what can happen in the emotion of a reading or performance and the end of a workshop, we also send reminders, as well as instructions for non-PCAP outside guests about the dress and behavior expected of them.

Troubleshooting

When Erin Connelly and her partner Ari arrived in the Education Building at the Ryan Correctional Facility one evening in February 2002, prisoners were clustered around the desk where they checked in. Al, a member of their theater workshop, was in a heated discussion with a young female officer who was new to the facility and to the job. Alone and scared about a possible escalation, she asked Ari and Erin to move aside and called for backup. A few days later our liaison, Pete Kerr, called to tell me about the report she filed. In an e-mail paraphrase I reported in turn to Erin and Ari:

> There was an argument between a prisoner and an officer at the desk downstairs by the gym. The officer told Ari twice to back away from the desk and Ari didn't comply. He twice refused a direct order to move away, thus placing him in danger if the situation escalated. Afterwards he gave a high five to the prisoner and (Pete thinks it indicates this:) to a couple of others. It doesn't say that the high fives were congratulatory or complicit with the offending prisoner, but Pete says that is probably the meaning of putting that in the report. Ari interfered with custody staff.

I added that Pete had spoken for Ari, but Assistant Deputy Warden Scott Nobles had been "adamant—that's it!" Ari was terminated. We could appeal, but Pete didn't think we would get far.

I solicited reports from Erin and Ari. They had said nothing about high fives or not moving away from the desk. I asked for more feedback. I learned that at first Ari had no idea what the argument was about and complied with the officer's request to leave the area by simply moving to the other side of the desk from Al. Later, when the backup had arrived and Al was removed, Ari heard that the choir group had been assigned to the chapel and stepped forward to inform the officer ("not in any aggressive manner") that the theater workshop regularly met in the chapel. He said he had greeted the men as he always does, with a handshake, not a high five. In workshop mode, he clearly had not sensed the officer's tension and continued to interact with the men as they came to the desk. In the workshop, when Al wanted to discuss his argument with the officer, Erin and Ari refused to talk about the matter, knowing better than to be involved in an altercation between a prisoner and staff.

What to do? According to Pete, Nobles was tough, strict on policy, sure of himself, and fair. He probably wouldn't bend. I wrote a diplomatic two-page letter, sharing Erin and Ari's descriptions and suggesting that "we have a situation of confusion, not at all an incident of intentionally disobeying direct orders from an officer." I cited Ari's three years "of loyal volunteer work at the Ryan Facility" and his previous work at the Adrian Temporary

Correctional Facility, all of it with "no history of incidents or complaints."

> As our mission statement (approved by Deputy Director Dan Bolden) says, we train our volunteers to work with the utmost respect for everyone at the facility where they volunteer. That is the training [Ari] received and it has guided his behavior.

I "hoped," since there had been no previous incident, that Deputy Nobles

> might see this as an inadvertent situation in which there was misunderstanding. If [Ari] could return, under probation, if that is best, I can guarantee that his incident-free record will continue and he will continue to provide the high quality volunteer work that Mr. Kerr has appreciated in him these several years.
>
> I will follow this letter up with a call. I am very willing to come out and join you and [Ari] (he has volunteered to do this) in a discussion of what occurred, so that he might understand the corrections officer's perspective in a situation that might have gotten out of control. If I can also be helpful in setting the terms of [Ari]'s return as a volunteer, I will be happy to do so.[17]

Nobles agreed to my offer to bring Ari in. With Pete present, he lectured Ari on the seriousness of the incident. Ari listened respectfully and took in the lesson. Even though the situation had been new to him, had he been more alert, he would have moved away from the desk area. We were able to negotiate between the two languages, recognize that the prison language must prevail, and gain Ari permission to continue with the workshop.

Generally I have been able to salvage such situations, but not always. Vanessa Mayesky and her partner Kristal, experienced PCAP members, had established a practice of asking in the bubble on the way out if they could carry out an item, putting the decision in the officer's hands. However, they had not yet asked when an officer discovered in their prop bag two T-shirts, a handmade gift from a prisoner.[18] I was able to reduce their termination to a two-month suspension. Unfortunately, Kristal was moving to North Carolina before they would be allowed to resume, and despite my offer to fly her back for the performance, the partners decided not to have the play, much to my regret.[19]

In other instances, wardens have been unable to reverse a punishment. Anna Clark and her partner brought a copy of a review of the annual exhibition to show the Poets Corner. One of the poets scribbled a note asking Anna to bring in more copies. In the flurry of leaving, Anna and her partner swept the note with other writing props into their bag. On their way in a novice officer had not asked them for a list of props; now, on the way out, a second officer found the note and a bracelet, which she assumed was a gift from the note-writer. The mistake was obvious and we had a program-oriented warden, but her response to my careful, detailed letter was a denial.[20]

But generally I find a way to negotiate between the two languages. What are the elements essential for successful troubleshooting?

A Strong Program

It is important to have done very good work from the beginning, to have a record of responsibility and success. This creates allies within the system who understand what the program does for the incarcerated. They can make a call, intervene, temper, and negotiate on your behalf. From nearly the beginning, we could call Bill Lovett in the Michigan Department of Corrections office and Wardens Luella Burke and Pam Withrow. Bill and Luella joined our first National Advisory Board[21] and gave our annual meeting a tough-minded perspective.

Respect, perspective, and generosity. My first partner in the Sisters Within Theater Troupe, in 1990, saw officers as demons serving an evil system. When they gave her a hard time, she filed grievances, a practice that would have caused a disastrous rupture had she continued in the workshop. Approach the staff as professionals who understand, as many of them do, the reasons for policies and who know the violence latent in prisons. Approach them as professionals who may be flexible and open to discussion, as many of them are. If they are complicit in the normalcy of mass incarceration—which means they are more like the rest of us than we like to think—they may still be professionals, trying to do their work well. It is within *their* workplace that we have to be strategic in order to keep doing what is so valuable to the men and women caught there.

Gather the full story and all perspectives. Then present a version that is neither belligerent nor arrogant, that both recognizes the system language and conveys the language of the outsider. Admit error. Listen very carefully, nod, and maneuver on behalf of the prisoners and PCAP members and students. Apologize, guarantee it won't happen again, compromise—which can mean agreeing not to shake hands with prisoners, agreeing to have an officer in the room or to be on probation or undergo suspension—so that in the end the butterfly can avoid the boot and soar, so that resistance to prison conditions and mass incarceration can continue through the exploration of creativity, voice, collaborative work, and celebration.

Recognize the enemy. One night in September 2007, I dreamed of a spirited rabbit, much like my daughter's childhood rabbit Timothy who would circle our feet in enthusiastic figure eights. Whoever we were in the dream, we loved this rabbit, because he represented our whimsical fun and our creativity. One evening, I opened a refrigerator and found that someone who hated us had put the rabbit inside, where it was freezing, barely still alive. I took it out and began to nourish it back to health.

The enemy is the one who, for whatever reason, cannot help but freeze the rabbit or stomp the butterfly. Such enemies may work in prisons, as elsewhere; some may even be drawn to prison work.[22] I have moments when I am like them.[23] I don't know if they are evil. They may be like the death camp commandants who, George Steiner tells us, could "read Goethe and Rilke in the evening . . . play Bach and Schubert, and go to [their] day's work at Auschwitz in the morning."[24] But, like those commandants, their work is evil. Their every decision, every word, represents a commitment to limit, clamp down, say no, damage the body, soul, and spirit of others. Elie Wiesel urges us to hate that thing in them that tempts them to destroy others.[25] There is reason to avoid thinking in terms of "enemies", but those under the boot experience enmity. As Lorna Dee Cervantes writes to "the young white man who asked me how I, an intelligent, well-read person could believe in the war between races,"

I believe in revolution
Because everywhere the crosses are burning,
sharp-shooting goose-steppers round every corner,
there are snipers in the schools . . .
(I know you don't believe this.
You think this is nothing
but faddish exaggeration. But they
are not shooting at you.)

I'm marked by the color of my skin.
The bullets are discrete and designed to kill slowly.

They are aiming at my children.
These are facts.
Let me show you my wounds: my stumbling mind, my
"excuse me" tongue, and this
nagging preoccupation
with the feeling of not being good enough.

These bullets bury deeper than logic.
Racism is not intellectual.
I can not reason these scars away.

Outside my door
there is a real enemy
who hates me.[26]

The rabbit freezers may destroy because they understand from others that that is their job. They may destroy out of theory: prisoners are scum, are dangerous, must be strictly controlled, the goal of prisons is to confine. They may have a vision of good and evil or a personal experience that makes them need always to retaliate, to bully, to get back, to tighten down inside themselves and give nothing. The effect is the same. People whose lives have been punishment from the start continue to be punished and alienated, prone to numbing, acquiescence, anger, and destruction or self-destruction. Many of the incarcerated are resistant and creative, but many succumb.

The enemy identified, what do we do? We continue to communicate with respect. We recognize that *somewhere* in most people is something that appreciates the dance of the spirit, the laughter and games of children, the new growth of their lawn after a good rain, the blessings at the heart of their faith. And so we seek the language, the entrance, that will get to that spot and enable an opening, a compromise.

That's first. It isn't always possible. And so we have to be strategic, find a way around them. The deputy warden at the Western Wayne Correctional Facility did all he could to thwart our work. We had a rich collection of videos of our plays; he forbade further taping. He stalled approving our scenarios and passing them on to his superior, remaining silent or making irrelevant excuses. He lied. And so we phoned the regional office, the regional administrator phoned the warden, and the scenario moved forward. When next the regional administrator and the warden told us to go through channels and he again stalled our next scenario, we phoned the warden on our Advisory Board, she spoke with the warden, the scenario moved forward.

This is very sensitive. It is dangerous to step outside the chain of command on which the volunteer is next link up from the prisoner. It has to be worth it. It has to be important enough. And sometimes it is. In the early days, when we had less understanding, I once went over the head of a warden to the Michigan Department of Corrections deputy director for programs and won, but the undying hostility of the warden later cost us losses.[27] When in 1999 Dan Bolden closed our workshops and we went outside the system to get them back, he never forgave me, but PCAP survived.[28]

THE TWO LANGUAGES

The enemy of the incarcerated also lurks in us, not only when we come abusively—to study the criminal mind, to enhance our resume, to get a grade, to be cool, to feel good about ourselves—but also when we are careless, immature, disrespectful, unprofessional, treating our enemy with hostility, our friends with disregard. So much is at stake that we must merge the two languages. We must be constantly alert at the same time that we are at our most relaxed and creative.

WHAT WE DEFEND

I believe almost everyone who works or lives in a prison hits moments when they are terribly hurt by what they see and experience, when the concertina wire rips at them and the walls turn steel cold, when they become worn and can't see their way out. And then:

Eric Shieh, a highly talented student from the School of Music, began in a youth facility in English 310, then, in PCAP, initiated a music workshop at the Parr Highway Correctional Facility. On December 4, 2003, he sent Professor Betty Ann Younker, myself, and some of his friends a message:

> Just wanted to drop an e-mail and let you know this evening in Adrian was one of those life-defining moments in my career as an educator. Basically, about half an hour into the workshop, nothing was going right in generating

this piece of music, we had hit a wall—and I did a big teacher no-no—and sat down and admitted I had no idea where to go with the project.

Then one of the guys asked if he could suggest something. Then another. That's when everybody started talking, arguing, and making suggestions. Pretty soon, we were trying out ideas and started moving forward again on the project—only this time everyone was on the same page. Afterwards a lot of people said to Suzanne and myself they felt today we had laid a foundation and they could see where we were headed. I myself felt I came to understand music and where it comes from at a much closer level.

It's funny—I had been trying so hard to make sure there wasn't a dull moment, and though all the musical ideas had come from within the group, I had kind of been talking over the silences and leading the generation of the piece. I realized when Suzanne and I finally shut up that much of the workshop had been a guessing game of where Suzanne and I were "going"—and thus some people were confused about what had been going on. In a sense, we had been silencing them. How easy it was to fall back on and get forced into this kind of work! But once we stood back and showed we had no more idea than they—well they took charge. "I feel you've been trying to orchestrate this thing" said one of the guys to me in the middle of the discussion. "We should be doing it." How embarrassing. And how right. I'm just glad these people were free enough to say that, and I had the opportunity to be showed that.

In a way, learning begins where the teaching ends.[29]

In 1999 Tracy Neal wrote in the autobiographical statement she submitted with her art for the Fourth Annual Exhibition of Art by Michigan Prisoners,

I have beaded, painted, and glued with sadness and anger hovering all around me . . .

Sometimes while I worked on "One Long Journey," I felt as if I were in a trance or somewhere else. One day I was working so diligently that I didn't hear the officer gruff my name over the loud speaker. When someone tapped me on the shoulder to get my attention, I felt as if I were being placed back inside of myself after standing on top of a mountain. I was gon'.

This project means so very much to me. It means so much because it is *me*. I have taken handfuls of my soul and shown you what it looks like and feels like. Can you feel me? "One Long Journey" represents how I have taken it upon myself to rise from rock bottom. It represents each and every woman that has been incarcerated, that is incarcerated, and will be incarcerated. It's not just about Tracy Neal. It's about a young woman, an old woman, a black woman, a white woman, a red woman, a brown woman. It's about a human being. It's about human beings. IT'S ABOUT HUMAN BEINGS. IT'S ABOUT HUMAN BEINGS. *IT'S ABOUT HUMAN BEINGS.*

We placed her statement on the gallery wall.

CHAPTER SIX

"This Is Our Bridge . . . and We Built It Ourselves!" The Annual Exhibition of Art by Michigan Prisoners

In January and February 2007 we travel as we have for the past eleven years, selecting art for the Twelfth Annual Exhibition of Art by Michigan Prisoners.[1] Traveling, we move between two problematically parallel universes, prisons and what prisoners call "the world," that is, between prisons and the towns depending upon them economically, or between prisons and a largely indifferent citizenry. Traveling, we know that in 1971 Michigan had four prisons, five small camps, and approximately 5,000 prisoners and now has fifty prisons and over 51,000 prisoners, and we are aware of the enormity of what has happened in this country. We move between these universes some forty times. Sometimes we see the art in the lobby. Mostly we meet the artists inside. This year we have spoken with over 150 artists.[2]

We park in the visitor lot, extract a portfolio from the trunk, enter the lobby, shake the snow off, present IDs to the officer on duty, secure our belongings, and greet our liaison, usually the special activities director. We pass through the metal detector, are shaken down, then cross the prison yard to a room in the education unit where the artists have laid out their work and are sitting around the edge, waiting. We are all expectant, quietly excited, and hopeful about our encounter. We shake hands, greet the artists we know, meet those we don't. This happens once a year: we are all aware of how precious our time is together. Some have worked all year for this moment, have developed new techniques and imagery and come closer to themselves in their work. Others are new, unsure what to expect.

The room is quiet as we look at the art. We ask questions, take everyone seriously. They leave the room while we decide, then we call them back one at a time for intense moments of discussion. We are moved by the emotion of artists accepted for the first time, eager to listen to those who have repeated, supportive of those we deny: we articulate their strengths and weaknesses, encourage them to find authenticity, suggest that they view the exhibition video we send each year and to seek tutelage from other artists. Many will submit next year more deeply felt or carefully rendered work and make it into the exhibition.

At the Florence Crane prison, we are stunned by three highly detailed, patterned colored pencil drawings by Frankie Davis, by the deepening of visual themes he first identified several years ago. Something very important has happened. When we tell him how much we love the work, he asks, "Can I speak?" He talks quietly, eloquently, about the drawings, wants to keep speaking, emotion brimming in his eyes. We acknowledge the care he has put into his work, his growth, and he responds, "It is because of you all." He must leave, but can't: it is hard to say good-bye to his work, to end this conversation, so rare in prison. We may see him next year, maybe not.

At the Straits prison, Shon Varner submits an image of hell seen through a keyhole. He hasn't submitted since 1996 because he has been going through the hell he now portrays in his painting. He thanks us for seeding the Straits workshop, for the exhibition, and again we see the brimming eyes, the search for words. We don't know his experience, but clearly this truly significant connection is keeping him going.

At every prison we meet a Frankie Davis, a Shon Varner, a Lessie Brown, a Cynthia Casey. We watch them converse with each other about their art, straighten with pride, light up with ideas, become so exuberant that they walk on air. Something electric is palpable as we meet, believe, and celebrate across universes.

Across universes. We intend the exhibition to connect inside and outside communities. Artists' artistic and biographical statements appear in a book for gallery visitors. Artists in their cells the night of the opening reception imagine what is happening, feel appreciated. Visitors, whose punitive stereotypes of prisoners have been broken by the range of beauty and talent they witness, write to individual and all artists in the visitors' book, and each artist receives the responses in a packet with reviews, fliers, and other items. The responses, charged with the magic and power of the exhibition, move some artists to tears. Individual artists receive letters from School of Art and Design students and faculty offering supportive, challenging critiques of their work. Later, a video of the opening reception and works exhibited arrives, and our liaison convenes the artists for a showing or screens it over the prison TV network, stimulating the artists to new development and risk. We write to the artists we haven't accepted, encouraging them. In the fall we send a letter inviting each artist to submit again. We have a small scholarship fund for artists who come home and a Linkage Project that connects returning artists with mentors. Oliver Evans, chancellor and vice president of Kendall College of Art and Design extends an invitation to all prison artists to apply for admission.

What happens in those selection rooms is significant. We respect and admire these men and women, are clear that like us they are trying to grow into powerful people. We believe in them. This is rare in prison, strengthening. And they are in a room *together* and before and afterward seek each other out, exchange ideas, apprentice and instruct, form workshops of their own with leadership from artists like John Lonchar, Ed Mast, Ray Gray, Jamal Biggs, Fred Ross, and Rod Strelau, and significant small communities are established in an alienating world where friendship and trust can be dangerous. Transferred artists find similar communities in other prisons: because of the exhibition, a general community of artists has sprung up across the system, producing art on a level and in an amount unprecedented in this country.

At the Newberry prison, one highly skilled but frightening drawing implies violence toward women, something we will not exhibit. The new assistant deputy warden listens intently as we explain our decision to the artist (who is incarcerated for forgery) and suggest alternative ways he might explore terror. She hears our respect and encouragement, hears us praise some beautifully rendered charcoal drawings of dark devilish figures that she had thought were bad, and she tells us that she has learned something important. We share with the officers at the desk what we are doing, share our spirit and respect, they look forward to our coming, and in a small way, now and then, this enlarges the community of support the artists build.

Family members enter the gallery, participate in our yearly panel of family members of the incarcerated, speak at the opening reception, purchase art, receive the unsold work in their homes, and something shifts a little. The son of James Gostlin, who has been incarcerated forty years, weeps when he reads on the wall his father's statement that art helps him control the overwhelming loneliness of prison. Danny Valentine's mother and sister hear about the exhibition on their car radio and come to the gallery and burst into tears.[3] Jerry Moore's mother looks down her Ypsilanti stairwell at her son's art and her eyes widen with new realization. Nothing is easy in this world of damage and pain, but at least here new understandings, new possibilities for connection.

The exhibition of 2007 is our twelfth, and 280 artists from 43 prisons submit over 1,100 works of art; 224 artists from 42 prisons exhibit 347 works; 3,526 people come through the gallery in two weeks. Of the artists with work to sell, 63 percent sell at least one piece; 57 percent of the work for sale sells. The total income for the artists is $17,974.

THE BEGINNING

Sometime in the early 1990s, Jackie Spring asked me to co-curate with her a tiny exhibition of art by women incarcerated at the Huron Valley Women's Facility. We placed about thirty works of very uneven quality around the wall in a small room in the Rackham School of Graduate Studies Building. I know now what it meant to those women to exhibit their work at the University of Michigan, but I did not know the artists and knew little to nothing about the project that had generated the art. I was in a support role. I was proud of the exhibition, but the major impact for me was that I learned that such an exhibition was possible.

When Janie Paul joined me in Ann Arbor at the end of 1994, I told her about that exhibition. We began to imagine something larger and decided to test the waters. With the help of Bill Lovett, we secured permission from Deputy Director Dan Bolden and on November 22, 1995, wrote to the wardens and other staff we knew at twenty-one prisons within a two-hour driving radius of Ann Arbor. We announced a February 20–28 exhibition of prisoner art and asked them to identify artists. We explained that we were looking for original two-dimensional work—paintings, drawings, collages—of any size, that we would mat the work and provide labels, that the work would be for sale if the artist wished, and that the income would go to the artist's prison account. We would deliver unsold art to friends or relatives of the artists, since once art left a prison, it was not allowed back in. In the two weeks following the deadline of January 14, we would visit the prisons to make our selections.

We were stunned by the response. Over seventy artists from sixteen of the prisons wrote us with great enthusiasm. We had had no idea that so much was out there. Anthony James challenged us with the right questions: who are you? will the exhibition be sensationalist, exploitative of prisoners? We sent a reply through his brother: this is an exhibition of *artists* who happen to be in prison, not an exhibition of the work of *prisoners*; we are taking no money from the sales either for the university or for our costs.[4] He entered his work and for the next five years was one of the best artists we would ever exhibit. When he came home in 2000, he served for several years as a member of our National Advisory Board.

We also had no idea of the quality we would encounter. As we traveled to Adrian, Coldwater, Detroit, Ionia, Jackson, Lapeer, Plymouth, Saginaw, St. Louis,[5] and Ypsilanti, we found major artists, Abdalla Ali, Billy Brown, Clark Brown, Otto Bryan, Scott Fabian, Anthony James, Tracy Neal, Cary Safarian, Danny Valentine, Martin Vargas, and Virgil Williams. Douglas Glover, Scott MacKenzie, Curtis Owens, and Monty Wade showed clear signs of what would emerge from them over the next years. Rick Ward's *Basement Apartment, Cadillac Bill,* and *When I was Young,* were painted with a mixture of instant coffee and glue. Virgil Williams had built his bas-relief *Tarbaby* out of layer upon layer of cardboard, the hair twisted pieces of toilet paper covered with shoe polish. Tracy Neal's brilliant untitled collage consisted of fragments of cloth, including her panties, and documentation of the sexual assaults she had suffered in prison. Martin Vargas had painted and framed a rendering of a murder he had witnessed at the Huron Valley Men's Facility some years before, a man bleeding in the snow with legs of prisoner witnesses all around. At the Ionia Maximum Facility we met a man who is one of my heroes. Herschell Turner, who is my age, had been an all-American basketball player at the University of Nebraska and a Harlem Globetrotter. Now the Michigan Department of Corrections paid him to teach art. He taught level 6 (highest security) prisoners through the windows on their cell doors or sometimes at a table in the unit, and he worked with level 2 artists in the studio space he had established. Many of the great artists in the system had come and would come under his tutelage. He fought for the integrity of his practice, he fought for prisoner art, he fought on behalf of the prisoners in Ionia, and he would continue to fight and negotiate over the next ten years until one day his patience finally wore out and he quit.[6]

At Ionia we had our first excruciating decision. At the Michigan Reformatory, where "young violent offenders," including adolescents assigned to adult prisons, were housed, our liaison laid the art out on a pool table in the large recreation room. We met the artists, except for one who was in a separate building. He had submitted two pieces. We rejected one because of its graphic violence against women. The other was more problematic, a small portrait of Rudolf Hess's face in part profile, half in shadow, with small swastikas patching the space around him. The drawing quality qualified it for acceptance, and it was possible a viewer might interpret it as a study of the ambivalent, haunted world of Hess. But our liaison told us this artist created Nazi art, and upon reflection the point of view seemed relatively clear. Janie and I worried and debated for half an hour at least and finally decided against. We were not opposed to art that reflected violence, but we opposed violence directed at specific groups. Survivors of the Holocaust live in Ann Arbor, as do many descendants of those who survived and those who died. It was also our first exhibition, and we did not want the press focusing on that piece. It was a difficult decision, the right decision for the first year, and perhaps a right decision in general.

Looking for work with some kind of edge in design or content, and seeking both to be as inclusive as possible and to maintain a high level of quality, we selected seventy-seven works by fifty artists. We knew what it would mean for men and women with disrupted childhoods and little family or school access to art to exhibit at the University of Michigan. The exhibition was free, funded by the University of Michigan's College of Literature, Science and the Arts, the Rackham School of Graduate Studies, the School of Art and Design, the Program in American Culture, and by hours and hours of dedicated volunteer work, flyering, gallery sitting, hanging and taking down the show. We invited the artists' family members and friends to the opening and closing receptions. At the closing they and purchasers could pick up unsold work.[7] Janie and Herschell spoke at the opening reception, as did installation artist and prison activist Richard Kamler, who displayed his work in progress, *Table of Voices,* which would later appear at Alcatraz.[8] Cary Safarian and Martin Vargas donated work for our raffle, and two attorneys contributed $250 each for awards for men's and women's art. Kamler, Ellen Plummer of the University Art Museum and Department of Art History, and Marinetta Porter of the School of Art and Design served as judges.

During the eight days of the exhibition, 462 visitors passed through the gallery. Thirty-three of the forty-five artists with work for sale were successful, and forty-three of the sixty-nine works for sale sold. The artists had set their own prices. Approximately 90 percent were in the $5 to $60 range, and the works that sold ranged from $5 to $300. Total sales, every dollar of which went to the artists' prison accounts, came to $2,267.50. It was a heady and euphoric time for us and the artists alike, clearly a beginning of something very big. Our one disappointment was the paucity of women's art. We knew of artists at the Scott Correctional Facility—we learned some names and wrote to them—but the staff made little effort to communicate with them and help them get their art to us. Only two artists submitted from the Florence Crane Women's Facility. We vowed to establish art workshops at the women's prisons and do all we could to get the word out.[9]

Gallery visitors were surprised and moved. Jessica Chaffin wrote in the visitor book, "A tremendous show of courage and emotion. A surprising and enlightening experience." Kimberly Yee added, "Thank you for sharing your art and yourselves with me. It has increased my awareness of a prison system that I normally don't think twice about. You are human beings who deserve respect just as everyone else does." D. Curtis found it "the most exciting contemporary art I have seen in a long while." And Ben McDonough: "This work is amazing. It wakes you up." We sent the gallery book responses, along with a list of artists and works, publicity fliers, and reviews in a packet to each artist. Year after year the artists tell us in their evaluations about the power of the gallery responses.[10] We hear of artists sitting on their bunks and weeping and of artists carrying the responses around and showing them to everyone, and Lionel Stewart, who in 2004 had persuaded Ritchie Weatherspoon to enter the exhibition, wrote to us that he found Ritchie in tears after reading the praise accorded him.

Having videotaped the opening reception, over the next four days we moved a camera and lights from work to work, zooming in for details. We added shots of visitors looking at the art and music layered under the images in a video that went to each of the participating prisons. A sheet listed the artists and works in the order they appeared.[11] In their evaluations each year since 1997, artists tell us that viewing the work done by others has challenged them, enhanced their sense of what is possible, and improved their own work. It is a significant factor in the improvement of overall quality year by year. Watching artists who have come home address the opening reception, they are inspired and write to us announcing their own out dates.

ARTISTS IN THE PRISONS

In the retrospective catalog for the Tenth Annual Exhibition, Janie Paul describes the situation of prison artists:

> Prison artists most often work in difficult conditions with many challenges. Some are bunked with 5 other people in a 12′ by 16′ cubicle. With people

"Prison," Anthony James, 2000

"Confiscated Goods," Bryan Picken, 2009

Opposite page, top:
"Omar's Brothers: The Throw Away Generation?" Jamal Biggs, 2005

Opposite page, bottom:
"Life and Death," Sheldon Murray, 2001

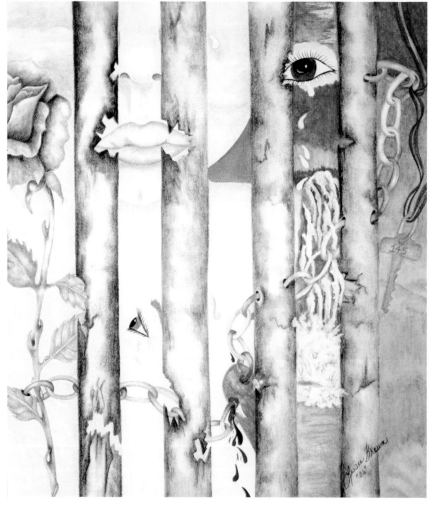

"Why My Baby," Dara Ket, 2009

Opposite page, top:
"Emancipation," Kinnari Jivani, 2009

Opposite page, bottom:
"Three Times Denied," Lessie Brown, 2007

"Clothing the Children," Lionel Stewart, 2006

"Free My Daddy," Wynn Satterlee, 2005

"Halloween: Fall Fun-time," Gary English, 2008

"September 11th, Twin Towers, World Trade Center," Frankie Lee Davis, 2005

"Everything's Alright I Guess," Cary Safarian, 1999

"Black Top Mourning," Martin Vargas, 2000

"Toxic Vacation," Daniel Valentine, 2009

"Ancient Gardens," Billy Brown, 1999

"Memory of Clark Lake Cottage," Fred Mumford, 2005

"Persona Non Grata," Duane Montney, 2005

"From a Sea of Lost and Living Dead II," André Watts, 2002

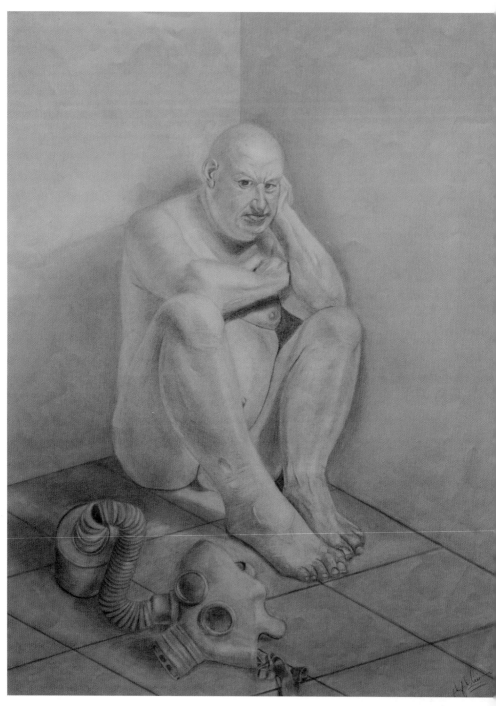

"Thoughts," John DiCiesare, 2008. After a painting by Ron Mueck, which
DiCiesare found on the cover of the February 2007 issue of *Discover*.

"Megan, Eleven-Years-Old, Retail Fraud. #520310," Nancy Jean King, 2000

"Middle Class 2028," Jack Boyd, 2008

"The Gift," Elizabeth Milosevic, 2007

sleeping at different times, it is hard to find space and light to work. Some work at a small desk. Some may work in the pool/gambling/tv room with bad light, smoke and people watching and asking questions. For most, materials are hard to come by either because the cost is prohibitive or the materials are not allowed in prison. While there is often support from other inmates and staff, art sometimes gets intentionally destroyed. There is hardly any storage space, so it is not possible, as it is for artists outside, to view the history and breadth of one's own work.

Many prison artists are new to art making. Some drew when they were young, and a few went to art school or practiced on their own. For most it wasn't until being locked up that art became an important resource. For some it starts as a way to keep busy and to earn income from making greeting cards, drawing portraits of loved ones from photographs, or drawing on envelopes. In addition, prison artists often sell their work to inmates who can afford it and to prison staff. Some prisoners start making art, not so much for the money, but as a way to relax or as an escape from the tension of surviving in prison. They may start by copying, or trying out a technique that someone else has used, or just doodling, and find that that takes them into a state of peace that is otherwise unattainable in prison. While many artists learn and work alone, experienced artists often mentor beginners and give them support.

Just as for artists everywhere, mastering a skill, getting recognized for it and feeling a sense of accomplishment develops into a desire to create something unique and personal. For many of the artists who continued to make art and exhibit in our shows, initial commercial ventures led to work that is artistically evolved and meaningful.

Many prison artists have carefully constructed a highly evolved process, worked out in hours of deep thought. Because reference materials, visual stimulation and supplies are limited, artists are forced to draw upon their own inner resources. In the repetition and refinement of their individualized process, artists can achieve a state of being that is sustaining and generative. Freely associating images, including things seen, heard or remembered, artists are able to connect back to childhood, people, and places, and to visualize feelings, ideas and longings. The urgent need to escape the difficult conditions of prison and return to this state of being results in the intensity that is such a remarkable quality of the work that we see.

Because the stakes are high in prison, artistic choices are made deliberately. Artists spend hours on the various stages of their carefully honed

Art Workshop, Western Wayne Correctional Facility, 1997. Janie Paul, Reuben Kenyatta (*back left*); Willie Birmingham (*front center*), Bill O'Guinn (*front right*), and two unidentified artists. (Unknown photographer.)

processes. It isn't only that prisoners have a lot of time to fill. Time must be transformed from dead nothingness into something active and alive. For a prison artist, doing time means transforming time. And for the visual artist, this is a process of transforming time into space. The space that artists create in dialogue with their work is a world within prison, in which they can live and find sustenance. The discovery of their unique process, the practicing and refining of this process and the repetitive execution of it is an active resistance to the deadliness of prison. And the final artwork is imbued with the spirit of this transformation.

Artists arrive at their imagery in many ways, which all have one thing in common: the thoughtful, inventive and emotionally charged relationship between artist and materials. Store-bought supplies and found materials are explored for all of the possibilities. The simplest of materials—pencil, charcoal or pen—can be used with extreme subtlety and attention to detail, exploring every nuance that the tool can give. The importance of this cannot be overemphasized. Prison intentionally strips people not only of possessions, but also of the experience of cherishing objects. While friendships between individuals and camaraderie in workshops can be strong, the pervasive atmosphere in prison is distant and guarded. In this context, the artist's relationship to their materials is special because it provides endless transformational possibilities and a give-and-take that is absent from most human contact.

There is little in prison to inspire aesthetic contemplation. So each artist must invent a way to generate imagery. Some work directly from their imagination, letting images emerge from the materials as they draw or paint. Others find images in photographs or artwork and integrate them into their own compositions. Many artists keep a file of reference materials gathered from magazines, books, newspapers, CD covers, and other visual materials. Some copy very literally from photographs, finding creativity in the accomplishment of technical skill.[12]

THE BUDGET

How do we pay for the exhibition? First of all, over the past two decades the University has increasingly realized that its mission as a public institution includes sharing its resources with beleaguered Michigan communities. As PCAP has grown and gained recognition for the quality and commitment of its work, the University in one form or another has provided enthusiastic support. From 2003 to 2008, our administrative position, which originated in an Access Grant from the National Endowment for the Arts,[13] was paid for by the Department of English and the School of Art and Design and is now covered by a three-year grant from the Provost's Office and the College of Literature, Science and the Arts (with continued assistance from English and Art and Design). University affiliation gives us access to free gallery space and free space for speakers, and as many as twenty units across the university have financed aspects of the exhibition. In addition to the Access Grant, we have attracted funding from a range of public and private sources, among them the Washtenaw Council for the Arts, the Michigan Council for the Arts and Humanities, the Kellogg Foundation, and the Rockefeller Foundation. We have also developed a loyal and growing patron base. In 2007, 222 patrons donated $14,909 to the Twelfth Annual Exhibition, and patrons respond annually to a summer mailing with another $3,000 to $5,000 for our staff positions. During funding crises, individual patrons have come through with sums from $1,000 to $10,000. In 2008–9 the economic crisis has brought us the fate of most nonprofits: contributions are down from 175 patrons and $12,924 at the end of May 2008 to 107 patrons and $6,668 by May 31, 2009. The exhibition is also funded by an outpouring of volunteer activity. Students and community members join the planning committee in the fall, make decisions, select panels and speakers, work on publicity, and then in the winter some of them join us traveling to select art, and newly recruited students put in hour after hour of hanging and taking down the show, daily flyering, gallery sitting, returning art to purchasers and to family members and friends of the artists. And eleven prisoner-run Inmate Benefit Funds in 2007 responded to our funding appeal with $1,160, an indication of the importance of the exhibition for all prisoners. It is the contribution we are most proud of.

HISTORY

Since that first exhibition thirteen years have passed. The exhibition is largely the same in form, but it has grown and grown and grown, from the 50 artists who exhibited in 1996 to 247 in 2006 and 229 in 2009, from 77 works in 1996 to 390 in 2009, from 426 visitors in 1996 to 4,203 in 2005 and 4,069 in 2009, from a total artist income in 1996 of $2,267.50 to $17,974 in 2007. The economic crisis took only a small dent out of artist income in 2009, bringing it up close to the $17,000 mark at $16,793.91.

And there are differences. In the second year, Bill and Pauline Stovall, parents of artist Lloyd Stovall, spoke at the opening reception, and other parents and children followed in the next two years. In the fifth year for the first time formerly incarcerated artists—Thom Baxter and Tracy Neal—spoke, and formerly incarcerated artists have spoken every time since. At the third exhibition, we added as a regular feature a series of speakers, panels, and events, in accord with our goals of demystifying, humanizing, and complicating prisoners and prisons and of providing analysis of mass incarceration. Our principal guests that year were Pat Bane and Sally Peck of Murder Victims Families for Reconciliation; Clementine Barfield of Save Our Sons and Daughters; Karina Epperlein, a dancer, performer, and video maker who had facilitated movement workshops with incarcerated women in California; Leslie Neal, a dancer who had initiated dance workshops in Florida prisons; Lateef Islam, a former New York State prisoner, educator, organizer, and social worker; and Barbara Zahm, one of the filmmakers who made *The Last Graduation,* about the termination of higher education in New York State prisons. Incarcerated youth presented choreographed poetry; Epperlein and Neal held an interactive dance workshop; former prison artist Jack Siegel and Janie Paul discussed prison art; former prisoners Blaine Crosby, Lateef Islam, Nate Jones, and Ahmad Rahman read from their own and other prisoners' writing; a recovering sex abuse survivor and an offender dialogued; two wardens talked about programs; Telisha Temple spoke about restorative justice, and Anthony Graham and his high school students from Colonel White High School in Dayton, Ohio, who had raised money to travel to Washington to oppose mandatory minimums, gave a presentation. Video interviews with Anthony James, Nancy Jean King, Larry

Kuligowski, Tracy Neal, Maurice Scott, Martin Vargas, and Charles M. Young ran constantly in the gallery.[14]

In 2002 construction in the Rackham Building forced us to move to the Media Union Gallery on North Campus, a more public space, where many students, faculty, staff, and community people pass through the adjacent corridor. This, plus increasingly smart publicity efforts and the exhibition's growing reputation, brought us much larger audiences.

In 2002 for the first time we offered artists the option of addressing a theme. In conjunction with Ardis Elementary School in Ypsilanti and the Matthaei Botanical Gardens we first exhibited at the Botanical Gardens and then at the Media Union Gallery works addressing the Great Migration of African Americans to the North from 1915 to World War II. In 2005 artists addressed themes of nature and the void of nature in prisons and inner cities and of prison programs that addressed the void; together with the Ella Baker Center we selected thirty works to be exhibited at World Environment Day in San Francisco the week of June 5. In 2009 fifty-four powerful renderings of the global crisis of climate change covered a wall and a half; the works had a second exhibition at Adrian College.

The exhibition's reputation in the prisons was bringing us more and more submissions, and after the 2004 exhibition we had to acknowledge a space crisis. The 343 works of art had more than saturated the walls and had spilled over into bins, where they had less exposure. I advocated adding the School of Art and Design's Slusser Gallery, just one building over, as a second gallery, but was roundly defeated by others on the planning committee, who were wiser than I: it would be difficult to double the number of gallery sitters and confusing for family members trying to locate their artist's work. We had already reduced from four to three the number of works we would accept from an artist: to go to two would be unfair to the best artists and their remarkable work. We contemplated becoming more exclusive, but knew it would thwart our goal of inclusion and discourage budding artists from submitting. We decided to ask the artists for unique and original work and give everyone a chance to step up. Janie composed the following statement for the October 20, 2004, letter that went to all previously submitting artists and to new artists who wrote to us:

As those of you who received the letter with last year's evaluation form know, we must be very selective this year. We have the same exhibition space, which was very crowded last year with 343 works of art, and we anticipate a higher volume of entries. Therefore we believe it will be helpful to you to know what we are looking for. As always, we seek work from both beginners and experienced and highly skilled artists, work that comes from the heart, that is unexpected, that we have not seen before. This does not mean that the subject matter must be new to us: as always, we are eager for landscapes, portraits, and other traditional subjects. But we want to be able to see the imagination of the artist.

We are not likely to select work copied from another artist, such as paintings or drawings found in a magazine, poster, book illustration, greeting cards, CD covers, tattoos or comics, etc. We understand that you may need to use photographs as references, but we are unlikely to select art copied entirely from a commercial photograph. On the other hand, working from your own, or from a friend's or family member's photograph is different. This would be a more personal use of photography.

There are many images that crop up frequently in the art from these shows, for example, hearts, flowers, teardrops, dragons, tigers, wolves, and eagles. If you wish to use one of these images because it really has meaning to you, use it in an inventive and personal way. What is important is your unique vision. And this is what we are eager to have from you, as always, your unique skill, your unique vision. And as always we are excited to see what you will submit. Because of your talent we are expecting the Tenth Exhibition to be by far the best ever!

In the prisons that winter we encountered artists who had taken the letter to heart. After showing us two conventional works, one artist, hesitatingly, said, "Oh, I have one more to show you: after I got your letter I tried something from my experience." He unwrapped a haunting painting of a man crouched by a wall under the bars of a local jail, with feet approaching in the darkened urban landscape. We selected it. When we were able to meet with the artists, we reinforced the message with those whose work we rejected or took with reservation. We would refer them to the video, have them reread the letter, and help them identify specific starting points in their own art that could take them to new places. The Tenth Exhibition surpassed all previous exhibitions in originality and quality, and, with our continued urgings, the Eleventh, Twelfth, Thirteenth, and Fourteenth have been progressively better. In their evaluations, artists have expressed gratitude for the push.

In 1999, as we have seen in chapter 4, Deputy Director Dan Bolden precipitated a crisis by shutting down PCAP's theater workshops. That fall he also set a new exhibition policy: if the art was prepared with materials or used staff time paid for by the Michigan Department of Corrections, it could be exhibited, but not sold. In practice, this was no problem: most artists purchased or found their materials, and, so far as we could tell, the policy was not monitored closely by prison staff. Unfortunately, the assistant deputy warden for programs at Florence Crane took the policy to mean that *no* staff time was to be expended at any time in any way: no staff person could bring the art to the front desk for us to make our selection. When we pointed out that the policy stated that the work could be *exhibited,* he remained adamant and was backed by the warden, who had become hostile to the women and to us. Since Bolden was also hostile, we were in a bind: we didn't dare contest the assistant deputy warden higher up—Bolden might impose his interpretation throughout the system, which would mean all artists would have to mail their art or have family members bring it to area community centers, all of which would lower participation substantially. We offered those options to the Florence Crane artists, but some were discouraged, some indigent, some without family members, and so we received fewer submissions than we might have. For several years we had to endure the assistant deputy warden's private policy, limiting the damage to one prison.

That was one form of censorship. In a few instances, prison staff have attempted to censor specific works, and in each case the Department of Corrections has affirmed its support for the exhibition and its recognition of our professionalism. The stories are instructive. They demonstrate the necessity of cool heads, goodwill, diplomacy, and connections.

In 2006, the end of a long day found five of us in the small muster room at Florence Crane (now a men's prison), where PCAP began. A pencil drawing of the Garden of Eden with Adam's penis extending far towards the ground was in poor taste and its purpose unclear, but it was unusual and its quality adequate for the exhibition. We debated then decided to take it, hoping the artist when he came into the room would illuminate the work (he didn't). Several days later the deputy warden phoned: the special activities director, offended by our selection, had notified the deputy, who requested that we not exhibit the drawing. Warden Howes and Director Patricia Caruso, who would be speaking at the opening, would take offense. I thanked him and promised to get back. Following a discussion with the exhibition planning committee, I called Warden Millie Warren, a member of our National Advisory Board, and we figured out what to do. In the previous two years because of volume, some first-time artists had their work only in the bins. The quality of the Garden of Eden piece made it possible to display it only in a bin. I left a message to this effect for the deputy warden, mentioning that I'd spoken with Warden Warren. There was no further effort to stop exhibition of the drawing.

In February, 2007, at the Deerfield Correctional Facility in Ionia, our liaison met us in the lobby and ranted about a violent work he had removed. The artist was Lionel Stewart, one of the exhibition's most interesting and versatile artists.[15] We stayed cool, selected the art, and went on our way. The next day at the Boyer Road Correctional Facility in Carson City, the special activities director told us that a lieutenant had forbidden another talented, prominent artist to submit a violent prison scene. We had completed our selections when the artist entered in a rage and declared he would remove all of his work. I slowed him down, told him that we had already selected two pieces, that we were backing him, as always, and that he should trust us on this. He thought about it and agreed to let us take the two works. Again, we didn't contest the situation while we were at the facility.[16]

When I returned to Ann Arbor, I phoned Warden Warren. She phoned the two wardens, who had not known about the censorship. They volunteered to mail the art to us, and one of them sent us an apology. The art arrived the following week, and we selected it for the exhibition. Lionel's piece was a two-panel display of prisoner weapons, some of them bloody. The other artist portrayed a prisoner standing over another prisoner he had just murdered.

On April 16, 2002, just after we closed the Seventh Annual Exhibition, Deputy Director Bolden's administrative assistant, Norma Killough, asked for a list of all participants and an accounting "for all works which were sold at the Exhibit, including the price that each item sold for and the amount of funds deposited into the prisoner's account." PCAP administrator Jesse Jannetta prepared a very thorough accounting, and we sent it in. It turned out to be a setup. Bolden, on June 13, within days of his retirement, wrote:

My review of [the information you sent] indicates that the volume of art work processed through this exhibition far exceeds the number which had been anticipated. Additionally, the manner in which the money from the sale of the art work was handled, as well as other funds distributed to prisoners through the Exhibition, is questionable.

By means of this communication, please be advised that the Michigan Department of Corrections involvement in the Prisoner Arts Program is discontinued.[17]

He was unhappy that so much art was being created by prisoners! His cryptic "questionable" in response to a very careful, professional, accurate accounting made it clear that this was a parting shot. Despite yearly invitations, he had never attended the exhibition. Since he was retiring, his action would have no weight in a department generally very favorable toward the exhibition,[18] so I didn't feel threatened, just sorry for him, that he had become someone who wanted to trample something so beautiful and positive. His decision was quickly reversed. However, his letter had been copied to the regional prison administrators and word trickled down to a few artists that the exhibition was canceled. Despite our annual letter to the prisons and artists in the fall, the rumor persisted and those few did not prepare well for the Eighth Annual Exhibition.[19]

You might expect that individuals upset that convicts have permission to make, exhibit, and sell art would oppose the exhibition. Once every few years a hostile comment turns up in the gallery book.[20] There have been perhaps two or three confrontations in the gallery. In the most dramatic, a woman exploded into argument with the gallery sitter, then proceeded to figure out how many of the artists had been convicted of murder, and wrote to the building director requesting she close the exhibition. She explained that someone had murdered a family member of a friend who worked in the building and that that friend was hurt every time she passed the gallery. The director responded sympathetically, but explained the values and goals of the exhibition. That was the end of it.

Otherwise, whatever opponents there are leave us alone. Apparently the quality of art, the depth of humanity, and the way we articulate the exhibition bring it widespread approval and celebration. I believe, too, that when most people have the opportunity to look closely, they both see the inequities in mass incarceration and believe that human beings have a right to grow beyond their worst moment.

TAXATION OF ARTIST INCOME

Another challenge we have faced is the Michigan Department of Corrections' gradual taxation of artist income. It began sporadically. While 10 percent of any prisoner income must go to the Inmate Benefit Fund, in the early years at first none and then only a few prisons applied this requirement to the exhibition. In 2002 it became MDOC policy, and a year or two later we were told to notify the cashier that the 10 percent must be taken out of the money order. In 2006, an additional 6 percent was assessed as a sales tax and in 2007 the IBF deduction rose to 15 percent, making a total of 21 percent of sales. For several years now we have suggested to the artists that they raise their prices accordingly. We do the calculation for them, adding either 15 or 21 percent to the price. Many artists have taken advantage. Rising sales indicate this is not hurting their income.

On March 31, 2000, Julie Southwick, Dan Bolden's administrative assistant, sent me a copy of a New York State Department of Corrections publication that revealed that 50 percent of prisoner income in the state-controlled exhibition went to the Crime Victims Board. Bolden was "intrigued" and wished to have my thoughts. Knowing that this tax had led most New York artists to refuse to exhibit, I sent an emergency e-mail message out to people around the country, including Tony Papa, a renowned former prison artist in New York, seeking advice, with excellent results. In my response to Bolden I was able to point out that many prisoners of their own volition contribute funds to Special Olympics, homeless shelters, and similar organizations and to point out that PCAP is very supportive of victims and their issues, citing the dialogue we had sponsored between a victim and offender and the participation of Murder Victims Families for Reconciliation in exhibition events. Second, were Michigan artists to be taxed in such a way, I urged that the artists have an option of contributing to organizations on a list furnished to them, which would include "organizations committed to restorative justice, and organizations that work with high-risk youth." I didn't hear back.[21]

SCAMMING

One might imagine that some prisoners would find ways to scam us, but, so far as we know, there has been very little of this, a result of their high regard for the exhibition, their personal connections with us, their awareness of the immense year-round energy and diligence we put in, and their aware-ness of how easily the exhibition could be closed down by the MDOC. In 2000, one artist recognized on the exhibition videotape that another pris-oner had submitted as his own a work that artist had sold him.[22] In a more serious incident, for several years an artist had other prisoners submit his work as if it were theirs, which gave him more work in the exhibition than the maximum three pieces and brought him, an excellent artist, more sales. He was taking space and money from other artists. We naively assumed that a school of art, under his influence, had risen at the prison, and so it took us a while to realize what was happening. Since MDOC exhibition policy, which we pass on to artists in our October letter, explicitly forbids artists from selling work not their own or exhibiting work created with the assis-tance of another, we had a punishable internal crime on our hands, possibly a felony. The other artists knew what was happening and hadn't said any-thing and were therefore complicit. We notified all artists at the facility and asked for a response. The artist in question accused us of lying—we weren't, we had done some conclusive investigation, but couldn't out our sources— and said he wouldn't participate again in the exhibition. After consulting with lawyers, beginning with the Thirteenth Exhibition, we require artists to sign a statement that the work they are submitting is their own and theirs alone.[23]

THE MEANINGS OF THE EXHIBITION

For the artists the exhibition means *visibility*. That we have imagined their creativity and walk into the space where they are warehoused, that we respect and admire them and talk with them about their art and their lives and select what they submit is huge. The public despises them, the prisons humiliate them, they have done damage in their families and communities, and we put their work on the wall in a prestigious university. An important and growing piece of them is acknowledged. Hidden away in prison, they learn that thousands of people will witness their expression of self, their images and ideas. As Nancy Jean King wrote,

> One aspect to this exhibit was having the chance to display our work to the community. Not only to share our thoughts, our talents and our dreams, but to say: "This is our bridge to you, and we built it ourselves!" Because, you see, many of us want to strengthen the rungs and come across to the other

side. . . . Expressing ourselves, sharing those expressions with a community we have been separated from, that is why we became involved. It would be such a beautiful thing if we could help to put cracks in the stereotypes and myths about prison and prisoners. If these exhibits serve to bring us and the community closer together, or make the community more receptive to us, what could be more wonderful than that?[24]

For the artists the exhibition means *stimulus*. Because of it art has proliferated in Michigan prisons. New artists apprentice to old, workshops spring up, the word spreads, artists spend the entire year preparing. When we wrote to the artists asking for unique and heartfelt work, the effect was profound. In a recent evaluation, Doug Hanna talked about how this request affected him and others:

> I know how hard it is to be on this side of the fence. I see people who are very well meaning doing their best to help. Most of them fail to be true to their mission. They seem to think that they can make us more to their kind of people. Your team tries to let us be ourselves. Asking us to tell people who we really are. . . . Perhaps the best service anyone could give a man in prison is to make him think . . . to let him know it is okay to think. It is sure most of the artists in prison will never get the chance to show anyone what they can do. They are not encouraged to think. It is discouraged more than anyone out there can ever understand. Your exhibition encourages us to think. I thank you for that.[25]

For the artists the exhibition means *a new image of oneself, new possibilities.* At Camp Branch in 2007 Lessie Brown entered the room. She looked at us. Janie wasn't there. She said, "Did I do it?" The previous year Janie had pointed out to her that her exquisite sensitivity appeared in isolated fragments and suggested that she extend it and create a whole world in her paintings. Lessie had taken it to heart. We saw a quantum jump in her work and now we told her she *had* done it. We selected both of her pieces. She glowed. Later she wrote to us:

> I just don't know how to describe how all this has made me feel. I guess if you consider a woman who felt like she was nothing, who felt she had no potential for anything, and would never be anything, then maybe you can understand just a little, what this has done for me. I now have a talent

that I can utilize to support myself, and give people pleasure, at the same time, it is so amazing to me! Then, to incorporate my art with my skills in Graphic Arts, eventually own my own business, and hire displaced women, train them, give them a skill, that they can use to support their children, and hopefully never end up in here, or in a Domestic Violence situation, well, it means the world to me.[26]

On April 27, 2008, we received an e-mail message titled "Letter from Grateful Mother":

I am the type of person who deals with life as it is thrown at me, taking no time to dwell or cry about what cannot be changed.

On a visit with my son who has been battling with depression and fighting the will to give up, [he] sat beside me with a gleam in his eye (I hadn't seen since he was a young boy) and told me as much as he knew about PCAP. Greg was all excited to enter a picture. He'd been drawing since he was just a tot. Just before your visit to the prison he was falling back into depression and self doubt and told me he wasn't sure if he would bother with entering his work. I told him he had nothing to lose and everything to gain so what would be the harm. Despite his depression he decided to do it, still having doubts but a little more excited after your visit and picking one of his drawings.

I went to the gallery with my husband, Greg's step-dad (who has always encouraged Greg's art). Silent tears filled my eyes and my heart to see works of my only son my troubled son hanging on the wall in an art gallery. I was so very proud. When we went to inquire about what the red dot next to the picture meant the young lady told us that [the work had been purchased].

You . . . have given new hope and new life to my son. Hope and confidence that I have never seen in him before. For this I want to express my greatest and deepest gratitude to you . . . There aren't enough words to tell you just how grateful I am, for someone other than his mother and sister to show him that he is a person and he does matter in this world means the world to Greg as well. It has given him the courage and strength to keep moving forward in life, to continue on with the self improvements he has made regardless of who tries to lessen who he is becoming.

On May 27, we received a letter from Greg, telling us that when he learned his work had sold, "I felt like I was on top of the world and that I can accomplish anything... I want to thank you for helping me realize that I can take something I love to do and make something of it."[27]

For the artists the exhibition can mean *survival.* In a letter that helped us secure the Access Grant from the National Endowment for the Arts, Danny Valentine wrote about that first exhibition:

> Totally shut off from the outside world, I had no other stimuli than what existed inside the prison walls; as a result, I became a zombie, numb to reality—all hope lost. Today, however, I can honestly say without reservation, that the U of M art exhibit for prisoners has restored my human spirit. Prior to my experience with the U of M, I was doing basic drawings which depicted a prison mentality boasting of criminal concepts (drugs, gang insignia, etc.). That was the audience of what little clientele I had [he is referring to fellow prisoners as the purchasers of these drawings].
>
> After the first exhibit, the U of M provided the institutions of the participants with a video. The video allowed the artists to see their work on television. That one single element of the whole process caused us to feel worthwhile again. . . . I personally witnessed the ambiance of restored humanity filling the souls of the other prisoners. Tears of joy welled in my own eyes for the first time in many years. A man crying in prison may not seem like a big deal, but a man in prison whose soul becomes hard and bitter, soon forgets *how* to cry. I guess that you would have to be here to really know what that is like.[28]

In other communications he has told us that the exhibition has kept him from suicide.

For the artists the exhibition and workshops can mean, F. Mumford writes to us, *"a kind of forgiveness."*

> My soul was wounded as I went thru the process of police interrogation, arrest, jailing, the court experience and finally imprisonment. The smiles and conversations with art student volunteers act as a balm for my wound. They are all held in high esteem. The letters written to all the artists and particularly to me, make me cry! I feel filled with gratitude and happiness after the show and read them thru and all the other things there in the packet.[29]

His letter triggered something profound in my own experience, and I wrote back,

I've long realized that what differentiates the workshops from anything else I've participated in is the unspoken spirit of forgiveness and even generosity in the room. Almost everyone incarcerated has done some damage—and most have had damage done to them—and you all know that about each other and at the same time know that most of you in the room are trying to grow, despite your demons, and to find what you can of real trust and community in a very hard place. If those of us who come in have thought at all about our lives, we know we've done damage too, and so we participate in the spirit of the room. There is something accepting in that which is powerful. The damage is real, some of the crimes are brutal, we aren't all wonderful and don't all get along. But in the face of all that, we give each other that acceptance, forgiveness, generosity, and willingness to help each other try to move forward.[30]

Years ago a student in my film course on U.S. prisons posed a question: "Can someone commit a brutal murder and still create beautiful art?" It isn't a new question, of course, as anyone knows who has struggled with the career of Leni Riefenstahl and other artists who have supported totalitarian regimes. And while the answer is no, in the end the answer is also yes, yes he or she can. A man can kill a woman and chop her body into pieces and still find beautiful landscapes inside,[31] and the landscapes will be beautiful to the viewer. We can't do anything about that. It is true. There it is.

In 2005 we received a letter from Andre Watts, whose work had been in the exhibition for three years. It was so moving that I turned it into a poem titled "My Story," which we published in the retrospective Tenth Exhibition catalog.

Born from the darkness of my mother's womb
into the darkness of this cold world of hard, and easy pain.
No father and a child in ago for a mother mix with man
with the characteristics of male animals
that eat the small males produced by another
so it had seem as they seen me and my mother as punching bags,
when subdue by the sweet burning taste of the devil's blood
running down their throats to their bellies
crying out hateful words grip by blinding self hate
which feeds its sickness like blacken wings of death
to the soul, heart and minds, to all who witness these painful acts.

But the worst was seeing the heated tears of betrayal falling time after time.
And inside of me lives my world of creation where pain isn't known,
where love shone none stop as if it was summer time each and every day.

So much created began flowing over unto paper to share with my mother
but it meant nothing but lines drawn on paper
not what I felt or wish for her to feel
instead of the pain placed over her eyes
where love should have filled.

And as I grew up these things, words burned inside of me
I couldn't speak out into sentence.
I did not know how to nor how to write them
but in Art it flowed, all my pain, hate want for love
loneliness and the wish for death.
The lie of my father leaving me when he was killed before I were born.
My unknown father, a man my mother to this day spoke not of,
is who guides my hand when I create, so I like to believe.
Even when I was unable to write nor read
I could draw what was in my heart from 5 years of age up to now.
And before now I lived like man had when he lived in caves
which no one could hear my cries for help.

But you the people who sees,
and comment on what's felt from what I created,
and this without knowing
how much has given me life in so many wonderful ways,
oh how I wish this was here in my childhood coming up.
But it's here now and I thank you for the tears of joy
you brought to my face and eyes which had only knew tears of pain.

So please know through your cares
happiness fills the hearts with humanity
and God knows we all need this in our lives
instead of longing for the kiss of death upon our lips
we so hunger for through lost hope.

Thank you for opening up a door

where we can be seen through feelings of Art and words
in which our eyes would have refused on face to face first encounters.

This is my story on how I became the artist you'll come to know
and hopefully love.[32]

Knowing Andre, knowing his powerful small pencil series connecting slavery, lynching, and incarceration, and working, as we do, on the exhibition and in the prisons, we deepen our knowledge of the complexity of the human animal and we gain, yes, a kind of forgiveness. Whether we know what someone has done or not (and usually we don't know), whether we witness harsh behavior or not, we are in the presence of what is worst in human experience, in the presence of physical, mental, and spiritual agony, in the presence of a child's scream and of the inner scream of that child grown up, in the presence of the violent results of economic injustice. And, if we are willing to acknowledge it, in the presence of our own capacity to do terrible harm. And because we are also in the presence of the best, the most creative, in human experience, we too, like F. Mumford, experience a *kind* of forgiveness, which must, of course, be distinguished from being forgiven.

And above all for the artists, and for us, the exhibition means *resistance.* Janie Paul, concluding her essay describing the conditions under which prison artists work, writes that "making art"

> is a form of resistance to the oppressive conditions of prison life. In resistance to the barrenness of prison, artists create images of beauty, joy, and celebration. In resistance to poverty of resources, there is inventiveness with materials. In resistance to uniformity, there is idiosyncrasy and freshness of vision. In resistance to the hidden devastation and violence of prison, artists depict harsh realities that we need to know about. In resistance to the coldness of prison, artists create images of love and tenderness. And in resistance to invisibility, artists create images of themselves.[33]

It is, of course, not only resistance to prison conditions, but resistance, for so many of them, to what they were given at birth: low standard health care and housing and schools; little access to employment; dangerous neighborhoods; unemployed, angry, negligent, absent, struggling, addicted, punitive parents; malnutrition; seductions of the streets, of drugs, gangs, prostitution; the heritage of violence. To become an artist, or an actor or a poet, to grow into articulation and originality and dignity, resists and overcomes what has been done to one and what one has done to oneself and others. It also means drawing on the resources that were and are there in those original families and neighborhoods,[34] makes further kinds of resistance more possible.

And because we learn from the artists, actors, and writers, young or old, who are incarcerated, because we become engaged in their world in the most democratic way possible, and because we ourselves have not and/or will not escape suffering and devastation in our own lives, being in the presence of Andre and his art enriches our capacity to understand, respond, speak, act, and resist what is done to us, what happens to us, and what we become. This enriched capacity makes further kinds of resistance more possible.

CHAPTER SEVEN

Is the Scapegoat Not Our Brother?

THE SIXTY-FOUR-YEAR-OLD POET DOESN'T REMEMBER
DOESN'T KNOW HOW TO REMEMBER RIGHT
WHAT SIXTEEN-YEAR-OLD ROBERT REMEMBERS

I don't remember being pistol-whipped
a block down the raw street
from my unlit shut-in house
with its dirty carpet
and only
two large awkward comfortable chairs
in the living room, I don't remember
leaving Chicago when my mother died,
don't remember that my father came by a few times
in my lifetime,
don't remember I have no wish to go back,
don't remember
that my childhood friends are so much dead,
I don't remember the Benton Harbor crime
that sent me to Boysville, don't remember
what my brother was doing with the gun
when they picked him up, don't remember
that this Friday I take the greyhound bus
across state as the day darkens
around the bright wounding colors
of the fall trees to see him

for the first time in two years,
behind a long wire fence and locked doors,
I don't remember that they won't let me go home
to my Benton Harbor aunt, don't remember
that they might be right. I don't remember
stumbling this morning over the uneven concrete blocks
that serve for steps, don't remember
catching the bus to emergency because of my heart,
don't remember the loneliness of trying to do right
in a town without friends, the loneliness of the house
hour after hour after hour all day all night

POEM BY AUTHOR AFTER A LINKAGE TRIP, OCTOBER 15, 2003

It was spring 2002 and our first role-play in the early days of our rehears-als for *When Can We Talk?*, a collaborative creation by former prisoners and PCAP members under the direction of Gillian Eaton. We stood in a circle in the Frieze Building on the University of Michigan campus, in an acting stu-dio inside the old Carnegie Library, and Gillian told us, "I've got bad news. It's that time again. One of us has to go. We'd better decide soon or they'll just come and grab one of us. If we can just decide which one of us is willing to be sent to the wilderness we won't have the usual battles and bloodshed. None of us are without family so I know it'll be hard, and I hate to draw straws. How can we choose who will go?" We were community goats. We needed to choose the scapegoat. And before the scapegoat was exiled, we would enact the ritual of Leviticus 16:21–22:

> And Aaron shall lay both his hands upon the head of the live goat, and con-fess over him all the iniquities of the people of Israel, and all their transgres-sions, and all their sins, and he shall put them upon the head of the goat, and send him away into the wilderness. The goat shall bear *all* their iniquities upon him to a solitary land and he shall let the goat go into the wilderness.

Nate Jones immediately volunteered. All too aware of his current weakness and despair, I spoke against sending him, trying to save him from such a personal step, but the others acquiesced. Gillian:

> I remember Nate taking the role willingly and with some insistence, and when he knelt down and the sins were placed on his head, the atmosphere

in the room became almost numinous—he either was re-living a ritual or creating the ritual for something that was extremely deep inside him. There was a shift towards real meaning in the room. Someone was connecting! And it was Nate.

It felt to me afterwards that Nate needed to acknowledge a role that he had consciously or unconsciously been playing in his life. That the role play we did was powerful for him. It may have been too powerful, because not long afterwards, he disappeared. I've only just thought about that—right now—and I hope it's not true, but the truth is a powerful force and I think there was truth in the room that day.

I do remember feeling the shift in the room and our wonder at Nate's willingness to play the role. I also remember that the sins we put onto his head were kinder than those society had burdened him with. Touché was the kindest, and the most moved—and represented, after Nate, the longest number of years spent incarcerated.[1]

Nate went to the woods. We spoke among ourselves a while, I don't remember, possibly about the temporary safety we had achieved by accommodating what the sheep wanted of us, probably self-justifying talk, covering our fear and guilt for what we had done to Nate. Then it was ten or fifteen years later: the scapegoat was to return and tell us what we had done and reveal to us who and what we had become, return as both exile and prophet. I volunteered to go to him in the wilderness, speak with him, and accompany him back as his advocate. Back facing the community, Nate faltered of course: caught in his misery, he had little perspective on what had been done to him. He had little of observer and prophet in him. To what he did manage to say, the other goats wouldn't listen, resisted, fought him off.

Six years later, that exercise haunts me, because of my recognition that those we refuse to acknowledge as our children, our brothers and sisters, those we cover with our cruelty, have an insight, whether they know or can articulate it, into our very souls.

I met Nate in April 1992, an actor in our first workshop at the Western Wayne Correctional Facility. In *Inside Out* he offered his Detroit East Side stories of childhood physical and sexual abuse. At the end of 1994 he left prison and enrolled in January as a University of Michigan junior, and in English 310 and 319 co-facilitated workshops at Henry Ford High School and Maxey Boys Training School. He went to the University of Michigan School of Social Work and became my course assistant in English 411, where once he cried in class at the sudden realization, triggered by another student's epiphany—"We want black people in prison"[2]—that all his life, right up to the present, everyone had told him he belonged in prison.

Over the years, his other stories emerged: physical abuse by his father, sexual abuse by his cousin, time in juvenile hall, two long bits for armed robbery, white men trying to kill him, jabbing a knife at his eyes, in a Georgia army barracks, his treatment of his wife and endangerment of his sons, the illiteracy of his father, who as a child had watched his own father murder his wife and kill himself. After receiving his masters in social work, Nate worked and lost jobs, drank and wrecked cars, sank into the morass of drug use, and fought back. We attempted an intervention, which almost worked. He fathered a girl and adopted her and her sister away from a traumatic situation, settled into an apartment with them. In the summer of 2006 he left a trembling message on my answering machine. He had been diagnosed with cancer of the esophagus, and in his last months I spent every week having breakfast or lunch with him while he laughed, told stories, cried, teased waitresses, and was terrified. When he passed, I wrote a letter to everyone who knew him, soliciting funds for the education of his daughters:

> When I arrived at his apartment in Romulus half an hour after his death—Janie, Gillian Eaton, and I were on our way to visit him—and saw him on the bed, hands over his chest, a bruise on his forehead where he had fallen, his face peaceful, I remembered a dream he had told me a month earlier. He had been in his casket in a large room, mourners walking all around, and suddenly his eyes sprang open, he leaned up in the casket, and cried "I'm alive! It was wrong, it wasn't true, I wasn't sick!" Now, in his bedroom, I notice a twinkle at the corner of his eye, and I wait, for long minutes, believing, knowing that he might in fact pull it off.
>
> Later, thinking about this, I realized that for so many of us that was Nate Jones, Nate in every space dancing suddenly to his feet, Nate taking us seriously and making us laugh, Nate somehow always coming back from whatever destruction had taken him on, a spiritual resource, an inspiration, for our own hard times.[3]

I recognized that he represented the resiliency of the people we worked with, the destroyed children who created poems, the abused women who created plays and filled rooms with their laughter and meaning, that he was the Prison Creative Arts Project at its most hurt and at its best.[4] I loved him, all of us who knew him loved him and his creativity and humor and spirit. On the one hand, I was always there for him, but, on the other, I didn't know how to help him, and sometimes I might have been more proactive. I was his brother. And not. After the scapegoat exercise he disappeared into some deep dangerous spot in a world I didn't know. In *When Can We Talk?*[5] I stood behind an empty chair and spoke a monologue about his absence, his talent, my anger for him and at him. He reappeared for our second performance at the Roeper School and came onto the stage as my monologue ended and improvised powerfully. He was back. And he spoke as the outcast. But he wasn't ready to take care of himself: he only gave the audience the reasons we should be angry *for* him.

Thanks to a conversation with Ruth Morgan while I was a Bridge Resident at the Headlands Center for the Arts in July 1998, when we applied for a Michigan Association of Community Arts Agencies Planning and Implementation Grant to hire Gillian and to fund the play, I knew I had to get Equity wages for the formerly incarcerated actors who would join us. What I didn't know was the difficulties these returned citizens would face in trying to get to work. Pilar Horner, Jesse Jannetta, Vanessa Mayesky, Kristen Ostenso, Janie Paul, and I, PCAP actors and technical assistant for *When Can We Talk?* (Josh White Jr. was our musician) agree that we learned more and were moved more by walking at the side of colleagues who were attempting to survive the return from prison than from all our years working inside the prisons. We lost Nate and we might have lost any of the others as well.

When Nate disappeared, we invited two other former prisoners to join us. We knew Jason Rios as an artist and as a solid, earnest, determined human being. We didn't know if he could act. He was home on tether with a nightly curfew in Monroe, an hour from Ann Arbor. If he went for coffee during a rehearsal break and anything brought police to the café and they checked people's IDs, he could be charged with escaping and sent back to prison. If his car broke down, he needed to phone his parole officer immediately. Toward the end of months of rehearsal, his parole officer's superior arbitrarily denied him permission to perform. If the parole officer had not courageously gone over her supervisor's head, and if her supervisor's superior hadn't been sympathetic, Jason would have been excluded from something in which he had become thoroughly invested. In *When Can We Talk?*, right after my monologue, while he performed his own monologue, "When Will the Punishment Stop?" three of us continually forced back to the floor a fourth actor, constantly trying to rise.

Nate Jones and his daughters, Patience Jackson Lussier (*left*) and Mi-nate Jones Lussier. (Photograph by Chris Lussier.)

Dave Hawkins was the other replacement for Nate, a large, powerful, earnest, decent man. After a Parnall Correctional Facility performance, he had talked with me about continuing acting at home. During the year of *When Can We Talk?* he and his wife were struggling with their marriage and he was fighting to find and hold work in economically devastated Flint, one of the most dangerous and challenged cities in the country. On his way to rehearsal one late afternoon, his car went over in a ditch. Luckily he walked away.

Tracy Neal was born and spent adolescent years in Flint. She had moved on to Detroit. Pilar and I worked with her in the Sisters Within Theater Troupe—she appeared in five plays from 1995 to 1997—and knew, later, the courage it had taken for her to be the named litigant in a federal lawsuit against the Michigan Department of Corrections. Personal problems during the time of our rehearsals led her with her two infants to Ann Arbor's Safe House, and the cast became her official support group. Her allotted time at Safe House up, Janie and I signed security on her apartment lease and lost the security deposit when she left early. In *When Can We Talk?* she and the other women spoke her agonizing story of brutal interrogation and forced confession, the most powerful moment in the play.

Touché (Jeffery Smith) took the culinary arts course at the Thumb Correctional Facility and was working in food preparation at the Adrian Temporary Correctional Facility when he began acting in PCAP plays. A risk-taking actor, he was a fatherly presence for our members. When he learned I was coming to a performance, he got permission to bake cheesecakes for the reception following the play. Ambitious to become a baker, he knew that a professor would, of course, know quality cheese cake. I ate a huge cherry topped slab, then another covered with blueberry, and pronounced their greatness. The rest is history. He had played high school football in Flint but had never attended a University of Michigan football game, a longtime dream. We got him tickets when he returned home after sixteen years away. He looked up at the 100,000 fans and vowed to make 100,000 cheesecakes. He has pursued that goal for years now, without benefits, without health insurance, suffering one broken down car after another: an ingenious, persuasive entrepreneur with too little business acumen, a supreme optimist struggling against fate. There is no one like him in this world. One night after a late rehearsal, he beckoned me aside: he owed another ex-prisoner $2,000 for CDs he had promised he would sell along with his cheesecakes: if he returned that night to Flint without it, he would be killed. I screamed at him . . . and gave him the $2,000.[6] In *When Can We Talk?* he acted out the scenes with this CD business partner, adding his daughter, and playing out the various voices in his head.

Clearly, Janie and I should not have given Tracy or Touché that money. Clearly, we should have done so.

Our civilization cast them out. Were they not once our children? How do their lives, how does Nate's life, reflect us? What might they, returned, say to us? What is asked of us? Is anything asked of us? Who are we? Wendell Berry, in *The Hidden Wound,* writes of his childhood,

> Within the language there was a silence, an emptiness, of exactly the shape of the humanity of the black man; the language I spoke in my childhood and youth was in that analogous to a mold in which a statue is to be cased. The options, then, were that one could, by a careful observance of the premises of the language, keep the hollow empty and thus avoid the pain of the recognition of the humanity of an oppressed people and of one's own guilt in their oppression; or one could, willing or not, be forced by the occasions of sympathy and insight to break out of those premises into a speech of another and more particular order, so that the hollow begins to fill with the substance of a life that one must recognize as human and demanding.[7]

In March 1996 I brought Michael Keck to the Florence Crane Women's and the Western Wayne Correctional Facilities to perform pieces from *Voices in the Rain,* his one-man play about the African American experience of incarceration.[8] In one monologue, a man just arrived back in town after years in prison stops at the local Y to ask about housing and a possible job. The manager offers him a cup of coffee and listens to him reminisce, describe his situation, and talk about how jumpy he got when two policemen sat next to him at a restaurant counter. In the discussions that followed the monologue, I heard in the voices of the men and women an anxiety I hadn't heard before. They were frightened. They had specific stories, they knew the odds. Their words mixed bravado and haunting uncertainty. The women talked about their individual, personal need to hold strong, and Sisters Within member Devora responded: Yes, but they needed to recognize that the *plan* was to

When Can We Talk? group photo. *Top row:* Jeffrey Smith (Touché), Jason Rios, Gillian Eaton, Buzz Alexander. *Middle row:* Jesse Jannetta, Tracy Neal, Janie Paul, Vanessa Mayesky. *Bottom row:* Josh White Jr., Dave Hawkins, Pilar Horner. (Photograph by John Sobczak, Lorien Studios.)

send them back; they needed to be organized on the outside, sisters who supported and fought for each other.

In 2000 the University nominated PCAP for a National Endowment for the Arts Access Grant and provided more than the matching funds required. By then I was wearing too many hats and was wearing down: it was clear we needed an administrator and clear NEA would not simply hand us an administrator. As grant writer, I had to come up with a new project. I remembered those prison discussions and decided that although PCAP's focus was on the incarcerated, we needed to address, at least in some small way, the anxiety I had heard. And so I imagined the Portfolio and Linkage projects. Because we were providing arts access to people who had none, we won the grant. I wrote to Jesse Jannetta, then in the Peace Corps in Armenia, and it turned out that the administrative position was just what he was looking for. Janie, Pilar, and I interviewed him when he came through town, at a South Main Market café. He was our best candidate. We were in business.

THE PORTFOLIO PROJECT

Through our workshops and the annual exhibition of art by incarcerated youth, we identify boys and girls who are discovering and deepening new sides of themselves through the arts and who wish to continue. Sometimes the Adrian Training School, Boysville, Lincoln, Maxey, and Vista Maria staff identify youth we haven't worked with.[9] Each term between seven and nineteen PCAP members travel once a week to those facilities and work with the youth to create professional art and writing portfolios complete with resumés, artists' statements, and a letter of recommendation from the PCAP member. Judges have praised the portfolios and sent the youth home early. At home they proudly show the portfolio to parents, teachers, and employers. In 2003 when Ariella Kaufman, Suzanne Gothard, and I arrived at step-down sites to establish linkage mentorships, the youth would enter proudly carrying their portfolios, eager to show us their new work. Robert, the youth in my epigraph poem, whose memories already are so different from mine, was one of them.

At the end of November 2007, Kate Richardson, a year and a half after graduating, was a paralegal in San Francisco with Rosen, Bien & Galvan, a law firm focusing on constitutional and civil rights cases. She was responding to inmate correspondence, interviewing prisoners, preparing documents on prison conditions and overcrowding evidence, and actively involved in a case on due process rights for youth on parole. It is, she wrote, "a tedious job at times . . . an exciting job at times."

When she joined the portfolio project in August 2005 and imagined entering a prison or juvenile facility, she felt intimidated, scared. She had "many preconceptions of prisons and the people they confined . . . conceptions . . . of murderers and rapists . . . of dark corners of atrocious human behaviors and malicious intent." Over the next year she worked one-on-one with Marcellus, Danny, and Ben at Maxey, "the faces behind my veil of misconceptions . . . young men who had grown up in broken houses, full of addiction, loss, turmoil and mistakes." Because of them she took her paralegal job and is headed toward a career in law. Reflecting on all this, she writes,

> I have a picture of Marcellus, Danny and Ben in my small cubicle now. The picture was taken right after their special performance outside of Maxey, on our campus, on my campus. They are artists, writers, and boys. And they are happy. I look at them daily and I don't mind that I sit under a pile of documents waiting to be reviewed, searching them for due process violations, searching for lengthy detentions and use of force incidents. I don't mind that sometimes I feel like the problem is so huge, so institutionally corrupt that there is no end in sight. I don't mind because the name and C[alifornia] D[epartment of] Corrections number on the document I hold in my hand has a face and a history and a family and a life. We too often remove the humanity from our work. Their picture is a constant reminder to me that I am working for a sense of human decency, respect, and right.[10]

Portfolio relations are not often easy. The youth tests the student, needs to trust her. Both sides feel out the power dynamics, even week by week. The haunted past and incarcerated present of the youth come into play. Trouble at home, a bad visit or no visit, old pain, tension in their living unit where they spend twenty-four hours a day with troubled peers they did not choose to live with: because of all this they may refuse to come to a session or turn up arms folded, head down, closed, and the student, who is so committed to the youth and to moving forward, has to figure out how to get through, how to listen. Then there is the institution itself. Our liaisons and most staff love the portfolio project. But sometimes staff on duty don't understand, are not excited for the youth, don't provide a quiet space. Sometimes there is simply no such space available: the room is agitated with noise, and other youth stop by the table to observe, to talk, to divert.

And there is the struggle that goes with all teaching: how to find exercises, how to listen, how to discover the words that enable the youth to tap into their lived experiences, so that the beginners can rid themselves of "friendship is" and "love is" list-poems or of traced cartoon characters, so that they, and the more advanced youth as well, can find their way to their *own* stories, language, lines, spaces, and images, to originality and power. For many there is the fear of performance, fear of failure. At the end of the term, often in front of all the facility peers and staff, the PCAP member introduces and celebrates the youth, and the youth then shows her art or reads his poems.

We recruit students for portfolio from PCAP and from other courses. Normally they receive independent study credit from either me in English or Janie in Art and Design. They are supervised by the Coordinator of the Portfolio and Linkage Projects, who is sometimes assisted by experienced PCAP members, also getting credit. The students keep a journal, which is read each week, they attend PCAP meetings and meet together for the last hour, they meet individually with the coordinator and sometimes with Janie or me, and they prepare and present a final creative, analytic project about their experience. When we have someone at lecturer or professor level, like Joyce Meier or myself, we teach the portfolio project as English 326, Writing in the Community, and add a substantial reading list. We insist that students work for credit so that during crunch times other courses don't take priority. Our bottom line is responsibility to the youth. After doing portfolio for credit, many students repeat without credit.

Anna Clark, eager for a new challenge beyond her workshop experience,[11] became an assistant to coordinator Ariella Kaufman, guiding other portfolio students, and taking on her own portfolio relation with Claire,[12] who "was a wonderfully open young woman who saw Anne Frank as her soul mate, inspiring many of her poems." With Claire she "centered on finding new forms and new words for her writing, to break out of the poetic molds she'd formed for herself" and "felt touched" when Claire started calling her "her big sister, especially when I knew she took her own role as a big sister so seriously." Working with Claire and the university students, she "learned a lot—about checking myself to not be pushy, about not trying to pressure someone's thinking to match my own, about respecting the pace and trajectory of each person's journey," lessons that have continued in her work as an advocate and organizer and in how she "interacts with others on an every-day basis." She writes me that she came to love the Portfolio Project

> for its focused attention on the talents of individuals; for its ability to foster deep one-on-one relationships; for the new kind of initiative and creativity and patience that it demands of facilitators; for its ability to draw new people into PCAP from many different realms at the University of Michigan; and for meeting a new need in both the people who are incarcerated and the people who come into that space.[13]

When Sari Adelson decided to take on an art portfolio at Vista Maria, she had "seen and been through a lot" in her short life and felt "relatively prepared for what I was getting myself into":

> I've been in psychiatric hospitals, substance abuse facilities, witnessed withdrawal from severe drug addictions, lost people close to me through suicide, dealt with self mutilation, eating disorders, and drug abuse. I thought I had seen and been through quite a bit, and although I know I'm not completely naive or ignorant, there are still corners of the world darker than what I've known.

Ashley,[14] her portfolio partner, at first meeting seemed "uninterested . . . apathetic."

> There was something about her though, something that struck me. She didn't laugh, she didn't smile, and she didn't seem to care one way or another, but there was this look in her eye suggesting that she was more excited than anything in the world. Her eyes were glazed over, and she was rather fidgety. She was either heavily medicated, or incredibly tired.

When they finally had the chance to talk for more than a few minutes, Ashley's "life fell into my lap, and cracked my heart."

> Her drug history, sex life, promiscuity, sexuality, self mutilation, depression, bipolar disorder, losing her mother, not seeing her brother, meeting her sister and real father for the first time in her life, age, different homes, placements, suicidal thoughts, medication, feelings about Vista. Her life was an open book, and by the sounds of it, she wasn't done talking. She's been in

the system since she was 12, moving from placement to placement, after running, self mutilating, drugging, and sexing her way out of the placements before. She talked of her life post Vista, about her dreams and aspirations, her desires to come to Ann Arbor, to attend the University of Michigan and get a degree in psychology. She's smart, real smart, well read . . .

Ashley wanted to knit, crochet, sew, and quilt, but wasn't allowed needles. So they worked with pencils, markers, and fine black pens, and Ashley started multiple pieces of art for her sister and father, who each time would be visiting the next day. But Sari didn't know what to do about the portfolio that required completion by the end of term. She hated having a structured plan, so she "abandoned the structure."

This project was about creating the space, allowing us to function organically, together. I wasn't teacher, or authority, I wasn't there to make her finish certain things at certain times in order for me to have something substantial to say at a meeting. This wasn't about a grade, or a final presentation, it was about her, and me, and things we discussed and did within that room with the two way mirror each Thursday. I brought numerous supplies every evening, and if they got used, awesome, and if not, if Ashley had had a rough day, and wanted to vent about staff, other girls on the unit, about her dad, about missing her mom, that's what I was there to do, to lend an ear to listen, and a heart to love.

They looked through her poems and worked on rendering them into art. One night they looked through her journals, full of "very detailed, vivid accounts of memories from her earlier years." Talking it over with Sari, Ashley decided to portray the memories visually and brainstormed one night, going through the journals, "finding the things she wanted for each page."

There would be a page, or a panel for each of these periods in her life, each page [composed of poetry and art] chaotic and colorful, depressing, yet delightful. With this her portfolio was born. That night I remember her telling me not only how excited she was about doing all this, she could see the images in her head, about how much it meant to her to have me there to help her get it all done. With a huge smile on my face, I told her of course, this is why I'm here!

"Ashley's life has been nothing short of hell," Sari writes, and

> she says she wants to share her life with other people, she wants people to
> see her work and know who she is, and what she's been through. . . . Her art-
> work, and the opportunity to be doing this specific portfolio, is cathartic,
> cathartic in the traditional sense, but also in terms of expressing her feelings
> and her demons in a form other than the words she's been speaking in psy-
> chotherapy for the last almost 10 years of her life. Ashley found great plea-
> sure in seeing the pages finished, as if a chapter had been officially closed,
> not because she got it out of her, but because she took something awful and
> turned it into art, something beautiful. I brought my computer in last week
> so she could see her poems typed up, and she was floored. She had said to
> me that "they look so much more . . . real, when they're there on the screen,
> than when they are in my notebook."

While Sari thought she knew what she was getting herself into, she
hadn't anticipated the pain and had not anticipated the relationship that
would come with the portfolio: "We learned, laughed, and loved. We were
friends, caring, honest individuals for one another. We were two people
looking to start something new."

Ashley told Sari toward the end, "I've always been able to talk about my
life, and I've always been able to make art, but not until you came along was
I able to do both . . . when I leave here, we need to stay in touch." "These are
the reasons," Sari adds, "I do this work."

> My experience this past semester at Vista Maria has been one of the most
> meaningful of my life thus far. . . . Ashley has taught me a lot about life,
> about trials and tribulations, about trust, honesty, and integrity. She reminds
> me that things aren't always as they appear, and that not everyone has the
> best of intentions, but the people who have been there since the beginning,
> the ones that never gave up on you; those are the ones you hold close. She
> has taught me to be strong, to fight for what I believe in, and always keep
> my head up. She is an inspiration and for this I thank her from the bottom
> of my heart. [15]

We are given so much by these hurt, beleaguered, resilient youth. Most of
all, as Sari says, we learn to be strong. And we take away, in their name, a

commitment to struggle, one way or another and in spite of our fears and limits, on their behalf for the rest of our lives.

"We need to stay in touch," Ashley says. "She started calling me her big sister," Anna reports. "I have a picture of Marcellus, Danny and Ben in my small cubicle now," Kate writes, "artists, writers, and boys . . . happy." For Kate, for Anna, for Sari: the scapegoat as brothers and sisters and permanent influences. For the scapegoats: Kate, Anna, and Sari, brothers and sisters who will continue as resources whether physically present or not.

THE LINKAGE PROJECT

In the spring of 2002 Terrell was mostly confined by his tether to his brother's tiny apartment on Detroit's west side. Jesse and I visited him there to talk about PCAP's Linkage Project. He brought out his sketch pad to show us his work. He talked about his job prospects and plans to attend Wayne State University's art school. We told him about PCAP's modest scholarship fund. Jesse and I agreed afterward that his environment and personal situation seemed stable enough for him to enter the linkage project and take on a mentor.

We next met with Detroit artist Michael Cooper and went over the Linkage Project requirements. Mentor and mentee must meet at least once a month. They respond to each other's work and develop their skills, with an emphasis on what the mentor can offer. The mentor seeks opportunities for the mentee: workshops, classes, other community artists or writers, venues for exhibition or performance. The mentor does not loan money, is not a social worker, avoids co-dependency or entanglement in any of the social needs of the mentee. That will be a challenge, and the borderline won't always be clear. The mentor receives a token fee of $500 for the year, paid in two installments. The mentee receives $300 and must submit receipts to be reimbursed.[16]

We arranged for Terrell and Michael to meet. After each communicated with us separately that they were compatible, the linkage kicked in. Terrell took advantage of our scholarship to take classes at Wayne County Community College and used his $300 to purchase art supplies from Utrecht. To supplement his income, he drew portraits at parties. Michael met with him frequently to help him develop his portraiture, charcoal drawing, and landscape skills.

At the beginning of this endeavor Jesse and I were on our own. Unexpectedly, the Linkage Project met resistance within the PCAP executive committee and indifference within PCAP. Some executive committee members resented that I had written the NEA grant without consulting them about ways it might stretch PCAP energies. Focused on their workshops and the annual exhibition, PCAP members seldom picked up on the anxieties of those coming home, and the project was invisible, with no easy way for members to get involved. Jesse and I were meeting great enthusiasm around the state from community artists and writers—they had been waiting for something like this—but it was difficult to convey that when we sat in the executive committee meeting room at the Ginsberg Center. Eventually Pilar Horner, a leader in PCAP who had worked with incarcerated girls, men, and women, but who had been one of the main skeptics and antagonists, chose the Linkage Project as her School of Social Work placement and became an enthusiastic convert. When we hired Ariella Kaufman as our first coordinator of Portfolio and Linkage, she, Suzanne Gothard (Jesse's successor as PCAP administrator), and I continued the lively trips Jesse and I had taken. We added numerous mentees, and the project took off.

The early years were exciting and full of promise. In 2003 and twice in 2004 we held conferences with linkage mentors and mentees, former portfolio youth, and PCAP members who had worked with them. In January 2004, thanks to our Rockefeller PACT Grant, we brought as participants and advisors Ellen Barry of Legal Services for Prisoners With Children in San Francisco, Rochelle Perry of Project Return in New Orleans, Benay Rubenstein, who supports returning women prisoners in their search for higher education in New York City, and Andrea Scott of Amicus in Minneapolis. Participants in the projects were bold in their suggestions for improvement in relationships, communication, and networking.[17] Mentees showed their art and read their poems. Some of them were eager to become mentors themselves.

The linkages were often dynamic and engaged. Tim, who had been in a number of our workshops at Adrian Training School, learned directing and stagecraft from Gillian Eaton at Performance Network in Ann Arbor and read his work publicly. Dave Hawkins, an actor at the Parnall Correctional Facility, studied playwriting under Bill Ward, director of the Flint Youth Theater. He auditioned and took a role in one of Bill's plays. India Sullivan, with the support of Barbara Pliskow, patched together a computer with her $300, wrote and read her poetry and exhibited prisoner art at a local café and in her own exhibition. Cathy Babcock helped Danny Biddinger create a small chapbook of his art and poetry. Donna Hiner helped Suzie Thompson break through her structured approach to art, and the two of them shared life stories and found they were kindred souls. Mentees spoke in front of University of Michigan audiences, and seven of them, at one point or another, joined our National Advisory Board.[18]

By November 2005 there had been sufficient activity for us to hold "Are We Free: A Linkage Exhibition of Art" at the Duderstadt Center Gallery. Curated by mentor Nancy Lautenbach and mentee India Stewart and organized by Jean Borger, it was a great success. Twelve mentors and ten mentees read, performed, and testified during the vibrant opening and closing receptions. Several of them told the audience that PCAP coming into the prisons had brought an unprecedented respect for prisoners as human beings and creators. "Then," they said, "we came home, and they were the same people." Nine mentees and six mentors exhibited sixty-two works of art: which included drawing, painting, scratch art, photography, mixed media, sculpture, ceramics, jewelry, fashion, and installation. Over thirteen hundred visitors attended the exhibition, and total income for the artists came to $2,115.

It was an ambitious and energizing time.

WHEN WILL THE PUNISHMENT STOP?

But the linkages were also difficult. Seven or eight months into his work with Michael, Terrell disappeared. Other cases followed. After eliminating a mentor interested only in assessing Will's "criminal mind," we found him Robert Stamps, an energetic playwright and author who fully committed himself to Will. After six months Will disappeared. We brought Melissa together with Michael Gillespie of Oakland University's theater department, but before they could start, her lost confidence as an actor, work complications, and visits to her children in Flint ended the linkage. As we were seeking the right musician for Billy, he reoffended, then escaped from prison. Mary returned home after twenty-six years to care for her dying mother and then her father with his gradually mounting Alzheimer's disease. Joan could not afford long-distance phone calls and had trouble keeping contact with her mentor. We had to suspend John's and Anthony's linkages because they began using again and were sent to rehab. Jerry admitted his felony on forty job applications and was turned down, then finally lied and was hired to caulk houses, developing pains in his arms and hands so severe that he was unable to hold a paintbrush. When they discovered his lie, he lost the job. James disappeared. Will Copeland watched one of the most talented poets we have worked with be reincarcerated once, then jailed. Theresa, raped by her lawyer employer, desperate, the same day reverted to an old practice of stealing credit cards, and returned to prison.

Men and women who have spent any substantial time in prison return home physically disabled, according to Mary Heinen, our current Linkage and Portfolio coordinator. Close quarters, heating and cooling conditions they can't individually regulate, noise that makes long periods of sleep diffi- cult, starchy diets, and often inadequate care for serious ailments take their toll. The Detroit House of Corrections, which became the Western Wayne Correctional Facility, housing men until 2000 and women until 2004, was built on a toxic-waste site and had methane detectors in the units. Before it was finally closed, the women in the horticulture program were told not to put their hands in the soil.[19] The Florence Crane Women's Facility, accord- ing to Mary,

> was built during the great depression as a state school for disabled chil- dren. [The warden] told me it had three wells. Two she had to close due to high toxin levels, including nitrates. She said she was worried she would have to close the third. One of the guards was a real estate agent in Coldwa- ter. She said she had been unable to sell property for miles around the area due to water and ground pollution from a chemical fertilizer plant nearby. The chemicals leaked into the farmlands/wells and were known to contain nitrates. Our water had a noticeably oily film on top of it in our coffee cups — when heated in the microwave the water turned foamy. It had white crystals floating in it cold or hot. The water was a major topic of discussion. We were not allowed bleach to clean because the old asbestos-wrapped pipes would rot from the caustics, officials told me.
>
> Bleeding was a serious problem for the women. Some had no periods for weeks. I learned nitrates are a compound found naturally in nature and I believe the pollution of the wells in Florence Crane came from the fertilizer plant toxic runoff in the area. The plant used bird droppings shoveled off forest floors for their mixtures. FCWF knew this and added bags of water softener to the water softening tanks in the basement, adding salt to a salt. Many of the women had strokes, raw ulcers that would not heal, cancers, seizures, headaches, bladder and kidney infections, and other terrible disor-

ders and diseases. Many of the women I knew have died from brain, breast, colon, lung, bone, liver and pancreatic cancer. Most of the lifers I knew in my age group and older developed cancer and died. Nitrates are used in the manufacture of paint, explosives, and farm products. Warning signs used to be up in the visiting room warning guests not to drink the water. Pregnant women were not allowed to transfer to Crane because of it. Some became pregnant there. We were forced to bathe in the water and eat food cooked in it. There were times there were open sewage pits in the yard from failed repair jobs. The place was crawling with rats. I was there from Jan. 25, 1989, until the day the pit of hell closed [it closed for women and became a men's facility in November 2000]. God save us from the consequences.[20]

And many return home mentally disabled.[21] Over the past three decades prisons and jails have become the principal mental health care facilities for those deinstitutionalized by the closing of state mental hospitals since the early 1980s and for those deranged by living on the streets as a consequence of Reagan economic policies. The afflicted do not easily follow instructions. They either isolate themselves in their rooms or go to the yard and act out. For those reasons they serve more time than others. Their illness deepens.[22]

Other prisoners suffer the results of what psychologist Craig Haney calls "'prisonization'—the psychological process of adapting to life in an institution, where one is neither expected nor permitted to make decisions; where trust is a liability and intimacy a danger."[23] Interactions with other prisoners and officers are often charged with violence, tension, and potential physical, mental, and sexual humiliation. Jerry writes that prisoners at his prison are requesting segregation, because current overcrowding is causing such random, frequent violence.[24] Judith Herman tells us that "a single traumatic event can occur almost anywhere. Prolonged, repeated trauma, by contrast, occurs only in circumstances of captivity." "One of the most intractable aftereffects of this kind of trauma, according to Herman," Nell Bernstein tells us, "is helplessness, or learned passivity. . . . Walking out the gates does not automatically reverse this process."[25]

Our state and federal legislators over the past three decades have voted to keep returnees feeling helpless and overwhelmed. Those with drug convictions (the majority of returnees) normally cannot receive student loans and may not live in public housing. If a family member takes them in, the family risks eviction. In most states those with a criminal sexual conduct conviction are restricted in where they may live, in some states so severely restricted that they find themselves under bridges or in isolated group houses in the middle of nowhere. They are also placed on permanent public lists and are subject to hounding and harassment. Returnees with felonies may not apply for a wide range of jobs. They are also much less likely to be called back for job interviews or attain employment than peers without criminal records, as Devah Pager has demonstrated in *Marked,* her study of Milwaukee employers.[26] If the purpose of mass incarceration was to create a caste of black high school dropouts whose life courses would be drastically altered and who would be eliminated from the workforce,[27] the effect continues unabated when they come home.

Because the federal Adoption and Safe Families Act of 1997 led to a 250 percent rise in termination of parental rights of the incarcerated, parents return to permanently dismantled families. "This will be known," Pam Martinez says, "as the great baby-snatching era." Ida McCray, founder of Families With a Future, notes that the tougher sentencing and child welfare laws that disproportionately affect black families have "set in motion 'the greatest separation of families since slavery.'" "The mood in prison," Philip Gentry says,

> is one of despair. Essentially what incarcerated parents are being told is that no matter what they do—how hard they work at overcoming the issues that put their children in foster care and brought them to prison—they cannot avoid having their parental rights terminated.

Bernstein concurs, alluding to women who have come home:

> For many women, losing the right to care for their children triggers a powerful despair—at their own failures, their children's resultant suffering, and the seeming omnipotence of institutions that many find incomprehensible, if not hostile. They treat this despair not with Prozac or Zoloft but with methamphetamine, heroine, crack cocaine—taking themselves one step further from the rehabilitation that is ostensibly the motive for incarcerating drug addicts.[28]

The problem in this country, Robert Moses says, is that "we do not think of others' children as our own." Now the incarcerated are unable to think of their own children as their own.[29]

And they return to families and neighborhoods damaged and wounded by their preprison behavior and by their absence. They had abandoned their children, and their children are loaded with grief and anger. They have been taunted in school. The families left behind have often lived in shame and, unable to pay for housing, have been on the move. The remaining spouse, if there is one, or the grandparents have suffered great economic and emotional stress. Returnees face high and often impatient expectations for them to reintegrate, take up parenting, and get a paycheck. They face people who hold them to their past, who stigmatize and distrust them no matter how much they have matured. And, especially in the early days and weeks, they face old associations, triggers, and temptations, which may deepen and seduce as they experience the mortifications of unemployment, housing denial, and health challenges. They face weekly (even daily) visits to parole officers who during the last three decades came to see their job as one of violating the returnee, sending them back to serve more time,[30] although in Michigan this is now shifting. With so few resources, such high levels of stress, and no health insurance, they are especially susceptible to illness.[31] In Michigan, which has perhaps the best-funded prisoner reentry program in the nation, they face the slowest economy in the country.

And so the exiled, disabled, returning citizen scapegoat remains disabled, remains scapegoat, sometimes truth-teller and prophet. Just as the Wayne County Court judge, lawyers, court officers, and stenographer froze when Jerry Moore spoke his powerful story, so do the rest of us turn deaf ears to the story about ourselves that our exiled relative reveals.[32]

It needn't be so. In an aboriginal sentencing circle in Canada, the elders apologize to the offending youth. "It is our fault you are here," they say: "we didn't raise you well." And they explain to him that they are seeking workable sanctions, because they *need* him in the community.[33]

THE DECLINE OF THE LINKAGE PROJECT

By the time of the November 2005 Linkage exhibition, we had established thirty-eight linkages. We had held three Linkage/Portfolio conferences by the end of 2004. As I said, it was an exciting era. Yet in the year succeeding the exhibition we added only one linkage, and between October 2006, when Mary Heinen became coordinator, and June 2008, we added only six more, none of them youth. And after December 2004 we failed to bring participants together for a sharing, assessment, and planning conference.

The consequences of this decline were evident in the second Linkage exhibition, "Are We Community," which ran from November 9 to January 30, 2007–8, at Focus: HOPE on Detroit's west side.[34] The opening was attended by 110 people, who, according to Mary, "were even sitting on the stairs going up to the third floor."[35] The spoken word presentations were lively, the mood spirited and celebrative. We paid formerly incarcerated people to design and create the programs, to do the matting, and to provide the baked goods. However, the master of ceremonies was not a linkage participant. One former mentor and no mentees participated in the spoken word entertainment.[36] The striking exhibition poster was by mentor Tony Bacon, not by a mentee. And of the six mentees exhibiting their work, two had already completed their linkages, three (one of whom had been home from prison for at least six years) had barely begun, and one was temporarily suspended, because he had relapsed and was in treatment.[37] It was a proud occasion but a far cry from the participation in 2005.

What happened?

Jean Borger in her first year as coordinator—late summer 2004 until summer 2005—added eleven linkages, vigorously committed herself to mentors and mentees, and organized the December 2004 conference and November 2005 linkage exhibition. But she also saw mentees struggling, hurting, and even returning to prison. Especially sensitive to what this meant to them and their loved ones, she felt inadequately prepared. Although a highly empathic listener, she knew she couldn't listen professionally like a trained social worker and couldn't easily provide or guide them to job opportunities, physical and mental health support, housing, drug counseling, family and other social services. She began to isolate herself within her role and gradually decrease her participation in PCAP meetings.

She hinted that we should add no new mentees unless we hired a social worker (we had no funds for this), and we suddenly noticed that she had in fact quietly added only one linkage during her second year. Her position was agonized, compassionate, and legitimate, but she was attempting a total reorientation of the Linkage Project to serve fewer people.

At the June 2006 Advisory Board meeting, she pointed out that although we tell the mentees "this is just an arts relationship . . . they come with life needs and ask questions because that's the lifeline." She proposed that we should focus on the handful to whom we were already committed and fund them for a second year, doing what we could to help with services and adding no new mentees.[38]

Michael Keck, recognizing from his own experience with youth that the borderline was subtle and painful, nevertheless urged PCAP to make our role clear to mentees, to set limits on what we can do, and to continue to offer linkages to people coming home. Janie remembered:

I visited an art project in a township art center in South Africa, where most of the participants were homeless and very needy in terms of services; the center only did art, and that was very exciting for the participants, it was a resource, a place they could be thinking, creating, and healing, and it was clear that working at something like this that they loved was enabling them to confront other needs.

Jesse Jannetta, now a board member, concurred: "A social worker may not be needed—the art can be the powerful thing, the thing that we focus on/do really well." Pat Gurin assented: "We don't have resources to help people who have nothing—art will have to be a part of helping someone who has other resources." It was a tough issue: if particular mentee circumstances took us over the border into their personal needs, we would have to struggle with that.

The consensus was to continue with new linkages and focus on what we could offer. But when Jean asked the Advisory Board point-blank to tell her *not* to add mentees, the members were silent. Since they did not actively instruct her to *add* mentees, the discussion remained in limbo, and it was her intention in the next year to add no new mentees. Since my intention was the opposite, we did not have a good match. Luckily, she found a better-paying job in September and moved on. I took on portfolio as an overload and worked with eight students. A month later we hired Mary Heinen.

In the next twenty-one months Mary added only six mentees. She was new to the position and to PCAP, needed to sort things out, was long on personal experience but short on connections to art communities around the state. I left on sabbatical in January 2007 and, although I stayed in town through mid-April, I needed to focus on this book and on the always overwhelming annual exhibition. Most of the remainder of the year I was away. In January 2008 I returned to intensive teaching, the exhibition, patches of focus on the book, and the growing PCAP demands that have come with our success. I was less available for Linkage than I once was, less able to travel the state to meet with potential mentors, with mentees.

Mary in the meantime, always a powerful speaker, diversified the coordinator position. She joined the Michigan Prisoner Re-Entry Initiative (MPRI) steering committee, attended and addressed local conferences, initiated a writing workshop with Washtenaw County returnees, and was left with too little time to pursue linkages. I insisted on a Linkage advisory committee composed of community members (including myself), but it met only twice in eighteen months and an August 2009 meeting was sparsely attended.

And all this while we were having a difficult time, as always, getting our members to see beyond their workshop experience to what returning citizens face. They did not think to identify committed actors, artists, and writers for Linkage, despite our periodic pleas.

Since 2006 Jean's concerns have been alleviated by the establishment of the Washtenaw County MPRI group under Mary King's and Joe Summers's excellent leadership. The group thoroughly researched local assets, contracted with agencies, and created a sensitive, dug-in program for prisoners returning to Washtenaw County, which in 2007 had the highest recidivism rate in the state. Mary is able to draw on the wealth of agency services MPRI has identified throughout the state.

And Linkage suddenly is coming back. Mary has taken it on now and has been persistent especially with exhibition artists we know are returning. From July 2008 through July 2009, she has added ten linkages, six in the visual arts and four in poetry and spoken word. Only one is a youth. We are required to go through the juvenile facility social worker to contact the caseworker. We can't make direct contact. So much depends on those individuals. I am gradually applying myself to this in support of Mary, and we have two youth linkages pending, both talented poets. A luncheon on May 30 to begin planning a November conference meant to reconsolidate and move forward was well attended by artist mentees and some mentors. Our next Linkage exhibition, in 2010, will be led by returned citizens.

Linkage is our most difficult project because for those coming home the punishment never stops. At its best it is a great resource, worth reviving.

THE LIFE OF LINKAGE

And here is why. This is the story of Wynn Satterlee.

In late January 2002 we stood in the lobby with Phil Klintworth, the great special activities director of the Southern Michigan Correctional Facility,[39] looking at the submissions for the Seventh Annual Exhibition of

Art by Michigan Prisoners. One was *The Lost Swimmer,* a haunting expressionistic piece: a hat floating, three figures in black top hats and dark gray shirts with vertical blue, teal, lavender, and purple stripes in various poses searching in the water. We decided to take it. Phil told us that the artist had terminal cancer and that our selecting his work might keep him alive a little longer. So we took two more of his pieces! They were more abstract, not yet Wynn's signature work.

Over the next years he stayed alive and developed his art. Now and then we would meet with him when we came in for selection, as at the Macomb Correctional Facility. One painting with several variations placed him in an open grave with many people gathered around. Janie and I own his piece with hundreds of floating hats, his depiction of prison mail-call time, his painting of four men sitting with their hands in their faces, a black splotchy hole in the floor, and perhaps my favorite painting of all I've seen over the years, *Free My Daddy:* fathers are locked in birdcages, and figures dressed like executioners restrain desperate children trying to get to the cages. He became one of the exhibition's best, most original, most moving artists.

When Wynn came home—a judge had reviewed his case and declared him innocent—now a cancer survivor, he spoke at the opening reception of the 2006 annual exhibition. He also purchased a motel just outside of Manistee, fixed it up, and opened for business. When we stayed at the motel during our art selection trip in 2007—Oaks Correctional Facility is in Manistee—we found him painting fourteen hours a day and filling his own quarters, three rooms, from floor to ceiling with his art, with other canvasses piled one atop another. I have never seen anything like it. It was brilliant, beautiful, determined.

We offered him a linkage with Donna Hiner, who had already worked with Suzie Thompson. He had his doubts about linkage, but agreed to meet with her. What follows is the story in their own words. It illustrates at its best what happens when we make a connection inside and carry it over into the world outside. First Donna:

Wynn . . . Wynn is great. We met at Big Boy and we were both I think a bit unsure of whether or not this would be a good match . . . however that was dispelled the first 5 minutes of talking with one another. I knew the moment I saw some of his art work that Wynn is an artist extraordinaire. I wanted him to show his art, he was reluctant, but over the months I began to see a willingness to begin sharing his art with the world. I think for some artists the work is so personal that the thought of someone looking at it and critiquing it is quite a scary process in itself. I downloaded all the New York galleries, addresses and phone numbers for Wynn. I felt that there were areas in and out of the country that would be more receptive to his art. Montreal would be a very good city to expose his art. I couldn't contact the galleries for him as I am guardian to my twin 3 yr. old grandchildren and struggle to find time for myself. But Wynn is a force in himself and if he could focus all [his] energies into one area, [he] would be a well-known artist. Wynn did begin to look at himself as an artist along with being a businessman. And I believe Wynn began to see the possibilities of making a living off of his art. We still talk from time to time, but with him in Reno [where he moved to be with his son], it is difficult to mentor in any productive capacity.[40]

I sent a message to Wynn, asking him (as I had Donna and other mentors and mentees) to tell me what he could about what, if anything, the linkage connection had meant to him. Here is his reply.[41]

Hello Buzz

It is a great pleasure hearing from you. I have thoughts *every single day* of my life that either you or Janie or Mary [Heinen] or simply the University of Michigan appear. Every day. *Every day.*

from that statement alone maybe you can feel the impact *that you all had and still have on my life.*

Mary always answers the phone when the rest of the world seems to be like a poison in front of my face. She has kept me on the ground more times than even she knows.

the support of all of you couldn't be replaced with blood.

I have an unexplainable love for all of you.

In a strange way . . . closer than family.

It was an incredible honor to be at your wedding. I was awakened in the moment and felt almost like a regular person for the afternoon.

even in your most personal moment in your lives you were still reaching out and healing this wayward soul.

I told Katherine Weider that her "chanting session" as part of your ceremony is without a doubt the most remarkable vision I have ever witnessed. It still moves me and it sets your wedding day out as the most remarkable wedding I have ever attended.

you guys are forever amazing me.

thank you for everything and your friendship.

now I will answer your questions to the best of my ability.

I did get motivated with Donna. It was hard for me as you know to accept any type of critique even knowing full well that I was not perfect . . . far from it. But I was so content on being "wonderfully naive" that I did not want the intrusion. If that makes sense.

I didn't care, but again reluctantly I gave in due mostly to Katherine Weider. She was interviewing me and she very delicately kept reasoning with me about the chance to just participate in the program. See where it goes. She has a way of influencing me . . . pretty women always do. So with her encouragement I proceeded.

Donna turned out to be wonderful. She came into my life and cared. Didn't push me around.

She drove out of her way and didn't complain. And I enjoyed every session we had.

Donna is definitely an asset to your program.

She also needs the outside attention from her other world and in its own way your program helps the mentor as well as us.

My humble opinion.

I faced so many adjustments [when I came home] that I am still facing them. Minute by minute, hour by hour, and of course the big standard day by day.

but in truth it is moment by moment.

the other day I was with my son and took him to the Dairy Queen. I ordered a chocolate ice cream cone just out of the blue. I don't eat ice cream. But I love chocolate ice cream.

I was eating it and my son said . . . dad that's not how you eat ice cream. I looked at him and he was serious. So I asked him how he ate it, he said you lick it and turn the cone.

I didn't know . . . or forgot, but I did as he said and turned the cone. It was good and fun. A simple pleasure.

I was down to the cone and without thinking I took a bite from the cone. I almost spit it out.

It tasted like old stale cardboard.

My mind went racing and came to a screeching halt.

After I realized that it had been over 12 years since I had an ice cream cone.

Reality checks that puncture the moment.

those are the defining scales that measure just how deeply damaged that time did to me.

I forgot that we are supposed to know the cone tastes like cardboard . . . and love it anyway.

golly grasshopper.

it can not be told in one story. Your impact on me goes far before I was released and has continued on just as this e mail I am now answering is in the moment.

you invited me to get involved and didn't get upset when I was unfit for human consumption.

I could step up as I wanted to but you always understood.

You still kept inviting me to be a part of things.

Thank god for your determination.

little by little I was re-entering the world.

It was just never again going to be the same world. I know that now. And I can live with it.

But not easily by any means.

I believe that if I had to say words to describe what you have done for me and for my life is

nothing short of a miracle.

You talk so highly of my art. You praise my efforts, but you don't fully realize that you gave me life years ago when you helped this sick man before you even met him.

It is called *hope . . . love . . . and forgivness.*

My art even shocks me after it appears on canvas. My art would not be here if it was not for you and the program. Period.

so what do you think . . . how important do you think you are in my life?

art is all I have now. It is a spirit that has taken over.

thank you again for that gift.

I will be glad to contribute more words if you need them.

I am not sure what more I can say but it is an effort from my heart to assist you.

please ask me more questions and I will answer.

hope to hear from you soon.

wynn

CHAPTER EIGHT

The Prison Creative Arts Project: Crafted Out of Newspaper, Modge Podge, Paint, and Glitter

PCAP's early days were freewheeling. No administrator, no executive committee, no national advisory board, very little attention from the Michigan Department of Corrections. A handful of us doing the work, usually fifteen of us in the living room of Sara Falls and Matt Schmitt's little house for a couple hours every week, committed, knowing what we were doing and inventing it as we went, working very hard, high on the excitement and growth of the annual exhibition. We weren't stringent, didn't have written policies. If someone needed to do a workshop and couldn't make it to regular meetings, that was not ideal but still okay. I made some decisions without checking with others, and we made decisions collectively as well. We were full of spirit, excited, very tight, and really knew each other well. Now and then there were tensions, and we struggled over the nature of the meetings, much as we do now with over three times as many members. But it was a heady time.

The year 1999 was a watershed. The catalyst was MDOC deputy director Dan Bolden summoning me to Lansing, demanding a mission statement, demanding that we submit play scenarios, shutting down our theater workshops, refusing to communicate with us.[1] Suddenly we realized more clearly than ever how much was at stake: we were under threat and could lose it all. We needed to assert ourselves. As the audience flowed out of Sister Helen Prejean's February 22 talk at the Fourth Annual Exhibition, we asked them to sign petitions supporting PCAP.[2] We also turned to state senator Alma Wheeler Smith and vice president for government relations Cynthia Wilbanks for help.

And we began to take new steps as an organization.

Bolden's behavior was precipitated by a warden learning that a veteran PCAP team had planned a scene in which a policeman is wounded. She phoned another warden and, I assume, Bolden, announcing that we were killing policemen in our plays.[3] PCAP was growing, attracting new members, and we learned here that a workshop could blow up or be terminated because of a simple error, a moment of inattention. We needed to monitor the workshops closely. We had already determined at the end of summer 1998 that "we would sponsor no workshops where people were unwilling or unable to participate in the weekly potluck discussions and support meetings."[4] Now, in the summer of 1999, we brainstormed and argued out a "PCAP Statement of Commitment and Understanding,"[5] for all members to sign.[6] Here are some key sentences:

I understand that PCAP is an organization whose vision is based on a commitment to social justice . . .

I understand that PCAP operates according to a particular value system, methodology, and strategy. We do not go into the workshops as teachers from above.

I understand that PCAP workshops are supervised. This supervision happens in the give and take of weekly PCAP meetings and in other planned meetings. I understand that I am expected to attend PCAP meetings. . . . I understand that if I do not participate in this mutual supervision, PCAP will no longer sponsor or take responsibility for my workshop and will notify the staff at my site that this is the case.

I understand that PCAP has many activities. I understand that it has the goals of witnessing and speaking of its experience and knowledge to the public and of demystifying prisons, prisoners, prisoner families and communities and the economic forces behind American punishment and prison expansion. I understand that being part of the PCAP community means assisting with activities beyond my own workshop.

I understand that PCAP is an organization of collaborators and friends, that we support and back each other, that we engage with each other, that we attend each other's performances and presentations, that we celebrate each other and celebrate together, that we feed each other and find occasions to check in and relax and generally just plain party together.

That summer we began to take nonattendance at meetings seriously. We told Carol King at Maxey that the workshop team there was no longer under PCAP supervision. She responded that they were then no longer welcome. The team began to come to meetings and continued the workshop. In another instance, Phil Klintworth at the Southern Michigan Correctional Facility said that he was fine with the poetry team continuing without PCAP supervision and understood that if anything happened, we would not be held responsible.[7]

Our second response to the crisis in 1999 was to form a speakers bureau to bring prisoner voices to the public, to bear witness to the causes, nature, and effects of mass incarceration, and to build support for our work by informing the public about what we do.

Our third response was to realize that we needed a strong National Advisory Board to help us move forward. We sent out letters in August inviting people to join. The letter included the following paragraph:

> Not everything is easy, despite our growth and the enthusiasm with which we are greeted by the youth and adults we work with and by the majority of staff at our sites. Last January our prison theater workshops were suspended for a month and our beautiful dance workshop at the Florence Crane Women's Facility, which had two excellent performances to its credit, was eliminated by the Michigan Department of Corrections. The theater workshops were given permission to continue, but have to operate under a new system of approval that has led to long delays at some sites and some censorship of content. We are seeking ways both to accommodate to this and to make the alterations that favor efficient and uncensored work. This has been hard, and we wish to draw upon the expertise and imagination of colleagues, peers, and friends of our work to respond in appropriate ways. We also need ideas for funding the new projects that constantly present themselves, assistance in thinking about our organizational structure, experience in staying energetic and avoiding stress and burn-out, and so on.

The board, we explained, would meet once a year and receive reports from us both before and after the meeting.[8]

We had an excellent response: four former prisoners (Jimmy Santiago Baca, Lateef Islam, Anthony James, and Tracy Neal—the last two had participated in the annual exhibition); three juvenile facility staff (Gary Coakley of Boysville, Carol King of Maxey, and Marlys Shutjer, director at Adrian Training School); two wardens (Luella Burke at the Saginaw Correctional Facility and Norma Green, former director of the Okimaw Ohci Healing

Lodge in Saskatchewan); one retired researcher and policymaker in the Michigan Department of Corrections (Bill Lovett); one high school teacher (Roberta Herter of Henry Ford High School); two PCAP associates[9] (Chiara Liberatore and Matthew Schmitt); Harriet Barlow, director of the Blue Mountain Center; Ellen Barry, director of Legal Services for Prisoners with Children; Bell Chevigny, editor of *Doing Time: 25 Years of Prison Writing*; Julie Ellison, professor of English and organizer of Imagining America; DeeDee Halleck, director of Deep Dish TV; Richard Kamler, installation artist and longtime activist in community-based arts; Michael Keck, an actor who works with incarcerated youth; Phyllis Kornfeld, author of *Cell Block Visions* and a prison art teacher; Leslie Neal, who had established dance workshops in Florida prisons; Susan Perlstein, director of Elders Share the Arts; Sister Helen Prejean, author of *Dead Man Walking*; Andrew Rubinson, codirector of Fresh Youth Initiatives and a student of mine in the early 1980s; and Andrea Scott, the executive director of Amicus in Minneapolis.[10]

Of all our 1999 responses, the creation of the Advisory Board was most important. The board is tough-minded with us and inspired by what we do. Its members provide perspective and push us to make sensible decisions that take us forward and (usually) do not overtax us. Alert to my exhaustion in 2000, they asked us to apply for major grants in order to fund an administrator. In 2002 they proposed a summer of guided visioning, which led to new self-definition and to our executive committee structure. In 2003 they helped us imagine the deepening of our workshop practice. In 2005 they advised us on seeking permanent university funding. In 2006 they helped us analyze our floundering Linkage Project, our dream of a national prison arts center, and an upcoming transition caused by my yearlong sabbatical absence, a new administrator, and high member turnover.

MY ROLE IN PCAP

I facilitate English 310 and 319, responding at length every week to each student's journal and meeting with each team on a weekly basis. I travel to their sites, attend their performances, and write long, considered, congratulatory and challenging replies to their final reflective papers. I am their advocate. I engage intensely in discussion with each of them, I strategize with them to confront our classroom issues and help us move forward. I do not dominate discussions, I do not lecture. I play a very active role that enables students to take on power and leadership.

My role shifts within PCAP. It is crucial that I am just another strong member. I can't discard my age, my university status, the previous role I have played with most members, my maleness, my experience, or my voice, nor do I want to, since much of that is useful to the organization. But I can minimize them. I never facilitate the general meetings. I am not a workshop supervisor, I don't read journals, I don't guide the discussion. I am in the circle, one voice in the room. I wait, I listen, I speak when I have something authentic to say, when I wish to advocate, ask a question, take a position. In my small group I join in eagerly, but again I don't lead or facilitate. I offer my experience when it is my turn to speak, and I listen carefully when others offer advice to Lizzy Baskerville, Jessica Brierly-Snowden, and Anna Paris, my current partners in the Sisters Within Theater Troupe, and me. In executive committee meetings I am a strong voice, but again speak in turn. Like everyone else, I advocate, advise, and struggle for positions and options I believe in, then wait for the decision of the elected members. Always I try to have the voices and lives of the urban youth and incarcerated youth and adults in my own voice and in the content of what I have to say.

My status is useful to PCAP and I tell PCAP to use me. As an Arthur A. Thurnau Professor, Carnegie/CASE National Professor of the Year, and founder of PCAP, a responsible organization that has sustained itself, grown, and established a national reputation over twenty years, I am in a position to negotiate and meet with university officials for support. When I call the prisons to ask for a new workshop or to troubleshoot, I am usually listened to with respect and am usually respected within the Michigan Department of Corrections. I am diplomatic and effective. I understand the work we do, know at bottom what it is about and who it is for. I know the ideas and forces that oppose the youth and adults we work with. I can answer arguments. I know who to turn to. I know how to work with the mission and goals of institutions while simultaneously establishing the PCAP mission and goals. I know when not to compromise. A number of PCAP members have similar skills and knowledge and step forward in similar ways.

THE COORDINATORS

We found small pockets of money in 1999 to fund Karen Goodyke and then Laurie Hess to help administer the annual exhibition and take some of the growing pressure off of me. In 2000 we found enough to hire Pilar Horner as part-time exhibition administrator.[11] But it was only with our National

Endowment for the Arts Access Grant in 2001 that we gained a full-time administrator. Jesse Jannetta led us through the 2002 visioning, worked hard with me to convince PCAP of the viability of the Linkage Project, and was a bold, engaged facilitator of our meetings. He laid much of the groundwork for PCAP's growth since 2003. Forceful, sensitive, deeply engaged administrators have followed: Suzanne Gothard for three years, Rachael Hudak for two more, and since the fall of 2008, phoenix Moore has held the position.[12] Thanks to them our work has grown and become increasingly efficient.

During our 2008 National Advisory Board meeting, we realized that our administrator was more than an administrator and renamed the position Coordinator of Exhibitions and Development. We renamed our project coordinator Coordinator of Membership and New Projects, a position currently held by Sari Adelson, and renamed Mary Heinen's position Coordinator of Community Programs.

These coordinators hold challenging, essential, and powerful positions in PCAP.[13] They are expected to be leaders and to be able to articulate our mission, values, and goals. In addition to specific duties like running our vast, complicated major exhibition and establishing and maintaining linkages, they play a strong role in general meetings, prepare for and often facilitate executive committee meetings, keep track of what needs to be done, and support executive committee members in their specific roles. They respond to local and national inquiries. They are available to PCAP members who need to talk about their workshops. They prepare documents and help document our work. They are often our public face and must have background in prison work and understand the complex experiences and voices of incarcerated men and women.

CELEBRATION

Celebration is central to PCAP practice. The youth and adults have struggled against multiple odds and insults to their souls to resist their conditions. They have looked inside themselves and have looked collaboratively for what they will create in the spaces open to them. We celebrate them and celebrate with them. The exhibitions and performances are more than individual pieces of art, poems, or plays: they celebrate what is possible when people work together across boundaries to resist the damage that has been done.

And within PCAP we celebrate. We celebrate the start of the fall with a retreat in someone's yard, at a lake, or at a center distant from Ann Arbor. We share summer stories and personal aspirations for ourselves and for PCAP. We look ahead and gather force. At the end of October, many of us gather at the Haehnle Memorial Audubon Sanctuary at dusk to watch sandhill cranes fly overhead from their day's feeding to the river estuary where they spend the night. Years ago we selected the sandhill crane as our logo because birds, who fly into and out of prisons (as the crane does locally), are symbols of freedom for the incarcerated.

When we received our Rockefeller PACT Grant, we held a slogan contest—"Out of the Cellar with Rockefeller" was the winner (we wrote it out on the cake)—dressed as gaudily as we could, and spent an evening over food and talk. When the provost and the College of Literature, Science and the Arts gave us three years of funding in 2008, the cake sported "Spare us the milquetoast; BOLD is our Provost." We dressed, we toasted, we talked. We celebrated our one hundredth prison play with a dinner at Paesano's, and to celebrate our four hundredth play overall and the Professor of the Year Award, in June 2006 we came to Janie's and my home, planted a memorial red oak tree, and dramatically read off the titles of all (by then) 428 plays. We are planning a symposium during the Fifteenth Annual Exhibition of Art to celebrate PCAP's twentieth year. We have sometimes gathered for an evening to present and celebrate our own poetry, art, and theater. And in late April we bring food and meet in a home or at the Wesley Foundation to celebrate our graduating seniors. That four-hour evening fills with stories, laughter, and tears as each of us speaks to the seniors, who then talk about their near future. We present them with a small gift, a PCAP mug, a special T-shirt. In 2008 the gift was a beautiful durable rose crafted out of newspaper, modge podge, paint, and glitter by prison artist Cynthia Casey for the occasion.

CONCERNS

In the early days PCAP was very committed, sure of itself, bold, aware of what was at stake, political and full of life, sometimes flamboyant, tightly bonded, funny, growing the organization as we went. When Dan Bolden tried to shut us down in 1999, we were outraged and ready to assert ourselves. Our beginnings resembled those of other vibrant, confident organizations created from the ground up and based in significant work.

We are still a unique organization and continue to draw members with that same spirit. Yet because we are also much larger, we have had to create rules and policies and firm up a structure, a fluid, lively, democratic structure, open to participation and rapid rise into leadership, but still a structure. We remain committed, sure of ourselves, and aware of what is at stake, but we are less bonded, perhaps less funny, less larger than life. Our work is much more demanding, because we are idea people who follow up on our ideas and because our local and national reputation draws people to us and we take the time to respond to their inquiries and requests.

Jean Borger, our Portfolio and Linkage coordinator, was critical of PCAP because it wasn't "professional" and didn't behave "like real nonprofits do." Resisting hiring from within, she urged hiring professional nonprofit administrators from without, people who would be more experienced in the general field, but with no experience of PCAP. I resisted this. Conventional nonprofits are fine, but I had no desire for PCAP to become one. Gillian Eaton, hearing of Jean's critique, wrote me that PCAP's success was based on its originality, passion, and openness to fertile chaos; on its refusal to talk about "clients," "volunteers," "teachers," "community service learning," and "rehabilitation"; on the equality, risk, and vulnerability with which its members engaged in the creative spaces they opened; and on the fact that it is "owned" by the youth and adults who enter those spaces with us. While we recognize that challenges come with hiring as coordinators recent university graduates and former members, we have known enough to hire remarkable people who understand that kind of success.

At our 2007 National Advisory Board meeting, Emily Harris talked about the need for a director of PCAP. This is a related issue. She and a few others would like to see me play a more controlling, more decisive supervisory role. But for me to become a director runs contrary to the role I have described above and would represent a troubling shift in PCAP. I prefer to work collaboratively with our administrators and with the executive committee as one strong voice among many. The shift may happen—I understand the perception and need—but as long as I am in the organization, I will both resist and negotiate it, wanting it to happen, if it must, in a manner that we maintain our spirit and versatility. Emily agrees with this.

PCAP has two tendencies. One toward stiffening, bureaucracy, stagnation, toward a loss of fluidity and originality, toward normal nonprofit conventions and practices, and toward a relative alienation and loss of trust that makes it harder for us to *speak* with each other, to be political, and to be out on the edge of what work in this field in an era of massive incarceration demands.

The other tendency is toward boldness, passion, and organizational and individual flamboyance that has us engaged with each other, laughing and full of life, and burdened with the voices of the incarcerated, in struggle against all that is hostile to them and their communities.

In the classes and workshops, we need everyone to figure out how to step up and participate, to take on roles, risk poetry and art, find personal levels of vulnerability, deepen what each person needs to say, and discover and give voice to the crucial issues affecting the person, the group, the families, neighborhoods, and futures. Within every aspect of PCAP we must treat each other with the same expectations, the same vitality and spirit. I am optimistic. PCAP members want this and struggle for it, brainstorming again and again how to make their time together more vital. During and after difficult times we recuperate and regenerate. Our high membership turnover[14]—a potential disaster for other organizations—is, given the nature of those who come to us in the classes and from outside, a constant source of new energy and leadership.

CHAPTER NINE

Failure

Ashley Lucas came to the 2008 Annual Exhibition of Art by Michigan Prisoners to perform *Doin' Time: Through the Visiting Glass,* her one-person piece about the family members of prisoners. On April 1 she visited English 319. We began with a talk circle, the students introducing themselves, saying what site they worked at, and sharing something on their mind about the work. They were just weeks from their performances, and I was struck by their doubts. They wanted to know how they were perceived. What meaning did they have in the lives of the prisoners, the incarcerated youth, the high school students? They had so little time with them. Sometimes those they worked with seemed not to care, and this hurt. Were they, really, having any impact on the boys, girls, men and women struggling with disturbing, often violent pasts and facing futures that held so little for them? Corey Blant, Tim Fillion, and the boys incarcerated at the Lincoln Center had co-created a lively, comfortable space, and when the boys spoke of their futures, they dreamed big. But Corey and Tim knew what the boys were up against and were disturbed at how the boys laughed off what threatened them. They both knew that the comfortable space and dreams, as Corey put it, "will all be shot down."

That week, troubled by all he had heard and by his own words and thoughts, Corey wrote in his journal that he had failed his boys.

We met on Tuesdays for two hours. The following Tuesday I read back from my notes what they had told Ashley and mentioned what Corey had written. Everyone turned to him. He explained. The boys had brainstormed a play that tied the recent closing of Detroit schools to the street life of school dropouts, but instead of guiding them into a meaningful exploration of this subject, he and Tim had gone along with their focus on being comic. Also, given the damage that had been done to the boys, the damage they had done to others, and all that waited them in the future, he had failed to give them anything that might be useful. He had let them down.

The others rallied to soothe him. Nan Howard in particular, who with Elise Rose was suffering through an extremely difficult workshop at another boys' facility,[1] reminded him that the boys live in tense proximity to each other twenty-four hours a day and that they have a pressured, disciplined week of classes and counseling connected to every aspect of their lives, including their crimes. That Corey and Tim had given them the opportunity to relax, run around the room, laugh, and have a great time was a gift, and sufficient.

Nan was passionate about this, and right, and wonderfully supportive of Corey, and of herself and Elise. After a while I told her so, but added: "And yet Corey still failed." Corey nodded, Hannah agreed, but most of the class was troubled, even outraged with our position. The final journals were full of contention, even anger, and several students returned to the subject during our closing talk circle the following week.

Becky McMellen worked at Cooley High School, Corey at the Lincoln Center, Christopher Rapisarda with men at the Cotton Correctional Facility, and Hannah with women at the Huron Valley Complex. They confronted themselves in their final papers.

At Cooley, Becky and Ashley Braun had two classes of close to forty students each, a mix of interested and disinterested students, highly inconsistent attendance, sessions disrupted by long announcements over the PA and interrupted by school holidays (including our own spring break) and standardized testing. Although discouraged, she was very happy at how the youth stepped up for the final performances. She savored the respect that developed between her and the youth and was proud of one particular accomplishment:

> I was worried about projecting too many of my own perceptions onto the play, so I tended not to give too many suggestions of my own. The students in second hour even began to catch on. After [my] deflecting all of the questions they asked me right back at them, one student said, "Can't you guys see? She wants us to figure it out for ourselves." I was really proud of that moment.

Ultimately, that is what I hope to have accomplished this semester in my workshops. Every Thursday morning, for approximately one hour, these students were responsible for their own decisions. The choices were not made for them by standardized tests or zero tolerance policies. I wanted each decision, from the story line to the title, to originate from their own ideas. In our class, during discussions, I was taught this same lesson. I was able to reach my own conclusions and make my own decisions, and was then encouraged to act on the issues I felt strongly about. In a smaller scale, through these theater workshops, I wanted to give this same opportunity to these high school students.

And yet she had also "failed." She hadn't fully crossed the boundary between herself and the students, had withheld something crucial.

I never attempted to really fix the simple little holes in the plot. I doubted the students' ability to work through these minor problems. This is a major failing on my part. I should never for a second have doubted their ability to work out any problem I presented to them. . . . I think some of my failures in my workshops came because I was afraid to attempt a more meaningful connection. I think in many cases, I stopped just short. . . . I did not always trust the students to be able to answer any questions I might have about their play. At times, I did not know how to answer the hard questions they had for me. In my workshop next semester, I hope I will be able to take a step further to make that extra connection with the people in my workshop. I want to be more invested in their well-being. I want to be more active in their lives.[2]

Christopher, Elizabeth Sinclaire, and Sarah Bennett worked with five men. In their play *Different Directions,* each of eight characters on a bus had a personal story. Dialogue on the bus would reference the story, then characters would step off the bus to act out a crucial scene. The university trio and prisoners had a spirited working relation and developed great mutual respect as they worked their way through various disputes towards the final product. And remarkably this fledgling group pulled off a performance before the largest crowd in our history: 270 prisoners and ten outsiders perched on bleachers in the prison gym, a daunting acoustical challenge, to say the least.

When I outed Corey in class, Christopher was "dumfounded."

First and foremost, Corey is a close friend and I assumed he would have come to me if he felt he and Tim were having any issues. But more importantly, I couldn't imagine how after doing the workshops that we as a class were doing, how could we fail? We were doing good, providing aid and a voice to a world that is all too often underrepresented and goes unappreciated. Wasn't that enough?

Over the next few weeks I searched for a possible answer. I realized that no, it wasn't. We *were* providing the men and women, boys and girls, an opportunity to be creative. We *were* giving these people a chance to be heard. But within our workshops, or at least mine, we didn't treat them as human or as equals, but we instead were willing to *settle*. I let my efforts to search for something deeper quickly evaporate because I didn't think it was worth feuding over. Or maybe my reasoning was that the prisoners just couldn't think or see things in a more complex way. Regardless of my intentions, *I* didn't push the men, *I* didn't challenge them, and *I* didn't trust them. For that, I failed them.

The five men had contributed very personal moments to the play: a funeral; an upcoming parole hearing after twenty-six years in prison; a visiting room relation with a wife; a confrontation with a daughter getting into trouble; and a longtimer's recent loss of his guitar because of a change in property regulations. Christopher, Elizabeth, and Sarah had not reciprocated, but played roles in the men's stories. Christopher, pretending to be trying out for *American Idol,* sang. Elizabeth performed slam poetry. Christopher:

I wonder why I never share those stories. Sure they are dear to my heart, tales that I opt more often to hide than share. But they are a part of me and vitally important in defining me. Maybe, just maybe, had I told a story from my past, my scene in the play wouldn't seem so awkward. Instead of an unnecessary audition for American Idol, I could actually have bonded with my fellow cast members and shared a small piece of what makes me me. Looking back, I suppose I was intimidated by the possibility that my story would sound far less significant than those of the prisoners. . . . I cannot speak for Sarah or Elizabeth, but I know that at least one of my regrets was not opening myself fully to this group. I shared details about me, but I didn't play fair: I expected them to supply the meat of the story and play without reciprocating and allowing the men to get to know the real me.

Like Becky, he resolved that his next workshop would be different.

If I can spend this first semester and learn how *not* to treat the men and women in prisons, or high schools or juvenile facilities, maybe the next time I will understand how to treat and respect them. Sure by the end of my workshop, I had the utmost respect for each and every member I had worked with over this semester. But the next time I will be aware of the fact that these, in spite of their decisions or circumstances, are all *people* and must be regarded as such.

For Becky it wasn't only that next time she would trust, respect, and connect. For her it went deeper, into her life choices.

I am angry that the school system is so unequal. I am angry that 1 in 100 U.S. adults are imprisoned. I am angry that the system is playing against minorities, and I am angry that people do not see that this kind of racism still exists. I am angry that according to statistics, only 1 in 4 of the students in my workshop is going to graduate.[3] I am angry that the narrator in my first play got suspended, and I am angry that one day, one of the students might end up in jail. I am furious that we invest more money in imprisoning human beings than we do in trying to educate them. With so many enemies, there is no way that I am going to be able to stop fighting against this kind of injustice. I feel like I can do nothing else but dedicate my life to trying to make some kind of a dent into the rampant dehumanization of so many people.

Christopher, working his way to the same place, faulted the class:

I feel we were too often eager to settle for this sentimental, easy overlook of the course and our work. Each partnership, whether they were going to a high school, juvenile facility, or a prison encountered some kind of issue. Some had to deal with an ever-changing number of members. Others had to deal with a lack of enthusiasm. For most groups, though, and all of us at Cotton, we dealt with a conglomeration of both and many others, depending on the week.

Then every time we would have a conversation in class about the sites, each group would share their varying array of difficulties. And although we have some differences, we try to find ways to console one another in class. But that's just it: not all of it is positive, not everything we are doing is good; the job is far from over. It is too easy to be complacent and take for granted what we've done. Far too often members of the class—myself more than most—will find the smallest positives in the gravest of circumstances. Instead, I should recognize the hardships and attack *those;* find the root of the issues and begin problem solving and evaluate what needs to be changed within the system.

Hannah too felt she had settled for less. "It's not enough to have a creative place," she wrote.

It's not enough to add humanity. That's all nice and really important too, but I think our mission was to do more than that and I was unable to [do that more]. . . . It takes little to make a theater workshop in prison, but it takes a lot to make it push the women and challenge them and myself to make it realistic and from their own minds and lives.

The play, about a high school reunion, "was decidedly about leaving the past behind and moving on with our lives for the better—an incredibly noble message for all the workshop participants[4] and everyone in general . . . [but] we absolutely lost it." Because many women lost interest and dropped out, Hannah felt she and Sarah Miller had failed to make the space significant. Like Becky and Christopher, she felt they had disrespected the women by not opening to them. She had created a wonderfully acted comic nerd, which "brought light and fun to a workshop that had become heavy and tense, [but] it added nothing to the content of our play," which degenerated into a relatively shallow and uninteresting comedy. Like Becky and Christopher, she hurt and learned: "In some ways . . . I'm glad I failed because it's a blatant slap in the face to make me keep working and acknowledge my own flaws."

The Lincoln Center group had named themselves CoNtRoLLeD CHaOS, and their play, *CoNtRoLLeD CHaOS,* was one of the liveliest, most varied, most energetic performances in 319. The boys danced, rapped, sang, and presented some very interesting characters and a plot with meaning and some depth. They broke all of Corey's stereotypes, and between that, the reading, and the class discussion, he wrote, "the amount of change that I have experienced this semester has been incredible." Most important was what he had learned about challenging himself.

It goes beyond what I had thought in the past, it goes beyond the idea of "seizing the opportunity" or stepping outside your comfort zone. The challenge is not about having fun, or laughing, things that our class took comfort in achieving. While we did take two of their hours a week and remove the routine and offer them the ability to create, that was not the challenge. The challenge is not about me, it is about something bigger than that. It is about responsibility, it is about failure, but more importantly it is about human lives. When I walked into that workshop I met 10 boys. I was in awe of their personalities and their energy, I understood that we weren't so different, I understood that society wanted them locked up and me to leave every Wednesday night and go back to Ann Arbor and forget about them. Unfortunately I succumbed to society, I didn't realize that they [the boys] wanted me to fight with them and so I laughed with them on Wednesday, thought about how I was going to challenge them the rest of the week and how we were going to fight next Wednesday, then went back on Wednesday and instead of fighting together we laughed. And then I left the Lincoln center for the last time on Wednesday and I really realized that I had missed the boat. These boys could die, they could end up back on the inside, it is now completely out of my hands. And while I can take comfort in the fact that we laughed together once, I cannot take comfort in the fact that I gave them all I had to give because I didn't.

He saw that "the most important thing that you can take from failure is the experience" and was eager for his workshop in the fall. And he had received a gift.

After our performance, Jeff[5] kept coming up to me, at least two or three times and putting his arm around me. Each time he would look at me and say, I can't believe you're eighteen. One time though he looked at me and said, "even though you're eighteen, I really look up to you. But you better keep straight man and keep doin' what you're doin', if I find out anything happens to you . . ." and we both sort of laughed and the moment was over. While I am not sure of what Jeff meant by that, I know one thing, he is right. It is not ok to stop, this is not over, it probably won't even be over in my lifetime. But what I am doing can make a difference and is appreciated and while I might not have done a perfect job, I did something and Pod E needed that something. Jeff appreciated this and I know the guys appreciated having Tim and me there. But more than anything it is important that

I continue, if for no other reason, I have to do it because I told Jeff I would and I intend to keep my word.

These four students and a majority of their 319 peers are demanding of themselves that they become authentic and effective activists. I admire them. They are far beyond myself at their age. Retirement, which I must face soon, is for me as for most people complicated and challenging, enticing and scary. One reason for my reluctance to enter it is that I will no longer be in a classroom with people like them. As I seek in whatever limited way to keep my hand in, I will continue to hear their voices acknowledging failure and moving on, and I will draw on their courage as I struggle against the infirmities that await me.

When Elise and one or two other students early in the term *insisted* that "one can never do enough," many of their classmates pulled back, perhaps frightened at what they had gotten into, but more likely and rightly offended at being given an absolute and denied the chance to shape their lives in any direction they chose. It reminded me of the English 310 discussion in which, working through the starfish metaphor, the students found a way to be generous with themselves and others and to value each other as allies,[6] and I was hopeful that we would recover and get to a similar point.

And Elise's insistence begged the question: what is enough? Given the enormity of what has been done in my name in my time, given the enormity of the privilege I was born into and the advantage it gave me over women and people of color, given the enormity of the dying infrastructures in megalopolises all over the world,[7] given the enormity of the wars, concentration camps, and massacres ahead as pure water disappears, saltwater rises along the coasts, and fires spread, given what others have been capable of during my time, given who I might have become, I am hauntingly aware that I have failed in courage, character, imagination, and intelligence. And of course I have failed in small ways, always, as well. And my students will always fail. And not. So sometimes I tell them a story that has always sustained me.

Marcel Ophul's documentary *The Sorrow and the Pity*[8] investigates the German occupation of a southern French town. He interviews many participants, including the occupiers; a local man inspired by Riefenstahl's *Triumph of the Will* to join the Waffen SS; Pierre Mendes-France, later French president, who escaped from a local prison where the Germans held him; farmers who became members of the Resistance and served time in concentration camps; and a pharmacist who was too frightened to join the Resistance. I haven't seen the film for years, but I can still picture him in his home talking to a circle of young people. He had continued his life and his profession during the occupation. But he somehow managed to keep two Jewish girls working in his pharmacy safe from deportation. And every now and then, he would wrap something in a pharmaceutical package, place it in his bicycle basket, and deliver it to a Resistance location outside town.

⧗

In August 2002, I wrote "Back Off," agonizing over my own place in the world and in Nate Jones's world, where Nate, despite his University of Michigan bachelors and masters in social work degrees, was in agony.

"Back off." I call from a roadside phone
on 72 and 33 heading north out of Mio.
We've been on the river an evening hour
and afterwards suffered a bad burrito
at the local pizza shop.
The tones are loud as I punch in the codes
making me hope a clear voice
at the other end will out-enunciate
the truck rush and cycle rattle fifteen yards away.
Barbara answers and I ask if she has news of Nate,
who disappeared again from where she watched him
through the night after he'd gone crazy
in the housing complex yard
while neighbors, horrified, called paramedics
and laughed. And Barbara replies, "back off,"
I mean
she says eagerly "I'll put him on,"
loving that her man
is back,
though she should have said,
"I've called the hospital, they're on the way."
I wait.
Nate comes on the line and says
"Back off,"

I mean
he barely enunciates in a thin voice
so full of the sadness of a lost life,
the sadness Tracy heard in the corridor
of city indigent
waiting to contest eviction,
"hello" and "I'm all right"
and, when I ask how he got home
hoping the police had found him,
"I walked,"
though he should have said
"drugs pulled me into the night
again"
and "I'm lost" and
"I'm hurting a good woman" and
"I've got to turn myself in."
And I,
angry at them both,
say "Back off,"
I mean
I say "Okay,
I'm just checking in"
and "goodbye,"
when I should have said
I don't know what,
told him to tell the truth or told him my anger
or gotten Barbara back on the line and shouted
or I don't know what.

By telling each other to back off,
we protected our territory,
saved our lives as they are.
Barbara held on to the co-dependence
on which she painfully thrives,
Nate held on to the downward spin,
the lie, the evasion,
that enable him to keep his habit.

And I

supported them in this, I held on
to the distance and relative peace
so important to continuing my work,
I avoided going to dark places and to conflict
I can't sustain.

We said back off and backed off
and continued forward, backward,
to more pain and sleepless nights.

Another poem emerged as I was writing "Back Off." And so I titled it "A Companion Poem."

The female tarantula
seizes four crickets at a time,
webs them up with silk,
sucks their insides out,
then is still again.

The female tarantula hawk,
hunts down and stings the fabled spider,
lays then buries its eggs
in the paralyzed body,
and leaves the larvae
to eat the tarantula alive.

SECONDARY TRAUMA

In November 2000 two close friends, Ellen Franklin and Raya Chyorny, revealed to me that I was suffering from secondary trauma. I had told them that ten years of working in prisons had put a new sadness in me, although I was still a happy person. I told them about my father's death three years before, about how Suzie DeWitt cried for twelve days after the parole board flopped her for two more years, about the arbitrary treatment Romando Valeroso suffered in prison, about my hurt that such remarkable human beings as he, Mary Heinen, and Sharleen Wabindato might never be allowed to come home.[9] Raya, who lived in Denver, suggested I go into counseling and offered to help me, through her connections, find someone back in Ann Arbor.

On the advice of the woman with whom I then did short-term therapy in 2001 and into 2002, I read Judith Herman's *Trauma*[10] and learned that trauma hits deepest when it disrupts one's worldview. If one views the world as a beneficial place, then the traumatic experience of war or torture or rape or incarceration shakes everything apart. In my case, perhaps because of my frightening experience of childhood bullying, I had an inordinate need for personal autonomy. I had built it early by becoming like my father, and in his last years we had built a very whole friendship. Having had the courage, finally, to end an inadequate marriage in 1990, with Janie I was in a fulfilling, loving, respectful, supportive relationship that we both intended to last until the end. And I had secured autonomy in my professional life, achieving a reputation, and a sureness, that gave me considerable control over what work I chose to do.

But I had stepped out of that cocoon to work in prisons, any one of which could eliminate me at any moment for a "breach of security." And I had chosen to work under the aegis of the Michigan Department of Corrections, which could also shut us down, as Deputy Director Dan Bolden in fact did for a month in early 1999, succeeding, even after he was forced to reverse himself, in crushing our dance workshop at a women's prison.[11] I had made myself vulnerable. More importantly, I had entered into work with and established friendships with talented vital people who were deprived of control over their movements, who were subjected to arbitrary treatment by fellow prisoners, corrections officers, and the parole board, and who were sometimes in physical danger with nowhere to flee. My empathy with them and my helplessness to do for them what I had done for myself got inside me, disrupted my own autonomy, and saddened me. In that August 2002 phone call, Nate, who called me his "best friend" and "only friend," was bringing up his and my helplessness and the fact I was responsible for some part of that helplessness. Was he not my brother? The companion poem illustrates how overwhelming and fatal this felt.

COMING HOME

In August 2002, we were in the final month of rehearsals for *When Can We Talk?* As I recounted in chapter 7, not only had Nate dropped out, but each of the formerly incarcerated actors was struggling.[12] Earlier that year we had begun the Linkage Project, committing for the first time to people who had worked with us inside and had come home. In this commitment we have experienced much success, and much sorrow. Inside "Back Off" are many lives and much disappointment.

When Steve[13] first submitted sketches of cheap nudes, we turned him down. He set to work and the next year presented us with wiry, intriguing, original drawings. Returned home, he entered the Linkage Project, joined our Advisory Board, and spoke eloquently about the importance of our prison work. The Michigan Department of Corrections website now lists him as "absconded." Why?

Troy, his art more and more intriguing each year, became clerk for the special activities director and an instructor of other artists. When he came home to Flint and dined with us, he was self-confident, well-spoken. He found work and had family support. He wished to develop his jewelry skills, so we linked him with a Detroit jewelry-maker and ordered him supplies. He didn't stay in touch. He returned to prison. I don't know the story, though we have talked by phone since he has again come home.

Morris, one of the very best of the thousand and more exhibition artists, would win a first-place award or honorable mention, then a week later be denied parole again. When he came home, his family couldn't bring him from Grand Rapids for the opening reception. We bought him a bus ticket and hotel room, then waited in vain at the bus stop. A day later he left a slurred message, saying he was now at the bus station. His cousin, at another prison, told me he was back on drugs. His wife accused him of domestic abuse. Why? Where do we come in? Do we come in?

In a famous Michigan case, an eleven-year-old boy convicted of murder as an adult was saved by his judge from adult prison. Several PCAP members worked with him in poetry and theater and a writing portfolio. Both the juvenile facility and his step-down house committed themselves to him. He came home thanking his judge for "taking that chance and believing in me," worked hard on his music and got a contract, and then, a year and four months after his release, was caught selling 250 Ecstasy pills in a parking lot. He received a four- to twenty-year sentence. Rochelle Riley, columnist for the *Detroit Free Press,* asked where his backers were, why they had let him down.[14]

So much is asked of so many of those who come home, and so much that is external and so much that their lives has burned into them stand in their way. And so many fail. And so many of us are so helpless. For all our good words, for all our goodwill, for all we actually do, we fail with them. It is systemic. It is also the human condition.

We come into the workshops together looking for what is missing in our lives. We pick up a pencil and look inside ourselves and make a drawing for the exhibition. Or we come to the prison and select art, and talk, and wear ourselves out fighting to keep the exhibition alive. We all act, write, sing, draw, love, fight, risk together, looking for strength, connection, a receptive ear, a kind of forgiveness. We come home. We welcome those who come home. We live in separate communities. We have our own lives. We are brothers and sisters. We are not brothers and sisters. We are torn apart. We choose, and don't choose, how we will live. Some are guided by faith, some by other resources, most of us also by our origins. We organize, we teach, we grow, we come out into the world, we send out into the world, we keep going. I am in awe of everyone's struggle, in awe of the voices they find, in awe of how they, how we, come back from failures.

⧗

If one of my students or a high school student or an incarcerated person or someone just come home asked me, or if I asked myself, what we should be doing on this earth, I wouldn't have a ready answer. Normally I would listen to them or myself as we talked further, trying to hear what they are telling themselves, trying to hear what challenges them and stands in the way, then say what words I can find to help them, or myself, on the way. But perhaps the answer is more clear now than it once was. I dreamed the other night, the night of June 26, 2008—stimulated by news of hundreds of lightning strikes and uncontrollable fires in California—that our entire country was swept with fires. I wrote another poem in August 2002.[15]

ENTERING PRISON

As I write this, rain falls through the tree
beyond my window while obscure birds
take suet from the log feeder hidden by leaves.
Water, a wet season in Michigan, the river flows.

And I have entered prisons so many times
that the first time blurs.
                    I recall only
the muster room and its foolish murals

of Snow White and the Seven Dwarves,
Disney style, for the children who came
by country road to Coldwater
to play with temporary mothers.

And today as I enter this prison to read this poem,
I know that every eight seconds a child somewhere dies
from drinking contaminated water.

In the muster room four of us began theater
with Mary and Joyce, we improvised and talked,
we felt our way together toward creation
of the Sisters Within.

I have entered prisons once a week
for thirteen years now,
                              and today
as I enter this prison to read this poem
I know that thirty-one countries
and more than one billion people
completely lack access to clean water.
I know that the earth's fresh water is finite,
less than half a percent of all the water in the world,
I know that fresh water, common property
of the peoples of the earth,
is increasingly controlled by private firms,
I know that when the people of Kwazulu-Natal
could not pay their bills
the company cut them off
from sanitation and water
and one hundred thousand
sickened with cholera,
I know that in South Africa women walk,
collectively, the equivalent of a road to the moon
and back sixteen times a day to fetch water
for their families,
                              I know that
Coca-Cola, Pepsi, Nestle, and others

mine and bottle our precious water
and sell it for more than the price of oil,
I know that they sold ninety billion liters last year
for a gain of twenty-two billion dollars,
I know that Perrier mines the water of Michigan,
I know that the Rio Grande no longer reaches the Gulf of Mexico,
I know that this is the crisis of our new century,
perhaps the final crisis of humankind.

And so I enter the prison today with questions for us all:
Should Sarah and I come to prison,
should any of us come to prison,
should we write poetry and make art
during this crisis that kills a child
every eight seconds across the globe,
or should we instead join
what may be the last
what may be the most important
struggle,
       join,
            so that,
                    perhaps,
if we fight together and well,
our brothers and sisters,
our descendants,
will have access to the life that is their due?

Or, should Sarah and I enter prison each week,
should we all come into this room, each week,
because here too we fight for water?

CHAPTER TEN

The PCAP Associates:
Places Like Rwanda

When in my doddering years my mind roves and dreams without control, the Ginsberg Center living room will be a frequent site of odd, intense events. Haunting figures will spin through the heavy wooden sliding doors that lead to the reception area and hallway, pirouette around the room, wave their claws, sink into the comfortable chairs and couch, or sit rigid and glare or grin on the curving bench occupied by latecomers or those who wish, like me, to stay especially alert. I'll be eager to learn what foods they'll put out on the center glass table. Since the formation of the PCAP executive committee in the fall of 2000, we have dined in this space nearly every other Wednesday night, easy or uneasy together, sometimes joyful, bonded, robust, and funny, sometimes struggling, fighting, and always moving PCAP forward, or not.

Tonight is our transition night. Newly elected members Emily Briggs, Cyan James, and Theresa Lindsay are here, Theresa accompanied by her beautiful third-grade daughter. Outgoing member Amit Weitzer is with us and continuing members Lauren Marshall and Alex Miller. Mary Heinen is unable to attend, but ex-officio members Rachael Hudak and I are present. The new members choose roles, learn some of the ropes.

And the voting members decide which departing PCAP members we should invite to become PCAP associates.[1] If those leaving us have engaged substantially in PCAP, and most of them have, it is automatic. Some of the new executive members don't know those who have left. We talk about them. They vote or abstain. Tonight there are no controversial cases. We go down the list: Mihal Ansik, Andrew Bronstein, Katie Craig, Anita Feingold-Shaw, Ollie Ganz, Emi Kaneko, Abbey Marshak, Andy Ramos, Kate Schuster, Julia Taylor, Amit. Easy, everyone nods, raises their hands. Others who have left and who did not engage, who missed meetings, are easy no's.

Associates—there are 165 of them now—stay in touch with us over e-mail and the phone. They stay in touch with each other and gather informally, sometimes formally, mainly in the major cities where they cluster. Many contribute financially to the exhibition and, in 2009, to sustaining Sari Adelson's Membership and Special Projects Coordinator position through the summer. We let them know of job opportunities and write them references or answer questions about them from employers over the phone. They advise us. Five of them serve on the National Advisory Board. We have invited them to speak as keynote speakers at the annual exhibition. We have invited them to speak on panels.[2] And they receive the biannual *PCAP Associates Newsletter,* which reports on PCAP, contains their current bios (what they are doing, thinking, observing, and feeling) and provides them with updated contact data. The *Newsletter* runs as many as sixty pages.

The first number appeared in the fall of 2002. Neela Ghoshal reported:

After graduating from U of M in 1999, I spent three wonderful, challenging, frustrating, inspiring years as a bilingual sixth grade teacher in Washington Heights, New York. However, I spent last summer in Guatemala, and one morning, squeezed into the back of a pick-up truck with fourteen other people and several sacks of beans, surrounded by mountains, the wind in my face, I made a pact with myself to return to Guatemala. I quit my teaching job in June and will be returning to Guatemala on November 9, to spend nine months as a human rights observer. I will be living in two indigenous villages in northern Guatemala which suffered massacres at the hands of the military in 1982, working with survivors of the massacres who are now serving as witnesses in a genocide case against two former Guatemalan dictators. One of my job responsibilities is to send out monthly updates about my work to friends and family in the U.S., in the hopes that building an extended network of *norteamericanos* who are informed about Guatemala will help to end impunity, so you all will be hearing more from me!

I added in the same number a subsequent message from her, with details of the massacre that had happened in one of the villages, a history of the genocide in Guatemala, and stories of her first days in the village.[3]

The following November, employed as an investigator for the criminal defense attorneys of the Bronx Defenders, she spoke with witnesses and gathered information. In November 2004 she worked with former street children in Children's Sunrise Village in Northern Uganda and accompanied peacekeeper Victoria Nalongo to a forum in Gulu between Acholi and Lango cultural leaders. She and her partner created an improv play with the residents of an urban slum in Kampala housing people who had been displaced from the war in the north. She then interned in Tanzania for the United Nations International Criminal Tribunal for Rwanda. On May 24, 2005, she wrote from Arusha, Tanzania,

> Some of you have wondered why I go to places like Rwanda, Northern Uganda, Guatemala, why I have chosen to spend nine hours a day for two months reading through testimonies from the survivors of genocide. It is because I believe we need to break through the net that artificially divides "us" from "others," when ultimately all of our lives, our fates, are inextricably intertwined. I believe that by listening to the stories of those who have lived through the darkest moments, and then retelling those stories, perhaps I can make a difference. We can't rewrite Rwanda's past—though of course there are many steps the U.S. and European countries could and should have taken at the time to avert genocide—but we can refuse to turn a blind eye to Rwanda's fragile future.

She returned to the States that summer to enter the M.A. Program in International Relations at Yale, focusing on civil conflict and peace building, mostly in East and Central Africa. That same year she organized a spring break student delegation to Guatemala, worked on getting Yale to divest from Sudan oil money, and tutored "a fabulous eleven-year-old." In the summer of 2006 she interned with the African Centre for the Constructive Resolution of Disputes in Burundi. During her final year at Yale, she initiated a video campaign enabling people across the country to speak up about the atrocities in Darfur. She now works with Human Rights Watch in Burundi and continues sending us her wonderfully personal, historical, political, observational, detailed dispatches, which I am sure one day will appear as a book.[4]

In the same first number, Joe Funt wrote from Mali, where as a member of the Peace Corps he was assisting a crafts collective develop and market their work, speaking both French and Bambara, and finding that "helping somebody is turning out to be much more complicated than I originally thought." In the summer of 2003, wrapping up his work, he wrote,

Only five more months to go. I'm tired and frustrated with my work, and the conditions in Mali are relentless. A lot of my goals as far as information exchange have been achieved and I feel good about that. In my mud cloth association, we are starting to see some tangible results from a few marketing projects. We have made some beautiful new products and found some buyers in the U.S. and also in the capital city here. I will be sure to bring some home. My main facilitation goals of creating a proactive and independent association have failed miserably. The business skills learned were not enough to create such a culture. From the beginning, I have received pressure from my artisans union in Mali and Peace Corps in Bamako to contribute financially to these associations. Instead of adopting my ideas of independence, my union has merely sought funding from different sources. Things have become a little strained between myself and these other involved parties. It's definitely time to step back and let the group work without Peace Corps for a while. I'm excited about the possibilities for the next phase in my life.

Back in the States he worked on a short-term project with the Smithsonian Folklife Festival Department, interviewed for a position with the Service Employees International Union, and ended up with Chemonics International, a contractor for USAID. Working on a Ghana trade project and a microfinance project in south Sudan, he was disturbed by social equity issues and by the small return on the vast amount of money spent by Chemonics. He resigned in 2005 to take an organizing job in Bushwick with the HomeBase Project, originally dedicated to preventing homelessness by intervening for families before they are actually in the street, then in addition trying to place the homeless in housing. Joe has risen to the directorship of the agency. He reports that HomeBase has been "able to obtain priority housing choice vouchers through a collaboration with an NYC agency for our clients" with the agency paying 70 percent of the rent, and that HomeBase has been granted "a job training and education program that facilitates employment and growth in a few career fields."

We are finishing a new office renovation that will have a classroom, computer training facility, client workstations, and lots of high tech stuff. We don't have a name yet, but it is more of a center. . . . The services we are currently offering are eviction prevention, housing relocation, general case management/social services, benefits advocacy, job training workshops, career counseling, job placement, GED classes, computer training, journaling workshops, tenants' rights workshops, and budgeting and savings classes.[5]

Liz Budnitz also reported in in the first number. She took English 310 in the fall of 1997, facilitated a small group in English 411 in the winter of 1999, and graduated that spring. For the next three years she worked for the Barnard Center for Research on Women, "doing programming and research on women's and gender issues." After meeting at the Critical Resistance East Conference (March 9–11, 2001) with Martha Raimon, a lawyer working on incarcerated mothers and children at the Women's Prison Association ("I walked right up to her and said 'I love what you do, how do I do that?'"), she decided to enter law school. While at Brooklyn Law School the next three years, she interned at the ACLU national office in their Women's Rights Project, working on the impact of litigation on national women's rights cases and attending meetings of the Coalition on Women Prisoners;[6] she took a clinic doing "post-conviction representation of death row inmates and prisoners in New York who have filed federal habeas corpus petitions, and filing petitions for writ of certiorari for prisoners in the Supreme Court; she worked with the Neighborhood Defender Services of Harlem; and she interned at the Brennan Center for Justice, "researching how foster care and adoption laws affect incarcerated parents."[7]

After graduation in 2006, she first clerked for a federal judge in New York, then took an internship in the Hague at the International Criminal Court, researching and writing on international criminal law for a judge. She returned in mid-2008 to the Brennan Center for Justice to work on their campaign advocating for the voting rights of prisoners and the formerly incarcerated. She finished her work with the Brennan Center in July 2009 and is facing the fact that in the current economy no legal nonprofit work is available.[8]

APOLOGIA

In what precedes and in what follows, I regret having to select some associates and not others and regret that I can't tell every single story in depth. Almost every associate has been my student and colleague, and most remain strong and often very close friends. When Janie and I married on a bluff above Lake Michigan on September 8, 2007, we asked Chiara Liberatore to read Mary Oliver's "When Death Comes." When a major traffic jam on the way from Chicago almost stalled her, ten associates present could have easily stepped into her place. Associates have common roots in the courses and in PCAP, in completing artistic tasks with people we were told are not our brothers and sisters, in what hurts us and what we come to know of the world, in our efforts to bear witness, and in our bonds with each other. When I see Hannah or Corey or Nan or Christopher or Sierra or Sarah in my present 319 walking across the campus, and when they see each other, a recognition and a greeting pass unlike what happens in other academic courses. When I think of associates Mikael or Mike or Laurie or Rachael or Eric or Alyssa, it is the same. When I think of Nate and grieve for him, when I think of Val and Shar and George in prison all these years and am haunted by my inability to bring them home and by the unforgiving brutal power that won't let them come home, it is the same. And it is the same for Rachael when she thinks of Kinnari, for Ollie when she thinks of DeWayne, it is the same for all of us when we think of those we have worked with and struggled with and loved. And so it is hard here not to celebrate everyone.

CAREERS

Some associates have only recently graduated and are feeling their way. Others are in graduate school. Others are now in their late twenties and into their thirties. Some have shifted their focus and moved into several fields. In the summer of 2009 we know what 153 of the 165 associates are up to.

> 31 are teaching in schools. 14 of those have been in or are in Teach
>   for America or another teaching fellows program
> 20 either have social work degrees or degrees on the way
> 14 are lawyers, in law school, or working with law firms
> 5 are entering law school in the fall of 2009
> 2 more are working as court advocates
> 12 are community organizers
> 2 are union organizers
> 5 are community outreach professionals in their agencies
> 4 either have medical degrees or are in medical school
> 4 are journalists: 1 is working in the urban field, another in labor
>   organizing
> 3 are professionals working with incarcerated youth and adults

2 are working in the environmental field

2 are leadership training professionals

2 are working with Human Rights Watch

2 are literacy work professionals

2 are in graduate school in international work

2 are in public health graduate school

1 is working with the New York Civilian Complaint Board

1 is working with the Fortune Society

1 is a case manger/counselor working with street youth in New York City

1 works at Mentoring USA as the Foster Care and English Language Learners' Program coordinator

1 is a research associate at the Urban Institute, focusing on prison issues

1 is working with an international aid agency

1 works with the Foundation for Sustainable Development in Kenya

1 is working in urban planning in Chicago

1 works at *Ms.* magazine

1 is in AmeriCorps, with Public Allies

1 is starting a Fulbright in India

1 is entering the Peace Corps

1 works at Planned Parenthood

1 is a nurse

1 works with ICF International, a Washington DC consulting firm, working with the Department of Education and Department of Human Services

1 is a program officer at the Charles Stewart Mott Foundation in Flint, Michigan

Others are research assistants at the Institute for Social Research in Ann Arbor (2), Sloan-Kettering in New York, and a Boston hospital; connected with the Children and Family Justice Center at Northwestern Law School; a psychotherapist who also has worked with homeless people with AIDS in New York; an artist; writers (2); a musician; a playwright/actor; a director/choreographer/performer; a filmmaker; editors (2); a stress management expert; a paralegal; and graduate students in photography, art, sociology and women's studies, occupational therapy (2), philosophy, and urban education.

Since graduation, nine have at one point or another worked with incarcerated youth, another twenty-four have worked with incarcerated adults, and eighteen presently hold positions that focus on issues of the incarcerated.

Let's take the lawyers and those working in law agencies.

Dargie Anderson is a student at Northwestern Law School and in 2009 "a summer associate at Skadden, Arps, Slate, Meagher, and Flom, a big corporate firm" with which she will work after graduation in 2010, doing transactional real estate or corporate work.

That may seem disconnected from anything I did with PCAP, but it actually doesn't feel disconnected to me. My experiences working and volunteering at nonprofits of various kinds, teaching at Michigan, and working in Americorps left me with a sense that there need to be people in the world who are conversant both with ideas about poverty and social change and education and also with corporate finance and accounting and management and business. So now I'm trying to learn about the second half so I can one day apply it to the first. I'm not sure where this path will lead, but I'm excited about it.[9]

Sarah Bergen, while a student at American University Washington College of Law, interned at the National Juvenile Defender Center in the summer of 2007 and that fall worked "at the civil rights, special litigation section of the Department of Justice, which handles, amongst other things, class action suits addressing unlawful conditions in public institutions, such as prisons, juvenile correctional facilities, mental health facilities, and within the police departments." After graduation in 2009, preparing for the Maryland bar exam, she is seeking child advocacy work, although the job market is forcing her to broaden her search horizons.[10]

Liz Budnitz I have written about above.

Mica Doctoroff is an investigator at the Southern Center for Human Rights. Her efforts there, she writes,

have focused on issues surrounding women in the criminal justice system in Alabama, including work on a class action lawsuit on behalf of all of the Alabama women prisoners for improved conditions, medical care and mental health care at the women's prison; lobbying for policy change at the Alabama legislature; coalition building; and organizing with incarcerated women. ... I have been working extensively on a class action lawsuit challenging the recent sex offender restriction law in Georgia, a law so severe that it had the potential to banish all of the people on the sex offender registry (approximately 12,000 people) from Georgia.

She is also "working with a coalition to reduce the number of Alabama women prisoners and develop a network of resources to serve as viable alternatives to incarceration; lobbying at the Alabama legislature to change a statewide practice that allows sheriffs to personally pocket any money that they receive for the feeding of prisoners in their county jails that they don't spend on food . . . ; working with our law school interns to advocate for Alabama prisoners at their parole hearings"; investigating a metro Atlanta area practice "by which parents are prosecuted in criminal court and sometimes incarcerated for their children's unexcused absences at school; investigating a practice in South Georgia by which indigent people are held in jail (sometimes for over a year) for not having enough money to pay child support."[11]

When Allie Horevitz graduated from the University of Michigan in 2005, she went to work for the Prison Law Office in San Quentin, California, "as a litigation assistant on class-action lawsuits that sought to improve prison conditions in California' state prisons." A year later she became a defense investigator for the Habeas Corpus Resource Center, an organization that provides legal counsel to indigent inmates on California's death row. In 2009 she finds her work at the Center encouraging her "toward the mental health profession—particularly working with underserved, immigrant populations and victims of trauma."[12]

After Emi Kaneko graduated from the University at the end of 2005, she continued with PCAP, even while attending Wayne State University Law School. Only recently did she agree to become an associate as well as a member. Over many years she has facilitated five poetry workshops (at the Gus Harrison, Parnall, and Scott correctional facilities) and an art and a theater workshop at the Parr Highway Correctional Facility. She served on the PCAP executive committee for a year and for four years, through April 2009, was a member and then an essential leader of the planning committee for the Annual Exhibition of Art by Michigan Prisoners. While at Wayne State, she interned at the Washtenaw County Public Defender and was law clerk for Trott and Trott, a real estate firm. Just graduated, she is for the moment practicing real estate law, but hoping to transfer to either public defense or public interest law.[13]

While in law school at the City University of New York, Joe Kudia interned at the Office of the Appellate Defender, working with indigent defendants who had been unjustly incarcerated, in an attempt to get their convictions overturned. He also worked in CUNY's Defender Clinic, "the only clinical program in the country that lets its student-lawyers represent clients who face the possibility of jail/prison time." He is now a public defender in the Hillsborough County Public Defenders Office in Tampa, Florida, working at first in the Juvenile Division and now in the Adult Felony division, "handling cases on a daily basis where people are looking at substantial prison time, including mandatory life . . . challenging work, very high stakes, but very rewarding nonetheless."[14]

In 2009 Emma Nowacki graduated from DePaul College of Law, focusing "on criminal law from both a defense and prosecution standpoint." She clerked at the Cook County State Attorney's Office "in the appellate division, juvenile delinquency division, felony trial division, and most recently in the felony domestic violence division," volunteered at the Cabrini Green Legal Aid Expungement Office "in order to assist individuals in clearing their arrest records and petitioning for clemency," and participated in the DePaul Death Penalty Clinic, "where I assisted in the defense of a federal defendant facing the death penalty for murder and bank robbery." She is studying for the bar and applying for "government public service jobs in all fields of criminal law." She writes,

> Despite my extensive work with the prosecutor's office, PCAP has certainly helped me to see the criminal justice system from not only the viewpoint of the victim, but also the accused. This perspective has influenced my desire to enter criminal law and serve justice either through prosecution or defense, without much preference or bias toward either side. For that, I am truly grateful to the PCAP organization, and to the incarcerated individuals who opened my eyes.[15]

Maggie Peck is a program associate in the Vera Institute of Justice Center on Sentencing and Corrections. Her primary role is to help "states nationwide reform their criminal justice policies to lower prison populations." Currently her "most exciting project" is with the New York State Division of Parole, creating new policies that "will provide parole officers with the tools to respond effectively to technical violations and new arrests without returning people to prison unnecessarily, which we all know interrupts the rehabilitation and transition process."[16]

Since June 2006, Kate Richardson has worked as a paralegal with Rosen, Bien & Galvan, a law firm that "focuses on constitutional and civil rights cases . . . with several large class action cases dealing with prisoner and parolee rights in the California prison system under the California Department of Corrections and Rehabilitation." She has been working specifically on juvenile parole due process rights and constitutional mental health care under class action compliance. Most recently, she worked "on a California prison overcrowding trial regarding mental and medical health care rights, which was held in front of a Federal Three-Judge Panel and may result in a prison population cap." She has moved to Boston to enter Northeastern School of Law and expects to graduate in 2012 with a focus on prisoner and human rights.[17]

Before she entered New York Law School in 2005, Lisa Ruff focused on mental health issues and in 2004 became a court-appointed child advocate in San Francisco. In the summer of 2006 she interned at Mental Hygiene Legal Service in Brooklyn, "an agency created through the court system that represents individuals involuntarily retained in psych facilities." After graduation and after passing the bar, she worked until June 2009 at Disability Rights California in their Oakland office on a temporary grant, serving "individuals with mental disabilities who were experiencing disability-based discrimination in areas such as housing, employment and public benefits." Currently doing contract work "for an attorney who represents individuals appealing their SSI and Social Security Disability claim denials," she is hoping the economy will pick up and enable her to find permanent work in mental health or disability law in the Bay Area.[18]

In law school at the University of Pittsburgh, Melissa Sachs established and cofacilitated a theater workshop at the Shuman Juvenile Detention Center, became president of the National Lawyers Guild chapter, and served as a legal intern for the Institute of Justice and Democracy in Haiti, whose mission is "to work with the people of Haiti in their non-violent struggle for the return and consolidation of constitutional democracy, justice and human rights, by distributing objective and accurate information on human rights conditions in Haiti, pursuing legal cases, and cooperating with human rights and solidarity groups in Haiti and abroad." After graduation she worked for "a plaintiff's side employment discrimination firm," but has left legal practice for a while. "Extremely interested" in the way social media "gives a voice back to those who have been neglected of opportunity," she has created an online magazine—http://nonpretentious.com, "a pop culture blog," though if you go "a little deeper," it is "a community for aspiring and inspiring writers to gather together to share tips and tools about the profession of writing." In a message to me she writes both that "I have not given up any fight" and "I'm admitting right now that I've stopped fighting the good fight."[19]

During her years at Hastings Law School, Nasha Vida worked with other students to raise money for summer grants for students wishing to enter public interest law and helped start the *Hastings Race and Poverty Law Journal.* She interned at the California Appellate Project, researching lawsuits against the California prison system, and worked at the Immigrant Legal Resource Center, developing "immigration law trainings for social service providers who provide services to domestic violence survivors." She also worked, her second summer, with the East Bay Community Law Center, which provides legal services to low-income people with HIV and AIDS. After graduation in 2003, she continued to work at the Immigrant Legal Resource Center "on a project training various social service providers in the northern valley counties on immigration laws so that they can better help their clients gain legal status," again focusing on survivors of abuse and violent crimes. After a hiatus with her husband in Italy, she is currently a staff attorney with the Federal Court of Appeals for the Ninth Circuit in San Francisco, assisting the judges in their decision-making process, working on immigration cases.[20]

Mike Ward entered the University of Pittsburgh law school a year or two after graduation and in his first year was thinking of a career in international criminal or human rights law. He applied for a summer internship with the Justice Department of the United Nations Mission in Kosovo. After graduation he moved to New York City and has recently joined an Internet company called The Legal Space, Inc., an online business development tool for attorneys. He hopes to find his way back to a social justice career.[21]

PCAP HUBS

After a social evening at a local bar Friday night, we circled up in a large Michigan League room on Saturday morning July 16, 2005, our bags cluttered against pillars or around the edges, holding coffee, water bottles, pens and pads. Our first Associate Gathering. Erin Aleman, Sara Bursac, Erin Connelly, Jean Fitzgerald, Joe Funt, Neela Ghoshal, Susie Harter, Laurie Hess, Jesse Jannetta, Chiara Liberatore, Vanessa Mayesky, Melissa Palma, and Ravi Ramaswamy along with some of the current PCAP members who were in town: Mica Doctoroff, Matt Erickson, Suzanne Gothard, Erin Kaplan, Brian Sellers, Alycia Welch, and me. We celebrated recent PCAP achievements, described the current PCAP, asked the associates questions and together discussed their answers. They advised us to respond to workshop performances with more critical feedback, they thought we might require members to attend one or two performances a year, and Neela wanted us to engage in more written witnessing of the kind required of her while living in the Guatemalan village.

Reconvening Sunday morning with the topic "Building on the PCAP Associate Network," we asked "What should we do with the network of Associates? How do we better connect Associates with each other and with current PCAP members? How do we strengthen the support provided to Associates and PCAP?" The group proposed associate "hubs (a group of associates living in the same city, meeting periodically, in cities where at least 2 associates reside)." Jesse Jannetta reported over e-mail and in the next newsletter:

> Though each hub would decide how it wants to take shape, the Associates present at the gathering would like to ask each hub to commit to the following: first, set up an initial meeting to gather and see where things go; second, to re-gather each time a new associate moves to the area to welcome that new associate.

He listed "the needs articulated by current Associates that necessitate building a 'hub' system":

1. Want a reason to gather with other Associates and talk
2. Connect multiple generations of associates
3. Build system that enables human contact, people meeting people, and cultivates ongoing discussion
4. Remind that we are all here, community of people with common experience
5. Energize each other
6. Remind each other of aspects of our life that we want to exist, but may currently be absent (ex. teaching, artistic work, etc.)
7. Support each other
8. Build system that sets us up to be ready to act on something larger,

organize nationally, stay better connected, collaborate on specific projects/future adventures

9. Build job network
10. Find and utilize smaller affinity groups within large base of Associates (geographic location, type of work, social issue, etc.)[22]

Current PCAP administrator Suzanne Gothard sent a geographical list to Chiara Liberatore, who recruited leaders and sent them a list of "potential topics for discussion at initial hub meetings."[23] Current PCAP members were expected to serve as liaisons, letting a hub know when a new associate was moving to their area. The next newsletter listed the hubs and those who had so far agreed to be hub caps (captains). Ann Arbor had twelve members, including three located in Atlanta, Germany, and Mexico, Baltimore/DC four members, Boston four, New York twenty-two including one each in Connecticut and Philadelphia, Pittsburgh two, Southern California five, the San Francisco Bay Area six, including one in Italy, and Chicago twelve, including one each in Denver, Milwaukee, and St. Louis).[24]

Associates had gathered before. In the fall of 2003 the Boston associates came together to plan a fund-raiser for PCAP and found, as Sara Bursac wrote, that "it brought us together and helped us revive this part of ourselves that is always there and really helped form what we are doing now."[25] In January 2004 the Chicago group brought in $600 for PCAP; on May 22 Naomi Milstein, working alone in Indianapolis, raised $721; and the New York associates held fund-raisers November 20 ($1,098.75) and again on June 7, 2005, this time in the home of Advisory Board member Bell Chevigny. They showed video documents of our work, and associates and Advisory Board members testified. During the same period Chiara, Jesse, and Matthew Schmitt, the three associate members on the National Advisory Board, had called around to other associates and raised another $1,075. In 2009, close to thirty associates raised over $1,000 to continue Sari Adelson's coordinator position through the summer.

Chiara's report from Chicago captures the spirit of the fund-raising events and of the 2008 event in New York that raised $1,300.

First of all, thank you *so* much to those of you who joined us last night to support the Prison Creative Arts Project. Beyond raising money for PCAP, we enjoyed an incredible night of dance, lyrics, art and dialogue. Through donations at the door as well as passing the bucket around after some of

Saiyid's inspiring freestyle sessions we were able to raise 380$. Around 1 am as I began to pack up for home, Nik, the bar owner stopped me and asked me to stick around until the end of the night so he could give me a percentage of the bar ring. He was very inspired by the spirit in his bar, moved by the artwork, and excited about the possibility of continuing to use The Tonic Room as a place to raise money for PCAP and other important organizations. He mentioned to me that his father spent some time in prison as a political prisoner for Che Guevara and then gladly gave me 120$ more to make our goal of 500$!!! This plus the money many of you have promised to send on through the mail should get us to a grand total of 600$ for PCAP. Thank You, Thank You, Thank You.

I'd like to share some highlights of the night with you . . .

1) A conversation I had with Gabriel, the lead MC, of the Dialects (the band performing) whom I had never met before. Having arrived to set up his equipment he studied the artwork closely and then immediately came up to me to introduce himself. "When Nik told me about tonight, I didn't realize this was what it was about. This is great. I know how important it can be for inmates to produce art. My dad was locked up for most of my life. He made me this (pointing to a necklace around his neck) when he was in prison and I have been wearing it for the last six years. I am going to give a shout out to him when we perform and ask people to give you money." Which he did. And they did.

2) The Freestyle sessions to the Artwork—Thank you Alyssa for borrowing a projector!!! Beyond the artwork on display, we set up a screen to show slides of the artwork throughout the night. This proved to be immensely helpful in drawing in those patrons who did not realize they were going to be at a benefit that night. Once some MC's had gathered, Saiyid announced the challenge. As each image appeared, the MC's would freestyle lyrics on their interpretation of the artwork. Saiyid worked his magic and soon we *had them*!! Heads that had been burrowed over drinks and cigarettes and *not* PCAP began looking up at the Art. After the session ended Saiyid asked people to give more money. Suddenly I had people dropping money in the bucket who had refused me at the door with "I'm with the band" or "prison inmates? I don't think so."

It never ceases to amaze me how this work connects people, gives them what they need and opens them up. Right now, when I say "people" I actually mean the non-incarcerated population of us. And once again, after years of doing this work, talking about it, searching for ways to communicate about it—I learned something new last night. During a moment of feeling protective of the artwork, the men and women who created it, Alyssa and I in our attempts to shout over loud music and talking to get people to donate, I questioned whether it was the right place to be. Is it ok to bring this work, which is so sacred and precious to those who understand it, into this loud place where people can shut it out through drinks and crowds? Wouldn't it have actually been better to be at home, in a small environment, where people could talk and where I could talk and talk and talk and convince them why this is important? Well sure, we can do that! And it would be great. But something happened last night that would have been missing in that scenario . . .

So I'm having this thought when my friend Gary showed up with his African drums. "Can I play?" "Of course!" So the live drumming begins, Saiyid is on the microphone, the DJ is scratching out beats, people got up and began to dance, and the room started to come together. Then arrives a man just released from a 12 year sentence who spoke with Alyssa, a "friend of the band" who had earlier seemed closed off asked me if he could buy Brent Harding's piece. People who had earlier refused donating began to drop money in the bucket and I realized why this place was important and different from a dinner at my house. Last night we made connections that we could have never made if the guest list was only hand picked. Last night the PCAP Artists got strangers talking, dancing, and connecting with each other. So one of the many walls that gets put up every day got taken down last night. Those of you who are in communication with the Artists, please let them know what they accomplished and thank them. And many, many thanks again to all of you who made last night happen. Thanks especially to my friends, who have known for years how important this is to me. We raised 500$ + for PCAP !! thank you, thank you!!!![26]

Since the July 2005 meeting, hub gatherings have been sporadic. Joe Funt brought six New York members together in January, 2006. Resolving to have rotating caps and meet every two months, they reported that "many of our reasons for establishing a hub were similar to those discussed at the Associates meeting last summer: a support network, to be a resource for new associates coming to New York, work on a project together, provide support for PCAP, hang out with like minded people, etc."[27] Meeting in Ann Arbor in March 2006, Sacha Feirstein, Vanessa Mayesky, and Melissa Palma discussed a beer-tasting fund-raiser for PCAP and volunteering for the annual exhibition "to alleviate PCAP member burnout."[28] Four members of the same hub barbecued in September of the same year, and others met in April 2008. Liz Chisholm and Alyssa Sorresso hosted a gathering of seven Chicago hub members in May 2007, attended also by three of us from out of town. At Habana's Outpost in Brooklyn on August 25, 2007, nine New York hub members discussed their goal as a hub, decided to start a hub newsletter, and planned what turned out to be a very successful February fund-raiser, bringing in $1,030, followed by another that raised $1,224 in February 2009. More recently, the flux of new arrivals in the Bay Area have been finding each other and met at the apartment of Emily Harris and Pete Woiwode on the night of September 28, 2008.

On August 20–23, 2009, twenty-six associates, Janie, and two PCAP coordinators came to the Ronora Lodge and Retreat Center in Watervliet, Michigan, for a gathering that had been a year in the planning, funded in part by the Office of the Provost, the College of Literature, Science and the Arts, and the Career Center. We didn't know what to anticipate, but knew that if nothing else, just the talk would be good, reminding, reinforcing, reinvigorating. We knew that every associate has an engaged life, new friends and colleagues, some have family demands, and all have aspirations and challenges, and so it was possible nothing larger would happen than what we already have. But there was also the potential for a spark, for recognition of a shared issue, for gathering of resources and contacts, for something to be organized, for new resistance.

We began with a two-hour round of moving introductions. Three intense visioning sessions were spread over the three days and were interspersed with equally intense specialized sessions on youth education, creative arts work in prisons and youth facilities, the impact of the financial crisis on mass incarceration, and career paths (community organizing, the arts, education, and policy and system change work), plus an evening of sharing our creative work and stories, mornings of yoga for early risers, and time for one-on-one or small-group connecting.

Looking back a month later, Jesse Jannetta found that

> there was a clear common feeling among those there that, coming from our separate and very different lives, we still need PCAP, need to be PCAP, and want to not only remember and reconnect with it, but continue the work of creating it.

Emily Harris observed that "a huge part of the weekend was about strengthening the support for each other so we can do this type of work for the long haul," and Chiara Liberatore remembered that

> it was mentioned more than once that people were pleased to find the group to be natural at organizing itself, that we accomplished quite a bit in the time we had together, and that we were able to be effective and productive without too much planning and structure. For me this was an indication of what possibilities we have to do more as a unified group.[29]

During one visioning session, attempting to define the PCAP associates, some of us proposed that we were characterized by a determination to "name the world" in the Freirean sense, that is, to be specific and very clear, to refuse to hedge our terms, in addressing the mechanisms of oppression and exploitation and the damage they do to those our work is associated with. Julia Taylor, who found the gathering "helpful in sustaining us," writes that "I also walked away really thinking of the idea of how we name the world, how we name our work, and the urgency in that."[30]

The associates agreed to strengthen the hubs; to organize their part of a letter-writing campaign to convince the University to make PCAP a permanent entity; to begin mentoring relations with university students seeking careers in social justice work; to address the national issue of incarceration of youth as adults without the possibility of parole; and to develop a *When Can We Talk?* play on a national scale.

THE ASSOCIATES

PCAP associates work in the hardest places, with battered women, homeless people living with AIDS, the mentally challenged, the incarcerated, men and women holding on on death row, foster care youth, unorganized workers, immigrants, William Martinezes and DeWaynes, the illiterate, runaways, gangs, beleaguered neighborhoods, people on the brink of losing their homes, people in refugee camps, urban and rural school children.

Some of the most troubling stories that come back are from the teachers. Kate Conrad:

Our school is in school improvement this year and if we don't meet state standards (i.e. *tests*—they don't care that our paint is peeling and the desks are broken and roaches the size of my big toe roam the halls) by the end of the year, the school will be taken over by the state. I'll have to reapply for my job, along with all other faculty, and I wonder if it will be worth it. If that happens, though, I imagine most other faculty will run for the hills and I think I owe it to the students *not* to give up on them.

One day last week, I dealt with two suicide notes, three students cutting themselves, an intimate encounter with an abusive parent and social services, a student taking his clothes off in class, a miscarriage, and a student yelling, "I hate white teachers!!!" (The student says I'm different. I say I'm a white teacher.)

As for my personal life, I don't have one. I sleep and eat and try to keep clean clothes. I'm going back to Warren to spend the holidays with the family and I look forward to that.

Our schools are in trouble. I'm frustrated and feeling helpless. Anyone in the same boat?[31]

Chrissy Brockett loves her teaching but writes,

We are not without our problems, some of them serious and troubling (as I write this, I am home because of school being cancelled after the shooting at another CMSD school), some of them the average outcome of stuffing hundreds of adolescents into the same building, all of them worth struggling with.[32]

Naomi Milstein, a graduate of the University of Michigan School of Social Work who has interned with youth in Mississippi and served as a Vista volunteer with youth in Indianapolis, writes from Indiana:

We have trips to Baltimore planned (visiting Baltimore algebra project, youth action research group and others) and possibly a trip to Chicago planned also . . . just trying to get our students exposed to some of the great youth organizing work happening across the country and to help build a network of young people they can turn to for support. And all of this in the face of a district that is suspending kids left and right for violations to the new uniform policy . . . stupid stuff like they get sent home if they have the wrong belt buckle . . . it's clear that domination and control of students is more important than academic achievement . . . more important than students feeling comfortable and excited to come to school . . . more important than student-teacher relationships.[33]

Jase Schwartz writes from Brooklyn:

Two of our clients have been killed since I began working with homeless youth in NYC, less than a year ago. I am 24 years old. Both clients were younger than I am. I stood at the grave site for the client who most recently passed away. Such moments make me question my ability to do this work for the long haul. I know there will be so many more funerals to come.[34]

Nasha Vida identifies the dehumanization in our institutions and practices:

I just wanted to say that I always think about my brief yet important time with PCAP. The more I learn about our immigration system the more I see similarities in the way immigrants and prisoners are treated in our country. Both groups of people are dehumanized and seen as deserving their plight— whatever that may be—without any understanding of the economic context and circumstances within which people make the choices that lead them to where they are today. There are so many immigrants who are detained, imprisoned and lost in the system. As we all know, navigating the legal system is a nightmare for anyone—try adding lack of English language skills, money or the right to an attorney (immigrants don't have the right to an attorney unless it is a criminal trial—and since most immigration law is considered to be civil—people who overstay their visa and get detained [imprisoned] must find their own representation).[35]

And Neela writes from Gulu in northern Uganda about the Internally Displaced People's Camps:

Another day, the whole conference piled into vans and headed out to visit two IDPCs, Unyama and Bobi. In both, the conditions were as miserable as anything I could have imagined. Huts are packed together, water is scarce, and women walk miles in search of firewood each day. Among the adults, there is a sense of despondency. These are people who historically have worked the land of their ancestors. In the camps, they have nothing. The children are another story. While many are visibly malnourished and ill, they lit up at the arrival of visitors and followed us along as we toured the camps, chattering at my side in Luo. I imagine that for the smallest children, the camps are like a giant playground—but at some point they grow older and realize they're living in concentration camps.

1.6 million people have been displaced by the war and up to 30,000 children have been abducted, though many have eventually found their way back home. Reintegrating former child soldiers will be one of Uganda's biggest challenges. What do you do with children who have been so brutally stripped of their innocence?[36]

Yes.

In English 319 a third of the way into the term, I speak briefly to the students about what they have read, heard, witnessed so far and include the following passage from Jonathan Kozol's *The Night Is Dark and I Am Far from Home,* the first book they read:

Boston, Blue Hill Avenue, ten days before Christmas: A child falls down in the middle of Grove Hall. She is epileptic, but her sickness either has not yet been diagnosed or else (more probable) it has been diagnosed, but never treated. Tall and thin, fourteen years old, she is intense and sober, devastated but unhating. Her life is a staccato sequence of *grand mal* convulsions: no money, no assistance, no advice on how to get a refill of expensive script for more Dilantin and more Phenobarbital.

This night, she comes downstairs into the office where I work within the coat-room underneath the church-stairs of a Free School: standing there and asking me please if I would close the door and hold her head within my arms because she knows that she is going to have an epileptic seizure; and closing the door and sitting down upon the cold cement while she lies down and places her head within my arms and starts to shudder violently and moves about so that I scarcely can protect her wracked and thin young body from the cement wall and from the concrete floor; and seeing her mouth writhe up with pain and spittle, and feeling her thrash about a second time and now a third; and, in between, the terror closing in upon her as in a child's bad dream that you can't get out of, and watching her then, and wondering what she undergoes; and later seeing her, exhausted, sleeping there, right in my arms, as at the end of a long ordeal, all passion in her spent; then taking her out into my car and driving with her to the City Hospital while she, as epileptics very often feel, keeps saying that she is going to have another seizure; and slamming on the brakes and walking with her in the back door where they receive out-patient cases, and being confronted on this winter night at nine P.M. in Boston in the year of 1965 with a scene that comes from Dante's Purgatory: dozens and dozens of poor white, black and Puerto Rican people, infants and mothers, old men, alcoholics, men with hands wrapped up in gauze, and aged people trembling, infants trembling with fever; one hostile woman in white uniform behind the table telling us, out of a face made, as it seems, of clay, that we should fill an application out, some sort of form, a small white sheet, then sit out in the hallway since the waiting room is full; and then to try to say this child has just had several seizures in a row and needs treatment, and do we need to do the form; and yes, of course you need to do the form and wait your turn and not think you have any special right to come ahead of someone else who has been sitting here before you. Two hours and four seizures later, you get up and go in and shout in her cold eyes and walk right by and grab an intern by the arm and tell him to come out and be a doctor to an epileptic child sitting like a damp rag in the hallway; and he comes out, and in two minutes gives this child an injection that arrests the seizures and sedates her, then writes the script for more Dilantin and for Phenobarbital and shakes his head and says to you that it's a damn shame: "Nobody needs to have an epileptic seizure in this day and age . . . Nobody but a poor black nigger," says the intern in a sudden instant of that rage that truth and decency create. He nearly cries, and in his eyes you see a kind of burning pain that tells you that he is a good man somehow, deep-down, some place where it isn't all cold stone, clean surgery and antiseptic reason: "Nobody but a poor black nigger needs to have an epileptic seizure anymore." So you take her home and you go back to the church, down to your office underneath the stairs, and look at the floor, and listen to the silence, and you are twenty-eight years old, and you begin to cry; you cry for horror of what that young girl has just been through; and you long not to believe that this can be the city that you really live in. You fight very hard to lock up that idea because it threatens all the things that you have wanted to believe for so long; so you sit alone a while and you try to lock these bitter passions into secret spaces of your self-control. You try to decontaminate your anger and to organize your rage; but you can't do it this time; you just can't build that barrier of logical control a second time. It's eleven o'clock now, and soon it's quarter of twelve; and it's cold as stone down here beneath the wooden underside of the church-stairs, and still you can't stop trembling. *Grand mal,* you think to yourself, means a great evil; it's twelve-fifteen and now you are no longer crying so you get up and you lock the door and the coat-closet which is the office of a Free School underneath the church-stairs; and you go up the stairs and turn out the light and then you close the door.[37]

Yes.

I have not facilitated a juvenile facility or high school workshop. Yet I have visited such workshops for years. I work with an individual, take a role in the play, write to the prompt, offer ideas, celebrate the group. And almost always in the faces, bodies, and words of the incarcerated youth, I see and hear the *hurt,* the diminished possibilities, the deep insults to the soul that their experiences have brought them. I intuit the same in some of the subdued and cowed younger high school students, so many of whom will drop out before graduation. I leave each time saddened, overwhelmed, and angry.

And I leave heartened. So often the room fills with life, with youth taking ownership of their poems, their images, their stories, risking a word; so often the room fills with laughter, with the excited ad-libs of improvised theater, with youth rollicking into character confrontation that spins into new scenes, into moments that plummet past mere action-filled plots. And my students riding the tide, provoking the tide, doubled over in laughter, learning courage, risking words, suddenly filled with awe, learning to work in the space, co-creating with the youth comfort, safety, respect, and even love. Gifts of resilience and resistance,which are also gifts for those courageous high school teachers and youth facility counselors who have committed and struggled so much, against such great odds, to enable at least some of these youth to grow into full lives.

And so I know those children who light up when visitors arrive at the concentration camp. I recognize Kate's frustration and helplessness and loss of personal life, her wondering if it is worth it, recognize Jase at the grave site unsure about the long haul, and know why Jase is in it for the long haul, why Chrissy sees the youth are worth the struggle, why Kate is clear she will not give up on the students and once again contribute the creation of a play to their imaginative and practical lives,[38] why Naomi travels to Baltimore and Chicago to expose Indianapolis youth to great youth organizing. I understand what Neela felt arriving at a Gulu night shelter that protected children from kidnapping by the Lord's Resistance Army, when dozens of children rushed out to meet her and her companions and sang welcoming songs and a boy told an Acholi legend, understand why she wrote in response,"children never fail to amaze me, somehow maintaining hope and positivity under the grimmest conditions."[39]

This understanding and resolve are in the room when the associates gather, it is what binds them, and binds them with others. It is rooted in their original work in the courses and in PCAP and in all they have done since. They either remember or simply know the final pages of Herbert Kohl's beautiful book on teaching, *36 Children*. As he reflects on the children who responded with such excitement and creativity to his trust and respect for them and who he now sees realizing—as Neela puts it—that "they're living in concentration camps," he writes,

> There is no point in continuing to document each child's problems and pains. Enough has already been said. The thirty-six children are suffering from the diseases of our society. They are no special cases; there are too many hundreds of thousands like them, lost in indifferent, inferior schools, put on the streets or in prep schools with condescension or cynicism. When I think of my work as a teacher one of the children's favorite myths, that of Sisyphus, continually comes to mind: the man condemned to roll a rock up a mountain only to see it fall back to the bottom, to return to the bottom himself and take up his unending task. Without hope and without cynicism, I try to make myself available to my pupils. I believe neither that they will succeed nor that they will fail. I know they will fight, falter, and rise again and again, and that if I have the strength I will be there to rejoice and cry with them, and to add my little weight to easing the burden of being alive in the United States.[40]

"Some of you have wondered why I go to places like Rwanda, Northern Uganda, Guatemala," Neela wrote to her family and friends and to the associates. It is, she says, because we must "break through the net that artificially divides 'us' from 'others'" and because she believes there is real value and potential in "listening to the stories of those who have lived through the darkest moments, and then retelling those stories."[41]

I don't want to romanticize or exaggerate the associates. Not all of them gather, not all of them are drawn back toward PCAP. All of them are everyday people like the rest of us, trying to figure out their lives, imperfect, meager, struggling with relationships and health, susceptible to doubts and despair, sometimes pathetic, sometimes afraid, often overwhelmed. But they are *in* the work, they cross borders, they risk, they bear witness, they have an orientation, they have each other, and they are in for the long haul.

APPENDIX

The Prison Creative Arts Project of the University of Michigan

MISSION STATEMENT

The Prison Creative Arts Project of the University of Michigan is committed to original work in the arts in Michigan correctional facilities. Our purpose is to enhance creative opportunities for inmates and to bring them the benefits and skills that come with each art. We attempt to provide the best possible and most positive programs and we work closely with each facility to ensure that this happens.

The Theater Workshops:

Into the theater spaces that our presence makes possible we bring complete respect for everyone involved, we bring a full belief in the ability of everyone to work together and create a play, and we bring a strategy of discovery, using warm-ups, games, exercises, improvisations, and discussion to arrive mutually at the stories that are told through theater. We build our plays through improvisation (a method of figuring out plot, character, and themes together and developing them as we go). Original music sometimes accompanies the plays. By participating in the workshop, the inmates gain skills in the conceptualizing, dialogue, casting, and blocking of a play, and they gain skills in working together, in creating ideas and images and putting them

---

Official Mission Statement for the Michigan Department of Corrections, approved by Deputy Director Dan Bolden in 1999.

together, and in speaking publicly before an audience. And the attention and praise of the audience, as well as the week by week growth in their ability to perform and work together, add to each participant's sense of his or her own possibilities. The themes vary considerably, but nearly every play centers on efforts to reestablish and form communities and reconstitute families, and on the effort of prisoners to have successful lives when they return to their communities; these plays often reflect the hard realities many prisoners have known, and they reflect the search for solutions, solutions which the actors consciously offer to their peers in performances. This reconstitution of community and family reflects both the desires of incarcerated people and the close-knit process of creation that leads to the plays.

The Art Workshops:

In the art workshops we create an environment in which participants can learn technical skills and create works which are personally meaningful. We bring in as much reference material as we can to provide examples and inspiration. This includes books, magazines, and hand-outs on topics such as perspective, drawing the head, and color-mixing. We work with a combination of structure and individual exploration. There are lessons on such things as color, portraiture, and shading. Also each participant is encouraged to work on their own individual project. Often these projects are inspired by the material we bring in. Sometimes an inmate comes in with a specific project and we work with him, discovering what skills and additional knowledge would be helpful.

The art workshops provide an environment that is conducive for both private introspection and shared appreciation of each other's work. We have seen wonderful examples of progress in artistic growth, and many of the artists from our workshops have participated in our Annual Exhibition of Art by Michigan Prisoners at the University of Michigan.

The Annual Exhibition of Art by Michigan Prisoners:

We understand this exhibition not only as a quality exhibition for the Ann Arbor and larger community, but as an event that breaks stereotypes and demystifies prisoners, revealing their talents, their perspectives, and their rich range of themes. We understand it as an annual event that encourages men and women in prison to develop their abilities as artists, and so in selecting the art our goal is inclusion without sacrificing quality. We also understand the exhibition as an event that connects two separated groups in the Michigan community. Visitors to the gallery encounter the work of the artists and biographical statements by the artists, and at the opening reception they meet both family members of the artists and volunteers who have interacted with the artists in the prison setting. The artists have more limited encounters with those outside prison: they receive a video tape of the opening reception which includes speeches, crowd shots, and images of each of the works on exhibition; they also receive copies of fliers and reviews and a copy of all the comments in the visitors' book; they often correspond with members of the team preparing the exhibition.

The Creative Writing Workshops:

We bring the same respect, belief, and process of discovery to the creative writing workshops. In these workshops, participants learn to develop their creativity and skill as writers, they learn to deepen their thinking and knowledge through writing about what they know, they learn to give and take honest and supportive criticism, and they learn to read aloud with the clarity and drama that can hold an audience. The revision and fine honing of their work and performance of readings held in the facility at the end of the workshop, which bring attention and praise, add to each participant's sense of their own possibilities.

The Dance Workshops:

We bring the same respect, belief, and process of discovery to the dance workshops. In these workshops, working closely with trained dancers from the University of Michigan Department of Dance, the participants learn to appreciate the range of their bodies' abilities to move, they learn to work together to choreograph original dance pieces accompanied by traditional, modern, or original music and sound or accompanied by the reading of poetry or creative prose. They learn to give and take supportive criticism, they learn the virtues of rehearsal and repetition, they learn to stretch themselves. And the act of refining a work until it can be performed along with the act of performance and the applause it receives, adds to each participant's sense of their own possibilities.

Training and Responsibility:

The student volunteers who come through the courses of Buzz Alexander and Janie Paul and other volunteers who work with us must interview to be in our courses or to work with us, they are carefully screened, and they are carefully trained. Our orientations on campus rival facility orientations in their strictness about rules and regulations and appropriate behavior at the facility. We work with complete respect for institution rules, needs, and personnel. We regard that as essential. Before our volunteers go to a facility for the first time, not only have they received an orientation at the facility, but they have received several weeks of training and grounding from us. Every volunteer who works with us must meet on a weekly basis to discuss the workshop and to receive supervision, either from Alexander or Paul or from other volunteers who have worked for a considerable period in the prisons.

We also maintain close links with the facility staff to whom we are responsible. We maintain a spirit of friendliness, respect, and cooperation with corrections officers, recreation, athletic, religious, and special activities staff, and with assistant deputy wardens, deputy wardens, and wardens. Our work is open and positive, and we are responsive to any queries or requests for documentation a facility may ask of us. We are proud of our work and of our collaboration with each facility, and we do everything we can to enhance and improve that work and that collaboration.

Because the official mission statement that Dan Bolden demanded in 1999 didn't get at the heart of our work, we developed our own mission statement and list of core values during the summer of 2000. It was ratified by the full membership that fall and now appears in our brochure and other documents.

Mission Statement

The Prison Creative Art Project's mission is to collaborate with incarcerated adults, incarcerated youth, and urban youth to strengthen our community through creative expression.

Our Core Values

We believe that everyone has the capacity to create art. Art is necessary for individual and societal growth, connection, and survival. It should be accessible to everyone. The values that guide our process are respect; collaboration in which vulnerability, risk, and improvisation lead to discovery; and resilience, persistence, patience, love, and laughter. We are joined with others in the struggle for social justice, and we make possible spaces in and from which the voices and visions of the incarcerated can be expressed.

PCAP Statement of Commitment and Understanding (draft)
(Summer 1999)

1. More than workshops

I understand that I am not merely joining PCAP in order to do a workshop in the arts in a prison or other institution. I understand that much more is involved.

2. Social justice

I understand that PCAP is an organization whose vision is based on a commitment to social justice. PCAP members are hurt, offended, outraged by the massive incarceration of Americans, by the disproportionate incarceration of poor Americans and Americans of color, and by the profit-making that is tied to this.

3. Strategy

I understand that PCAP operates according to a particular value system, methodology, and strategy. We do not go into the workshops as teachers from above. We bring skills, exercises, and knowledge to our workshops, and we are able and eager to share these. But we do not dominate the workshops with *our* skills, exercises, and knowledge. We don't go with the purpose of implanting or "teaching" what *we* know. Our main purpose is to establish a space that is open, trusting, honest, respectful and exploratory, where those inside, including ourselves, can find out what it is we want to say through our art, music, dance, writing, and theater.

There *are* other viable strategies: classes can be taught in prisons, prisoners can be lectured to and examined, prisoners can be considered students and can be given texts and instructed on how to perform someone else's play or to write in specific styles. But those aren't our strategies. Those who prefer to use them should find other routes into the prisons.

4. Supervision

I understand that PCAP workshops are supervised. This supervision happens in the give and take of weekly PCAP meetings and in other planned meetings. I understand that I am expected to attend PCAP meetings and that if those meetings happen the same time as my workshop, I and my partner will make arrangements to meet on a weekly basis with another member or members of PCAP.

I understand the importance of this supervision. Our work is sensitive and vulnerable. Much is at stake. If we fail to obey the rules and regulations at our sites, we may lose our workshop and PCAP workshops could be entirely closed down. We exist in a conservative climate and under a very conservative legislature which constantly takes rights and privileges away from prisoners and narrows their options for communication, growth and creativity. We must do everything we can not to make mistakes that the forces hostile to our workshops can seize upon. This takes vigilance, and we must be cautious, polite, grateful, non-confrontational. We need to talk with others in PCAP about our workshops so that others may hear us and pick up on vibes we may not be recognizing. We need to check in when we have a problem or when we are harassed or when we have made a mistake that could be problematic, so that we can get advice, support, and trouble-shooting on our behalf. We cannot be out there alone doing our workshops: too many prisoners and incarcerated youth and their families are dependent upon our being in touch and knowing what we are doing. That is the bottom line.

I understand that if I do not participate in this mutual supervision, PCAP will no longer sponsor or take responsibility for my workshop and will notify the staff at my site that this is the case.

5. PCAP activities

I understand that PCAP has many activities. I understand that it has the goals of witnessing and speaking its experience and knowledge to the public and of demystifying prisons, prisoners, prisoner families and communities, and the economic forces behind American punishment and prison expansion. I understand that I am expected to assist where I can with activities beyond my own workshop.

6. PCAP relations

I understand that PCAP is an organization of collaborators and friends, that we support and back each other, that we engage with each other, that we attend each other's performances and presentations, that we celebrate each other and celebrate together, that we feed each other and find occasions to check in and relax and generally just plain party together.

Prison Creative Arts Project: Member Statement of Commitment and Expectations (Fall 1999)

As a member of PCAP and a workshop facilitator, I will:

- Establish a space that is open, trusting, exploratory, honest, and respectful in my workshop.
- Go in as a facilitator, not a teacher.
- Participate in mutual workshop supervision by attending weekly PCAP meetings or other regularly scheduled meetings.
- I will follow institution policy, including dress code policies, and manifest procedures.
- In the facility/school I will be cautious, polite, grateful and non-confrontational.
- I will communicate about my workshops. This includes its joy, but also when I have problems, when I am harassed, or when I have made a mistake.
- I will strive to be a member of the PCAP community. This includes celebrating together and supporting other people's work.
- I will recognize when, for whatever reason, I am not meeting the expectation of a workshop facilitator, and I will actively seek solutions.
- I will maintain contact with my site liaison.
- I will attend all scheduled workshops at my site, except in cases where my absence has been discussed and agreed upon.

As a member of PCAP and a workshop facilitator, I can expect:

- Occasional "skills nights" to learn new games and exercises.
- A thorough orientation to working in a prison, juvenile detention center, or high school.
- A supportive community who will hear me when I need to talk about my workshops.
- A regular opportunity to problem solve with other workshop facilitators.
- An opportunity to discuss the larger personal and political issues underlying my work.
- Chances to engage in other PCAP activities beyond my workshop. These include: annual art exhibitions for prisoners and incarcerated youth, speaking engagements and planning and management.

PCAP Structure and Policies

Executive Committee

In the summer of 2000 we generated a proposal for an executive committee. Anna Clark, Pilar Horner, Ariella Kaufman, Kristen Ostenso, and Janie Paul were elected in September and became a vital, wonderfully contentious first committee. Administrator Jesse Jannetta and I as founder served as ex-officio members. Several years later, we began to hold staggered elections at the start of the fall, winter, and spring/summer terms in order to guarantee that we always have seasoned committee members.

The five elected members now have specific duties. Three are new member coordinator and trainer, Speakers Bureau coordinator, and coordinator of the bi-weekly full membership meetings. A fourth assists the administrator and edits the PCAP Weekly, an e-mail news letter which consists of updates, upcoming events and performances, reports on executive committee and full membership meetings, job opportunities, and articles and reports that are food for thought. The fifth meets with members proposing new projects—in 2008, for instance, the new annual *Review* of prisoner writing—and helps them think through the energy, resources, and timetable that are necessary.

We meet every second Wednesday. The first hour is a closed dinner meeting, which allows committee members to work efficiently and intimately and to deal with sensitive matters concerning members or sites. The second hour opens to all of PCAP[1] (with shared dessert). In both hours we discuss proposals for new activities, new or evolving policies, ideas for the general PCAP meetings, and other business. Any major issue goes out to the entire body.

General Meetings

All members meet from 6:30 to 9 pm alternate Wednesdays. At the first meeting each semester we creatively introduce new members and hold elections. In the meetings that follow, two PCAP members lead a program from 6:30 to 8:00. We interact with a speaker or respond to a film, share creative ideas and exercises, discuss the implications of our work, seek ways of deepening our practice, and look at larger economic and political issues. In the summer of 2008 we discussed a theme — the United States phenomenon of sentencing adolescent offenders to natural life.

From 8:00 to 9:00 we break into small groups of 4 to 6 teams which remain constant throughout the term, to talk about ongoing workshops, listen carefully to each other, and give advice. This is a continuation of the course team meetings and is *essential*. PCAP currently has 55 members. They come from the community or from the courses at different times and are together as a whole body only three hours a month. We work hard at communication, trust, and deepening relationships, but it is not easy. And so the intensive small group discussions are where rapport is most frequently developed. Any workshop can be a struggle, any facility can raise unexpected challenges, any team may fail to recognize what is happening. Each group has veteran members who can identify dangers and help a team move forward and who themselves are open to guidance.

And so the general meetings are mandatory. If someone misses two meetings, one or two members of their small group contact them and arrange to meet. If they miss three meetings, two members of the executive committee meet with them. The goal is to enable them to return to PCAP, to welcome and embrace them, not to castigate and purge. Recently an older member who had graduated from the MFA Program in Creative Writing and was working full time felt that the young members of PCAP had little to offer her. Three of her group members met with her, listened, urged her to think of herself as someone with a lot to offer to the membership. She came back, is now very engaged, and has taken on a new project which has everyone very excited.

If the absent member cannot attend or has a casual attitude toward the meetings, we ask them to leave PCAP. In these cases the workshop either closes — a situation we wish to avoid at all costs — or the other partner, permitted to go in alone for two sessions only,[2] must find another partner. This policy constantly has to face new challenges.

Other Policies

You cannot join PCAP without our formal training. If you come in without the benefit of the courses, you receive a PCAP host and mentor and are required to shadow two other workshops before you begin. Your partner may not be another new member. When outside guests come to your performance, you inform them about dress and behavior. If you have an incident, you immediately notify the PCAP leadership and, when appropriate, the authorities at the site. When you host formerly incarcerated youth (especially) and adults, no alcohol, no campus parties, and no identification of youth as formerly incarcerated. Because of the sensitivity of our work, we carefully review other organizations' requests for endorsement for participation in their activities. We decide what publications we will appear in[3] and have our own publication policy: we check in to be sure we haven't jeopardized our work and haven't been insensitive to the voices and experiences of the incarcerated. To avoid proliferation of group e-mail messages, information goes to the member in charge of the PCAP Weekly unless timing makes it necessary to get out a message immediately (and even then, we usually check in for approval).[4]

All PCAP policies derive from our mission and values. The youth and adults we work with need us to be responsible. We have a high turnover of university students who have many needs, situations, and issues: they need us to stay on top of things. They need our structure to bring them opportunities for leadership, personal and group power, creativity, community, and growth. We are eager for input from members and from the incarcerated. Our policies are both set and welcoming, both firm and open to discussion and revision.

Note: Additional resources and supplemental materials are available at www .digitalculture.org/books/is-william-martinez-not-our-brother. Additional information on the Prison Creative Arts Project can be found at www.lsa .umich.edu/english/pcap/.

NOTES

Introduction

1. This and the following description of public scholarship are based on the following texts: Harry C. Boyte, *Everyday Politics: Reconnecting Citizens and Public Life* (Philadelphia: University of Pennsylvania Press, 2004); Jeffrey C. Bridger and Theodore R. Alter, "The Engaged University, Community Development, and Public Scholarship," *Journal of Higher Education Outreach and Engagement* 11, no. 1 (2006): 163–78; Julie Ellison, "The Humanities and the Public Soul" in "Practicing Public Scholarship: Experiences and Possibilities beyond the Academy," ed. Kathryn Mitchell, special issue of *Antipode: A Radical Journal of Geography* 40, no. 1 (2008): 463–71; and Judith A. Ramaley, "Community-Engaged Scholarship in Higher Education: Have We Reached a Tipping Point?" presented at the Community-Engaged Scholarship for Health Collaborative Invitational Symposium, February 21–22, 2007. Available at http://web.uvic.ca/ocbr/assets/pdfs/community-engaged_scholarship.pdf (accessed February 2010). "Overemphasis on critique"—Ellison is quoting William Paulson (*Literary Culture in a World Transformed*); "arenas of deliberation" (which he criticizes when they are detached from work and government) is from Boyte, 66.

2. "Engagement agenda" comes from Bridger and Alter, "Engaged University," and is commonly used. Bridger and Alter mention D. C. Korten's discussion of enabling spaces. Boyte discusses free spaces, *Everyday Politics,* 60–62, 67, 85, 91. See my own advocacy of "creative spaces" in "Creating Spaces: Two Examples of Community-Based Learning," *Praxis I: A Faculty Casebook on Community Service Learning,* ed. Jeffrey Howard (Ann Arbor: OCSL Press, 1994, 41–56; in "Creating Spaces," *Praxis III,* ed. Joe Galura (Ann Arbor: OCSL Press, 1995), 161–73; and in "Creating Spaces at Western Wayne Correctional Facility," roundtable discussions by Western Wayne Correctional Facility staff and inmates and University of Michigan faculty and students, *Praxis III,* 297–321. Boyte and Ellison frequently talk about public goods.

Chairs in a circle—Boyte, 91, is here sharing a point made by Michael Kuhne. "High tolerance . . ." comes from Ellison in the original talk upon which her essay is based, as does "relentlessly multiple" (she is quoting David Scobey). See http://www.imag iningamerica.org/IApdfs/Ellison.HumanitiesPublicSoul.pdf (last accessed February 3, 2010).

3. Boyte, *Everyday Politics,* 67.

4. For Boyte and Ellison "public work" is a key phrase. "Connections across lines of difference" and "sense of ownership" are Boyte, *Everyday Politics,* 165. Public Achievement, Boyte, 186. Public Achievement exists in many states and abroad: see Boyte, 88ff.

5. Ramaley, "Community-Engaged Scholarship," np; Boyte on Imagining America, *Everyday Politics,* 175. From the Imagining America website: "Imagining America is a national consortium of colleges and universities committed to public scholarship in the arts, humanities, and design. Public scholarship joins serious intellectual endeavor with a commitment to public practice and public consequence."

6. See Stephen Hartnett, *Incarceration Nation: Investigative Prison Poems of Hope and Terror* (Walnut Creek, CA: Altamira Press, 2003) and Austin Sarat, *When the State Kills: Capital Punishment and the American Condition* (Princeton: Princeton University Press, 2001).

7. I was the only one who had invited my students to be part of the conference.

8. Of course civic engagement has not always been supported on every front, nor is it always supported now. It is often in tension with demands for more traditional scholarship, which is prioritized in tenure decisions.

9. I could go on and know I must be leaving people out. Other faculty members in the College of Literature, Science, and the Arts and in other schools and colleges were also breaking new ground. In my own department, English Language and Literature, Lemuel Johnson and Alan Wald from the early 1970s on brought to their courses new texts and voices and fought for inclusion of other traditions in our curriculum. Faculty in other disciplines were also pathfinding. PCAP is housed in English, where it has found my colleagues and chairs Sidonie Smith and Patsy Yaeger beyond supportive, which is true also of Dean Bryan Rogers of the School of Art and Design. For five years English and Art and Design picked up the yearly tab for our key administrative position and continue to financially support that position.

10. I mention here only those I have worked with most closely and who have been supportive of PCAP in deeply significant ways. They each deserve their own chapter for what they have brought to the University.

11. Undated letter (summer 2008) to the author from Gregory Taub.

12. Formerly the Neighborhood Arts Program National Organizing Committee, the Alliance for Cultural Democracy (1982–94) supported "community cultural participation," believed in "cultural pluralism," was committed to struggling "for cultural, political, and economic democracy in the United States," and argued that "the

most important initiatives for cultural democracy take place on a grass roots level in communities, neighborhoods, and among activist artists and other progressive cultural workers." "Cultural Democracy means that culture is an essential human need and that each person and community has the right to a culture or cultures of their choice; that all communities should have equitable access to the material resources of the commonwealth for their cultural expression; that cultural values and policies should be decided in public debate with the guaranteed participation of all communities; that the government does not have the right to favor one culture over another." *Cultural Democracy* 33 (1986). See Doug Paterson et al., *We Are Strong: A Guide to the Work of Popular Theatres across the Americas* (Institute for Cultural Policy Studies, 1983), 6–7, 195.

13. See my brief article "Muerte al Polio!," *Tonantzin,* July 1988.

14. Among my sources: Jorge A. Huerta, *Chicano Theater: Themes and Forms* (Ypsilanti, MI: Bilingual Press, 1982). *Theaterwork Magazine* ran from November–December 1980 to July–August 1983. Ross Kidd, "Popular Theatre and Popular Struggle in Kenya: The Story of the Kamariithu Community Cultural Centre," *Theaterwork Magazine,* September–October 1982, 47–59; "From Outside in to Inside Out; The Benue Workshop on Theatre for Development," *Theaterwork Magazine,* May–June, 1982, 44–48, 50–53; "From Outside in to Inside Out (Part II); "People's Theatre and Landless Organizing in Bangladesh," *Theaterwork Magazine,* January–February, 1983, 29–39. Paterson et al., *We Are Strong.*

15. William Alexander, *Film on the Left: American Documentary Film from 1931 to 1942* (Princeton: Princeton University Press, 1981).

16. See my article "Clearing Space: AIDS Theatre in Atlanta," *Drama Review* 34, no. 3 (1990): 109–28.

17. I quote him in my chapter on Everyday Theater in my unpublished manuscript, *More Verses to Write: or, Lost and Presumed Dead.*

18. Lillian Smith, *Killers of the Dream* (New York: W. W. Norton, 1994), 25, 27.

19. The figures on Holy Cross Children's Services (Boysville) are for 2007 (http://www.easyschoolssearch.com) and are from the Michigan Department of Education. NAACP, "Juvenile Justice Fact Sheet." The figures are for 2002–4; 58 percent were African American. Among youth in adult prisons, 75% are youth of color: http://naacp.org/advocacy/research/facts/Juvenile%20Justice.pdf. 40 and 20 percent: The Sentencing Project, "Facts About Prisons and Prisoners," http://www.sentencing project.org/doc/publications/inc_factsaboutprisons.pdf. On August 11, 2009, this URL was damaged; an alternative is http:cltlblog.wordpress.com/2009/04/06/facts-about-prisons-and-prisoners/. The statistics are for 2008 and the source is the Bureau of Justice Statistics.

20. Adam Liptak, "U.S. Imprisons One in 100 Adults, Report Finds," *New York Times,* February 29, 2008. Source for the article: "One in 100 Behind Bars in America 2008," Pew Center on the States' Public Safety Performance Project, February 2, 2008.

21. Boyte, *Everyday Politics,* 83–84, 49, 55, and 177.

22. Jonathan Kozol, *The Night Is Dark and I Am Far from Home* (New York: Simon and Schuster, 1990). In a talk at the Lensic Theater in Santa Fe in early 2008, Kozol called this his best book, because in it he had told the truth.

23. Paulo Freire, *Pedagogy of the Oppressed* (New York: Continuum International Publishing Group, 2007).

24. Myles Horton with Judith Kohl and Herbert Kohl, *The Long Haul: An Autobiography* (New York: Teachers College Press, 1998).

25. Words to that effect. This is from memory, since the film is not currently available for viewing anywhere.

26. Noam Chomsky, "The Responsibility of Intellectuals," *American Power and the New Mandarins* (New York: Pantheon Books, 1967), 323–66. His immediate context was the war in Vietnam.

27. Elie Wiesel, "An Appointment with Hate," *Legends of Our Time* (New York: Schocken Books, 1968), 131–42.

28. Horton, *The Long Haul,* 8.

29. J. M. Coetzee, *Age of Iron* (New York: Penguin, 1990). See particularly pp. 14, 131, 135–37, 143, 145.

30. Giles Whittell, "Welcome to Hell—Investigation—Corcoran State Prison in California," *The Times (London),* July 25, 1998. My other sources here are Mark Arax and Mark Gladstone, "State Thwarted Brutality Probe at Corcoran Prison, Investigators Say," *Los Angeles Times,* July 5, 1998, and the film *Maximum Security University,* produced by California Prison Focus. Unless otherwise cited, quotations are from Whittell (the quotation about "home boys" is from Tom Quinn, who was an investigator looking into a killing at the prison). Many thanks to Dawn Wilson and Nasha Vida for getting me to the sources.

31. Arak and Gladstone, "State Thwarted Brutality Probe."

32. This is Whittell's conclusion in "Welcome to Hell" and my own. The footage, broken down into slow motion and analyzed, can be seen in *Maximum Security University.*

33. Whittell, "Welcome to Hell."

Chapter One

1. For a full account, see the article Tom Philion and I wrote: "Students Support Fired Projectionists with Street Theater," *Labor Notes,* July 4, 1985, 4, 14.

2. At one point Mary told us about the death of Darlene Lake at the Huron Valley Women's Facility years before; I had her repeat it while I took notes, and we turned it into an action theater piece that we performed in two university classrooms, one of them taught by Susan Fair, a formerly incarcerated lifer who also earned a University of Michigan degree while in prison. While Susan lectured, suddenly five women

interspersed in the class began to gasp for breath while a heartbeat sounded on a drum in the back of the room. The five became just one woman, who stood, struggling for breath, while other women went to the wall and simulated pounding on their cell windows while—during shift change—no officers paid attention to Darlene's collapse in the yard. Officers had taken her asthma medicine the night before. The heartbeat stopped, two officers strolled over, a wheelchair was slowly brought out, and Darlene, already showing rigor mortis, was lifted into the chair.

3. O-33 is the major disciplinary ticket given women for what an officer determines is inappropriate, intimate touching of another woman. We were not doing such touching, of course, but the improvised scenes allowed for touching that might have been seen as problematic elsewhere in the prison. We didn't share this name for the group with anyone. It was during a discussion on October 13, 1991, that the women decided to name the group the Sisters Within Theater Troupe.

4. In this exercise, we determine a place, people choose roles, we place costumes and props on the floor, they choose from them and begin the improvisation. Sometimes we disrupt the action by handing notes to individual actors giving them unexpected instructions.

5. Cristina discusses this in her University of Michigan Ph.D. dissertation, Maria Cristina Y. Jose, "Women Doing Life Sentences: A Phenomenological Study," 1985.

6. In 1995, the Michigan Department of Corrections created a new policy that drastically reduced the number of visitors to Michigan prisoners (for instance, a child could visit only if a prisoner's name was on that child's birth certificate). Upon appeal, the United States Supreme Court upheld this policy. Before the policy change, I could arrive at a prison, put someone's number on the desk, and visit that person. Now everyone must fill out forms, and I am permitted to visit but one prisoner in the entire system. It eliminated one of my support roles. Mary Heinen: "I lived through this mess. It was awful. Some women were never able to visit with members of their families again, caused by the rules, death, separation, etc. Many were unable to visit with brothers and sisters they had previously seen. We went through a long grieving period. The trial and court proceedings were agony" (e-mail message, June 11, 2009). In a recent conversation, Department of Corrections Director Patricia Caruso gave me permission for one-time visits after gaining the warden's approval.

7. We later learned that the protagonist, played by one of the finest comic/serious actors we've seen, also had AIDS, which he had been keeping to himself. Later, we were able to help him get out of prison when he had been unfairly placed in quarantine.

8. Debra's father, Ken Goodman, had written an important book about holistic education, *What's Whole in Whole Language* (Portsmouth, NH: Heinemann, 1986).

9. Ralph's strategy to get it through (he wasn't sure how popular a "community service" course would be) was to give it the dignified name of Discourse and Society. If I think about it, I can see how that applies to what we do, but we call the course

by its subtitle, "The Henry Ford High School Project" (in 2009 "The Cooley High School Project") and know it simply as English 310.

10. The specifics of what had happened with the fathers are from memory and may not be totally accurate.

11. See Roberta Herter's University of Michigan Ph.D. dissertation, "Conflicting Interests: Critical Theory Inside Out," 1998.

12. The story of *Inside Out* and the interactive theater project that follows is told more fully in my article "Inside Out: From Inside Prison Out to Youth," *Drama Review,* Winter 1996, 85–93.

13. I am struck here by the lived situation that permits these great questions. Any of us coming into the prisons from outside—my students, myself—may be very curious about these matters, but, unless we are insensitive, we realize that a lot of trust must be established before we have a right to ask.

14. The University of Michigan Regents Award for Distinguished Public Service.

15. E-mail message, April 2007.

Chapter Two

1. Quoted by Marc Mauer, *Race to Incarcerate* (New York: New Press, 1999), 1.

2. Nkechi Taifa, "Laying Down the Law, Race by Race," *Legal Times,* October 10, 1994. Quoted by Mauer, *Race,* 118.

3. Mauer, *Race to Incarcerate,* 142–43.

4. Randolph N. Stone, "The Criminal Justice System: Unfair and Ineffective," paper presented at the Chicago Assembly on "Crime and Community Safety," November 19–20, 1992, 2–3. Quoted by Mauer, *Race to Incarcerate,* 134.

5. In writing this section, I am indebted to more writers and thinkers than I can name, though I will name some here, including some I don't cite: Nell Bernstein, *All Alone in the World: Children of the Incarcerated* (New York: New Press, 2005); Nils Christie, *Crime Control as Industry: Towards Gulags Western Style?* 2nd ed. (London: Routledge, 1994); Kozol, *The Night Is Dark;* Kozol, *Savage Inequalities: Children in America's Schools* (New York: HarperCollins, 1992), and *The Shame of the Nation: The Restoration of Apartheid Schooling in America* (New York: Crown Publishers, 2005); Terry Kupers, *Prison Madness: The Mental Health Crisis Behind Bars and What We Must Do About It* (San Francisco: Jossey-Bass, 1999); Mauer, *Race to Incarcerate;* Marc Mauer and Meda Chesney-Lind and the authors in their *Invisible Punishment: The Collateral Consequences of Mass Imprisonment* (New York: New Press, 2002); Jerome G. Miller, *Search and Destroy: African-American Males in the Criminal Justice System* (Cambridge: Cambridge University Press, 1996); Christian Parenti, *Lockdown America: Police and Prisons in the Age of Crisis* (London: Verso, 1999); and Bruce Western, *Punishment and Equality in America* (New York: Russell Sage Foundation, 2006). I am also indebted to all those who have

thought about the arts in prison and those who have committed to describing their world through art, to Judith Tannenbaum and the poets in her *Disguised as a Poem: My Years Teaching Poetry at San Quentin* (Boston: Northeastern University Press, 2000), to Bell Chevigny and the authors in her *Doing Time: 25 Years of Prison Writing* (New York: Arcade Publishing, 1999), and to all the authors, artists, and actors in Detroit high schools, Michigan juvenile facilities, and Michigan prisons whose work I have been allowed to take in and whose words in person have been among my teachers.

6. In 1999, Mauer (*Race to Incarcerate,* 1) wrote that the then (only) 1.2 million prisoners "represented a societal use of incarceration that was virtually unique by world standards."

7. Christopher Shea, "Life Sentence," *Boston Globe,* September 23, 2007.

8. The Sentencing Project, "Facts About Prisons and Prisoners," December 2007. This is "the highest reported rate in the world, well ahead of the Russian rate of 624 per 100,000."

9. Mauer, *Race to Incarcerate,* 4.

10. Adam Liptak, "To More Inmates, Life Term Means Dying Behind Bars," *New York Times,* October 2, 2005. "Indeed, in just the last 30 years, the United States has created something never before seen in its history and unheard of around the globe: a booming population of prisoners whose only way out of prison is likely to be inside a coffin." He points out that "almost 1 in 10" of the nation's prisoners "are serving life sentences."

11. Quoted by Shea, "Life Sentence."

12. This paragraph is an arrangement of Mauer's history in the third chapter of *Race to Incarcerate.* The statistics at the end of the paragraph are on p. 34.

13. Howard Croft (professor of urban studies at the University of the District of Columbia), "Whether or Not We Want It, They All Get Out," talk at the George Mason University Conference "Behind Bars: Prisons and Communities in the United States," March 30, 1996. He said, "I have fantasies as an African American of the police coming for me like the slave traders of old on the Gold Coast, not to put me in the cotton fields of Virginia, but in contemporary prisons."

14. Parenti, *Lockdown America,* 29–38.

15. Barry Bluestone and Bennett Harrison, *The Great U-Turn: Corporate Restructuring and the Polarizing of America* (New York: Basic Books, 1990), 92. Quoted by Parenti, *Lockdown America,* 39.

16. In 1983–84 my students and I made a video with Detroit's Locals Opposed to Concessions, an effort by progressive members of the UAW to resist what was happening.

17. This discussion is drawn from Parenti, *Lockdown America,* 38–44. "Swallowed by taxes": he is quoting George J. Church, *Time,* October 10, 1988.

18. Michel J. Crozier, Samuel P. Huntington, and Joji Watanuke, *The Crisis of*

Democracy: Report on the Governability of Democracies to the Trilateral Commission (New York: New York University Press, 1975), 113. The phrase is Huntington's.

19. Mauer, *Race to Incarcerate,* 12.

20. Parenti, *Lockdown America,* 46. The source from which he elaborates is Steven Spritzer, "Toward a Marxist Theory of Deviance," *Social Problems* 22 (1975).

21. Mauer, *Race to Incarcerate,* 1, 9–10.

22. In 1987, "Assistant Attorney General William Bradford Reynolds sent a memorandum to key leaders within the Justice Department, 'A strategy for the Remaining Months'; the memorandum proposed that the administration attempt to 'polarize the debate' on a variety of public health and safety issues—drugs, AIDS, obscenity, prisons, and other issues. Reynolds suggested that 'we must not seek "consensus," we must confront . . . in ways designed to win the debate and further our agenda.'" He "feared that . . . 'the voices of those who say we need fewer prisons and more "alternatives" to incarceration' would rise and advocated attacking by name those who took that position. 'Overall, of course, we must make the case that public safety demands more prisons.'" Mauer, *Race to Incarcerate,* 63. Media frenzy, Mauer, *Race to Incarcerate,* 171–77.

23. Parenti, *Lockdown America,* 47–48.

24. Parenti, *Lockdown America,* 50. Both Mauer and Parenti write thoroughly about these acts.

25. Parenti, *Lockdown America,* 57.

26. Mauer, *Race to Incarcerate,* 59. He adds: "Within a few years of their adoption, the guidelines provoked widespread criticism and dissent from those charged with implementing them, leading sentencing scholar Michael Tonry to describe them as 'the most controversial and disliked sentencing reform in U.S. history.'"

27. Parenti, *Lockdown America,* 57–60.

28. Mauer, *Race to Incarcerate,* 71, 169–79. Nearly $8 billion was for prison construction, $1.8 billion for incarceration of illegal aliens, $2.8 billion for policing. This Violent Crime Control and Law Enforcement Act also "eliminated the awarding of Pell grants for higher education to prisoners" and created incentives for states "to toughen penalty structures in order to qualify for funding" and "to increase prison terms through its 'truth in sentencing' provisions" (77).

29. Mauer, *Race to Incarcerate,* 74–75, 77.

30. Julie A. Hagstrom, Cedrick Heraux, Emily Meyer, Lori A. Post, and Kimiko Tanaka, "Measuring Disproportionate Minority Contact in the Juvenile Justice System: An Examination of the Michigan Relative Rate Index," University Outreach and Engagement, Michigan State University, submitted March 17, 2005, 7–9. After African Americans, Hispanics experience the most disproportionate contact ("Disproportionate Minority Contact," 9). http://www.michigan.gov/documents/DHS-dmc-appx-h-06-142986_7.pdf.

31. Hagstrom et al., "Disproportionate Minority Contact," 1.

32. "Easy School Search," Michigan Department of Education, 2007, http://www .easyschoolsearch.com/. I will be calling Boysville by this name. The proper name, given to it recently, is Holy Cross Children's Services, Boysville campus.

33. This was July 2006. In July 2008, Jerry wrote to tell me that he had been given parole. He felt the letters we and the PCAP Advisory Board wrote for him made the difference. When I tell historian Peter Wood about the court turning deaf when Jerry recounted his life before being taken from the mother of his baby and the baby, Peter tells me that he was hearing a slave auction.

34. William J. Sabol, Todd D. Minton, and Paige M. Harrison, "Prison and Jail Inmates at Midyear 2006," U.S. Department of Justice Office of Justice Programs, June 2007 (NCJ217675). See also the *Los Angeles Times* study showing that black crack cocaine users from 1988 to 1994 were charged in federal courts, where they received longer sentences than white users, who were charged in state courts. Mauer, *Race to Incarcerate*, 156.

35. "One in 100 Behind Bars in America 2008," Pew Center on the States' Public Safety Performance Project, February 2, 2008, http://www.pewcenteron thestates.org/uploadedfiles/8015PCTS_Prison08_FINAL_2-1-1_FORWEB.pdf (last accessed February 10, 2010).

36. Various sources for this paragraph. In addition to Mauer, *Race to Incarerate* and Parenti, *Lockdown America,* also Mauer and Chesney-Lind, *Invisible Punishment;* Christie, *Crime Control as Industry,* and Miller, *Search and Destroy.* The Detroit dropout rate: "Cities in Crisis; A Special Analytic Report on High School Graduation," EPE Research Center, April 1, 2008. The report was issued by America's Promise Alliance. Black urban youth: Western, *Punishment and Equality,* 29–30: "systematic incarceration . . ." is his quotation of David Garland, "Introduction: The Meaning of Mass Imprisonment," *Mass Imprisonment: Social Causes and Consequences,* ed. David Garland (London: Sage, 2001), 1. Bernstein, *All Alone,* 191. Glen C. Loury says we have created "a racially defined pariah class in the middle of our great cities . . . a racially defined nether caste" (*Race, Incarceration, and American Values* [Cambridge: MIT Press, 2008]). Mauer, *Race to Incarcerate:* "no other democratic nation bars ex-offenders from voting for life or keeps such a significant proportion of its citizens from voting as a result of a felony conviction" (187).

37. Mauer, *Race to Incarcerate,* 19, 198.

38. See Gary Hunter and Peter Wagner, "Prisons, Politics, and the Census," *Prison Profiteers: Who Makes Money from Mass Incarceration,* ed. Tara Herivel and Paul Wright (New York: New Press, 2007). The book is an excellent source for everything I mention in this paragraph, and much more.

39. Editorial, "Michigan Must Escape from Rising Prison Costs," *Detroit News,* April 17, 2008. See also Gary Heinlein and Charlie Cain, "Prison Costs on Agenda," *Detroit News,* May 2, 2008, available at http://www.capps-mi.org/prison%20costs %20on%agenda.htm.

40. Mauer, *Race to Incarcerate,* 111–13, 157.

41. Christie, *Crime Control as Industry,* 16.

42. There are numerous sources for this. I recommend David M. Oshinsky, *"Worse than Slavery": Parchman Farm and the Ordeal of Jim Crow Justice* (New York: Free Press Paperbacks, 1997).

43. Mauer, *Race to Incarcerate,* 198. Emphasis is mine.

44. For me this is equal to those senators who clearly understood what the Bush administration was doing yet voted nevertheless, for political reasons, to support his invasion of Iraq. They have a lot of blood on their hands.

45. Mauer, *Race to Incarcerate,* 92 (and on p. 55 he quotes sociologist Dario Melossi on the "general moral malaise of society"—"Gazette of Morality and Social Whip: Punishment, Hegemony, and the Case of the USA, 1970–92," *Social and Legal Studies* 2 [1993]: 266). Kozol, *The Night Is Dark,* especially chapters 1 and 2. Christie, *Crime Control as Industry,* 161–63 (Bauman's *Modernity and the Holocaust* [1989]).

46. Wiesel, *Legends of Our Time,* 189. Simon Wiesenthal, *The Sunflower: On the Possibilities and Limits of Forgiveness,* 2nd ed. (New York: Schocken, 1997), 57.

47. Jessica Mitford, *Kind and Usual Punishment: The Prison Business* (New York: Knopf, 1973). She ends her book with that question. Cited in Christie, *Crime Control as Industry,* 105.

48. Mauer, *Race to Incarcerate,* 116.

49. I use quotation marks here because I mean to generalize William Martinez: I know nothing of his particular childhood or family.

50. Peter Sacks, *Standardized Minds: The High Price of America's Testing Culture and What We Can Do to Change It* (New York: Da Capo Press, 1999), 7, 8, 201–20.

51. M. M. Matney, *First Year Student Survey 2006: Entering Student Profile* (2007). Summary data from the Cooperative Institutional Research Program (CIRP) (Ann Arbor: University of Michigan Division of Student Affairs).

52. Freire, *Pedagogy of the Oppressed,* 103–24 (but see all of chapter 3).

53. Another composite picture came out of a small-group discussion in English 411 and was shared with the class: a stark scene of a man alone behind bars, his head in his hands, and divided with forceful lines from that scene, a scene of a girl in a suburban yard playing with her dog. The separation is revealed in another way in an exercise I do in my English 239, a prerequisite course to the English concentration, the week before we read Jimmy Santiago Baca's *A Place to Stand* (New York: Grove Press, 2001). I ask the students to write on a piece of paper the image that comes to mind when they hear "prisoner." Each student then reads what he or she has written. With some important exceptions, the portrait is overwhelmingly as follows. A prisoner is male, scruffy, unclean, alone in a cell, either depressed and beaten down or violent and dangerous with no relation to loved ones or family, no talent, employability, or career. Generally the students avoid race, though my sense is that in their imagination, it breaks down fairly evenly between black and white. I should use the same exercise

in a juvenile facility or prison, asking for an image of an elite college student. In my prison film course, English 411, I bring in former prisoners early on. For three years—in a more enlightened and liberal time—wardens permitted me to carry out a video dialogue between 411 students and two lifers first at the Western Wayne and then at the Saginaw Correctional Facility; Romando Valeroso participated each time.

Chapter Three

1. It isn't always easy to remember where we got an exercise that we've used many times. I believe I learned this at a Theater of the Oppressed conference in Toronto.

2. This exercise I learned from Pregones during a workshop that was part of a collaboration with a group of citizens and Muhlenberg College in Allentown, Pennsylvania.

3. This is my variation on an improvisation I learned in a workshop with Robert Alexander. He paired us off as blind and sighted in an institution for the blind. At the end the director of the institution announced that government funding had been pulled and the institution would close that night. We had the final five minutes to negotiate what that meant.

4. I learned this conversation/acting exercise from John Malpede of the Los Angeles Poverty Department, in a workshop he led in Ann Arbor.

5. I have told the students that the journals are theirs. They are to write in them whatever relates to the course for them. Some restrict themselves to the workshops, texts, and discussion, while others range into politics, faith, family, friends, their own growth as group facilitators, as people. I am able to hear in the journals warning signs about workshops—although the students may not recognize them as such—and am able to respond in a way that prevents the problem from growing.

6. I am especially strong on all this, because, unfortunately, not all of our liaisons, including counselors, special activities directors, and even assistant deputy wardens, are as tough and clear in their orientations as they need to be.

7. This "telling on" is hard for students to contemplate. I explain that it is expected of us, for very good reasons. I add that if we don't do it, gossip among the youth will probably bring it to the counselor's attention and we will be in serious trouble for not reporting.

8. And the notebook should be left lying around, so that suspicious participants can assure themselves the team is not making personal observations.

9. There are many variations of Freeze. In one, two people start a dialogue, then a third person cries "Freeze" and they freeze in their positions; the third person then replaces one of them and starts an entirely new dialogue, based on the frozen positions. I don't know where I learned the next two. In Kitty Want a Corner, one person goes around the circle asking each person in turn, "Kitty want a corner?" and is told, "Go ask your neighbor." While this is happening any two people who meet

each other's eyes have to run and exchange places, and the first person tries to get in the spot one of them has vacated and that person becomes the person going around the circle. In Apples, Oranges, and Bananas, everyone sits in chairs in a circle, with one person in the middle. Everyone, including the person in the middle, is an apple, an orange, or a banana. The person in the middle tells a story, and when she says the word "orange," for instance, or any two or all three fruits, the people who are those fruits have to get up and find a new chair, while the person in the middle tries to capture a chair. The person left without the chair becomes the next storyteller. Bear and Woodcutters is the same as Augusto Boal's "the bear of Poitiers" in his *Games for Actors and Non-Actors* (London: Routledge, 1992), 79. Everyone except a person representing a bear is cutting wood. When the bear roars, all fall to the ground and play dead. The bear then moves around telling stories and making noises that may provoke individuals to laugh or wince or show signs of life. Once they do, they become bears and engage in the same practice until only one person remains.

10. Untitled booklet edited by Suzanne Gothard and Megan Shuchman, brief essays addressed to Buzz Alexander by his students and former students on the occasion of his receiving a 2005 Carnegie Foundation for the Advancement of Teaching and Council for the Advancement and Support of Education Professor of the Year Award (2006), 5.

11. Leslie Marmon Silko, *Ceremony* (New York: Viking, 1997); Elie Wiesel, "My Teachers," *Legends of Our Time*, 14.

12. Kozol, *The Night Is Dark*, 91–93. For the passage itself, go to chapter 10, pp. 267–68.

13. Raya Chyorny first told me of the "bone game" exercise, which I adapted. See Michael Brown, "The Bone Game: A Ritual of Transformation," *Journal of Experiential Education* 13, no. 1 (1990): 48–52.

14. Years ago I realized that if I learned group skills, I would be a better teacher. I asked my colleague Dick Mann from the Department of Psychology to form a group, which I advertised to my colleagues in the Department of English. A lecturer and several graduate students signed up and we met four hours a week for a semester. One of the most important things I learned from Dick was to listen for those who brought energy and need to the group and to make sure they got attention and to see where it led.

15. Helen Lewis, introduction to Horton, *The Long Haul*, xix–xx.

16. See discussion of this play in chapter 1. The statements in this paragraph are by Nate Jones and Romando Valeroso III.

17. Herbert Kohl in *36 Children* (New York: Penguin, 1988), 45: "I listened, hurt, bruised by the harshness of the children's world. There was no response, no indignation or anger of mine, commensurate to what the children felt. Besides, it was relief they wanted, pronouncement of the truth, acceptance of it in a classroom which had become important to them. I could do nothing about the facts, therefore my words

were useless. But through listening, the facts remained open and therefore placed school in the context of the children's real world." Also see p. 191.

18. See note 14 to this chapter. Dick, by example, also taught me to wait until my speaking would be grounded and authentic. This has served me very well.

19. In this class I asked if any of them had been taught by a "Kohl" in grade or high school. This question became a refrain for several weeks and in some of the journals throughout the term. Only one person could identify that she had been taught by a Kohl. Others had had remarkable classroom teachers who were very committed to them personally, but only she had had a teacher who wanted her to understand that she was in relation to others in ways that were political, economic, and troubling. Kohl in an noninsistent but vital way had brought that to his connection with the children.

20. Untitled booklet edited by Gothard and Shuchman (see note 10), 26.

21. They carried this out, with mixed results and much learning. In April 2007, when PCAP held its annual potluck dinner to say good-bye to seniors, Julia and Karen and others came back to that moment, that discussion, with Karen's sudden leadership and Julia's change as a key moment in their own growth and sense of possibility.

22. Many students from this class joined PCAP, and a number of them, including Karen, were key organizers in my English 411 (a film course on prisons) the following term. The students in that class, after struggling with each other, suddenly took on a number of activities, including a fast supporting Texas death row hunger strikers, guerrilla theater on prison issues in other classrooms, and two demonstrations in the middle of the campus Diag, one an acting out of an execution by lethal injection, the other a long line of chained-together orange-suited prisoners chanting figures about health care in Michigan prisons, with a petition to be signed by passers-by.

23. I sometimes ask my students what the incarcerated and urban youth and prisoners, if they really thought about it, would want from us. It is a hard question for them. Most focus inside the workshops and talk about the kind of people the participants would wish us to be as we interact with them. Some see that what they would want is that we take the plunge and fight for the justice so many of them have been denied.

24. Later, when the room was empty, she came back, to throw her coffee cup in the wastebasket, not wanting to litter, and told me, "I will never forget this class." Afterward she checked with her supervisor and was assured that her speaking in class had been, under the circumstances, appropriate (e-mail message from Kate, June 16, 2009).

Chapter Four

1. On May 16, 2007, I was able to watch a performance of Shakespeare's *The Tem-*

pest at the Racine Correctional Institution in Racine, Wisconsin. In the audience were family members of the performers, including their children. The interactions were very powerful and moving, and of course seeing their prisoners engaged in such a positive activity was very healthy for the family. We had similar beautiful interactions until the Michigan Department of Corrections eliminated this option for families in the 1990s.

2. In 1993 I took the video of *Junkie* to the homes of members of the Sisters Within Theater Troupe and was present while it was screened. The audience was glued to the screen, fascinated by the experience of seeing their family member engaged in a very positive activity and of knowing them beyond the visiting room and long-distance calls. Again, this was very healthy, and I regret that videotaping performances was stopped by Deputy Director Bolden. In the fall of 2008, we finally received permission to document our work again and began with the Sisters Within Theater Troupe's *Bodies on Slabs . . . We Can't Open the Door* in December. But we are not allowed to make the work accessible to family members.

3. I tell the story of *Y2K and the Wicked Stepmother* later in this chapter. In the other two, a warden required us to have word-by-word scripts; our response was to have the men at the Cooper Street Correctional Facility write monologues based on a common theme and memorize them. Each play then told a story through blocking, movement, and the sequence of monologues. The warden actually sat in on a rehearsal once, script in hand, making sure they didn't miss a word, which they didn't.

4. Our workshop is one small moment in an arduous, challenging week. Also, some staff see us as just one more student volunteer group coming in to provide recreational time, taking the girls off their hands for an hour and a half.

5. The presence of an officer or special activities staff person is required only in level 4 prisons.

6. The first scene we improvised for *Seasons* (July 1996) had a drug dealer tempting an athlete in front of his high school locker, a situation based on the experience of both actors. By the time we performed the play months later, at least three actors had replaced each of the original two, adding their own nuances to the roles.

7. In one case, in the late 1990s, we learned that one of the actors in the Western Wayne Players had attempted suicide. I wrote him a letter in which I did not acknowledge the attempt (since he may not have wanted me to know), but told him that whatever he was going through, he should remember what a positive space the workshop is for him. I also sincerely praised him for his acting, which was in fact excellent. He responded by returning to the workshop. Although the letter was strictly professional, about the workshop, now I would not send it on my own (since we are not supposed to communicate with prisoners in a facility where we are working). If I thought we had a liaison who would be sensitive about the suicide attempt, I would ask him or her to convey the letter. That way the decision would be

a professional decision by someone responsible within the facility. We have gradually learned the parameters of the permissible and have learned from our mistakes (see chapter 5).

8. See Jean Trounstine, *Shakespeare Behind Bars: One Teacher's Story of the Power of Drama in a Women's Prison* (Ann Arbor: University of Michigan Press, 2004) and for Kurt Tofteland's work the DVD *Shakespeare Behind Bars* (Act Now Productions, 2006). For Jonathan Shailor, see "Humanizing Education Behind Bars: The Theatre of Empowerment and the Shakespeare Project," *Empowerment or Incarceration? Reclaiming Hope and Justice from the Prison-Industrial Complex,* ed. Stephen Hartnett (Champaign: University of Illinois Press, 2010) and http://shakespeareprison project.blogspot.com/. For Agnes Wilcox, her website: prisonperformingarts.org.

9. Of course those working with texts have some of the same issues. In the recent performance of *The Tempest* at the Racine Correctional Institution, Jonathan Shailor took on a minor role to replace an actor who had transferred. The group had also scrambled when actors chose to leave the workshop part way through rehearsals. Luckily the population is relatively stable at Racine; many of the actors had performed in all three plays so far. Most remarkable, at least from our experience in Michigan, one prisoner was allowed to delay his going home and another his transfer to a lower-security prison until after the performance. I was extremely envious of that. For a while at Western Wayne, the deputy warden would put our participants on hold against being moved, but mostly no one asks if something important is happening for someone in a workshop, and prisoners are moved when the system determines.

10. In a dramatic scene lit with a strobe light, the grandmother leafs through a photo album and behind her the four deaths are enacted; a black-robed figure (her aborted son) in a Peruvian devil's mask (from Paucartambo) writhes over her shoulder.

11. In *Rico's Story* (February 1995), a play about how to get out of a gang, we had decided not to end the play with the ritual beating sometimes accompanying departure from a gang; it didn't work aesthetically and it wasn't the message we were trying to give; however, at the end of the second and last performance, the actors carried it out anyhow. Smitty, a Vietnam veteran who had aspired to medical school, loved to play a doctor. He would invent diseases and treatments while on stage and was loathe to leave the scene; finally another actor figured out what to do—he would don a lab jacket, come on stage, and tell Dr. Smitty he was wanted in emergency!

12. The women were being moved to the Western Wayne Correctional Facility in Plymouth (the lifers were sent to the Scott Correctional Facility, also in Plymouth, and so we lost Shar Wabindato for several years). The men from Western Wayne were dispersed, which ended my years of theater with men; when the women arrived in 2000–2001, we continued the Sisters there.

13. Normally we simply carry out leftover programs, but on this occasion we were

told we would have to manifest them out. I could have left them inside, but I was offended and decided to ask for the manifest. When I went back inside to get the official signature and programs, I was treated with such hostility that I had the very distinct sense that had I been in a death camp, the officers and captain would have been very happy to have me executed.

14. I originally learned this exercise in a Detroit workshop led by Robert Alexander of the Arena Theater.

15. Lauren Rubinfeld, term paper, English 319, April 2001.

16. Tait Sye, English 319 journal, February 1994. Tait is currently the media director for Planned Parenthood in Washington, DC (e-mail message, July 2, 2009).

17. Kozol, *The Night Is Dark*.

18. Our understanding was that Bolden had supported the exhibition in part because he had played basketball in a Grand Rapids Community Center established by Herschell Turner, who became the art instructor at the Ionia Maximum Facility, and a close associate of ours in shaping the exhibitions. The team won two championships in community competitions. Phone conversation with Herschell, July 1, 2009.

19. I am not totally sure of the timing. It is possible that she had called him before I was summoned to Lansing and that he intended to close down the workshops anyhow. The word got around and for years after, staff at various prisons mentioned the police wounding ("killing") we had permitted.

20. This and the following quotations are from English 319 journals. Of the PCAP associates in this group, Samarrah Fine in 2009 received her MSW and is "coordinating a network of homeless service providers and helping . . . homeless clients obtain housing" at a New York settlement house; Liz Grubb, now Liz Idris, in 2009 graduated from University of Maryland nursing school and is working on the cardiac floor at her local hospital; eight and one-half years ago Lee Shainis cofounded Intercambio, which has served 5,000 adult immigrants and trained over 2,000 volunteer English teachers, and much more. In two cases, I have not been able to reach former students, and so I have referred to them as "another student" when I quote from their journals.

21. Ryan was one of the facilities that had not noticed Bolden's directive and had done nothing to cancel the workshop.

22. We learned to shift "the couple fought," in a situation where the context made it clear they were merely arguing, to "the couple had a verbal altercation," and we learned to have shootings overheard, take place behind a screen, be described vividly by witnesses.

23. "The dance workshop focused on creative thinking and expression through movement. We worked on choreographing dances using improvisational movement exercises. For example, the participants would all pick three things they felt strongly about such as one thing they loved, one thing they hated, and one thing they feared.

They would make gestures to illustrate each of these words. This would form a short movement phrase, which would progress into a longer phrase as the participants shared their gestures and taught each other. When music is added a self expressive dance is created. The end result is participation in creative communication and expression through dance. We have done many different choreography and improvisation exercises, all focusing on creativity and communication. In the workshop we try to expand our ideas on what dance is, and move beyond what is seen everyday in music videos and dance clubs." Amy Martin, letter to Deputy Director Dan Bolden, March 24, 1999.

24. Judy Rice, letter to Dan Bolden, March 24, 1999.

25. Author's letter to Dan Bolden, March 29, 1999.

26. Letter from Julie Southwick to author, April 2, 1999. We actually began to take him up on the dance theory offer. We received permission to have such a class at Florence Crane, taught by two students from the School of Dance who had experience in English 319. We would show videos, have discussions, and have the women illustrate ideas by performing within the class dance movements and short dances. Because of the schedules of the two women and eventually because of the move from Florence Crane to Western Wayne, we never got beyond a couple of class sessions.

27. This quotation is from her English 319 journal.

Chapter Five

1. From a conversation at the time with Luella Burke, who was the first warden at the Baldwin Facility. The turnover rate of officers was high: they would train at Baldwin, then apply for higher-paying officer jobs in the state system. We know that youth sentenced to adult facilities have a higher rate of committing later crimes than youth sentenced to juvenile facilities. See the Campaign for Youth Justice, "Youth in Adult Prisons Fact Sheet," February 2005, http://www.act4jj.org/media/fact sheets/factsheet_26.pdf; and the MacArthur Foundation Research Network on Adolescent Development and Juvenile Justice and their book *The Changing Borders of Juvenile Justice: Transfer of Adolescents to the Criminal Court,* ed. Jeffrey Fagan and Franklin Zimring (Chicago: University of Chicago Press, 2000).

2. I have altered the punctuation and tightened a little, for the reader's sake; the content is not changed.

3. It has been as many as fourteen. Two prisons have closed and others are being consolidated into single prisons. If we traveled an hour and forty-five minutes, in summer 2009 we could reach twenty-six prisons and camps.

4. The confiscation, or forbidding, of costumes, including wigs and masks, is justified by the fear that prisoners will keep them and use them as disguises to escape. With 244 plays to our credit, this has never happened. It is probably very rare in gen-

eral and is very unlikely to happen with us, because of prisoner support and defense of our workshops.

5. My reading, what prisoners tell me, and the fact that I do not live or work in a prison means there is more to be said here, aspects I don't know. The messages the institution gives the incarcerated are different from those we get, if related in some ways.

6. See chapter 2, note 53.

7. Unpublished poems written in the Poet's Corner at Southern Michigan Correctional Facility, 2004.

8. In Susanna Moore's *The Big Girls* (New York: Knopf, 2007), 96, Captain Bradshaw says "corrections officers are the dentists of the law."

9. Here I am talking about oriented and trained students from English 310 and 319, Art and Design 310, and PCAP members. I am not describing students from other projects who are generally less well trained, who generally are getting pass/fail credits for participation, who are taking required lab courses, who enter in clumps, not in pairs or (now and then) trios, as we do, who are, on the whole, more naive and less well motivated. Generally we are seen with more favor by officers and liaisons, and yet . . .

10. See Sacks, *Standardized Minds*.

11. In Michigan, we can write to prisoners who have been transferred to other prisons and can write to prisoners in the prison where we have worked, as long as we have no plans to return to that prison.

12. Recently someone from the ACLU approached us to see if we would pass out in juvenile facilities and high schools material asking youth to identify situations in which they felt they were being misused, for the purposes of finding cases to litigate. Some members of our executive committee were enthusiastic and wished to participate. This would have jeopardized our work: no principal or head of a juvenile facility would accept us helping youth litigate against them. Wiser heads prevailed.

13. The word *Gestapo* kept popping into my mind as I watched, and still does. The student wasn't prosecuted, but the university imposed sanctions: one was a requirement that he come to my office and have me explain to him the effects of his action. Our talk left me mostly certain that he was not actually trying to bring drugs into the prisoners. But who knows?

14. A rule of thumb is always to consult with the special activities director or a corrections officer—if, for instance, an incarcerated youth or adult wishes us to carry anything out or, say, bring in educational materials. It puts the onus on the staff member, who is also able to make a professional judgment. We don't ask if it is a personal note from a prisoner or youth; we simply refuse the note and not involve staff. But if the workshop group has written a card as a thank-you to us at the end of a workshop, we ask staff. Failure to ask in one such case led to our being banned from the prison for three or four years because the special activities director was hostile.

It gave her the excuse she wished, and until she finally took another job, we were unable to persuade her superiors, who had to work with her, to overrule her and let us continue workshops at the facility.

15. We use this term sometimes in our communications when it serves our purposes. But normally we avoid it, because of our critique of volunteerism. Beginning with the Reagan and first Bush administrations, which were eliminating and scaling down social services, public officials began to put a great emphasis upon Americans as "volunteers," successfully obfuscating the effects of their economic practices in beleaguered communities. The money those administrations put into stimulating volunteerism gave opportunities to activists and took people into environments where they might be politicized, but generally the work was piecemeal, charitable, and without an economic or political perspective. Also see Boyte, *Everyday Politics,* 14–15, 57–58, 66–67.

16. E-mail letter from author to Christina Bates, January 18, 2006.

17. Letter to Assistant Deputy Warden Scott Nobles, February 28, 2002.

18. It was an unprecedented, and clearly risky practice, for them to be waiting until the bubble to ask. They should have asked either the special activities director or officer while they were in the room. Vanessa, a PCAP associate, has worked in the nonprofit sector for twelve years and is currently the development director of an adult literacy program. Kristal is a high school teacher.

19. I was disappointed not only because the experience of performing is so important to the participants, but because our work represents resistance to circumstances and is an important lesson for both prisoners and PCAP members and students: no matter what happens, no matter how we are treated, we step up and perform and perform with exuberance.

20. Anna is now a writer, journalist and teacher in Detroit, mentoring a formerly incarcerated girl in PCAP's Linkage Project. Her partner asked not to have her name used.

21. The National Advisory Board was formed in 1999–2000 and had its first meeting in May 2000. All of these people have been remarkable guides, friends, and collaborators. Pam in 2001 was named Warden of the Year by the American Corrections Association. Warden Millie Warden replaced Luella on the National Advisory Board in 2005 and in 2009 was also named Warden of the Year.

22. Hannah Arendt's study of this phenomenon, which can appear anywhere and which can be widespread and indirect (through toleration of oppressive behavior by others) is suggestive and helpful. She says Eichmann "merely . . . never realized what he was doing." She is fascinated by "the strange interdependence of thoughtlessness and evil," distinguishes "sheer thoughtlessness" from "stupidity," discusses the self-deception "normal people" are subject to, the relation of "normalcy" and "orders," and analyzes the role that "language rules" and convenient "stock phrases" (what many call consensual language) play in the banality of evil. *Eichmann in Jerusalem: A*

Report on the Banality of Evil (New York: Penguin, 1994), 25, 26, 48–49, 52, 55, 85–86, 287–88.

23. I am always haunted by Tarrou's observation in *The Plague* that all of us are plague-stricken and murderers: "Yes Rieux, it's a wearying business, being plague-stricken. But it's still more wearying to refuse to be it . . . All I maintain is that on this earth there are pestilences and there are victims, and it's up to us, so far as possible, not to join forces with the pestilences." He adds a third category, true healers, but one doesn't "come across many of them." He "decided to take, in every predicament, the victims' side, so as to reduce the damage done." Albert Camus, *The Plague* (New York: Alfred A. Knopf, 1957), 222–30.

24. George Steiner, *Language and Silence: Essays on Language, Literature, and the Inhuman* (New York: Atheneum, 1974), ix.

25. Wiesel, "An Appointment with Hate."

26. Lorna Dee Cervantes, "Poem for the Young White Man Who Asked Me How I, an Intelligent, Well-Read Person Could Believe in the War Between Races," *Emplumada* (Pittsburgh: University of Pittsburgh Press, 1981), 35–36.

27. The programs deputy overruled the warden who was trying to eliminate our workshops. It worked, but I wouldn't do that now. Later the warden put up obstacle after obstacle. Three PCAP members, Samarrah Fine, Nadja Hogg, and Colleen Urban, had, with PCAP advice, agreed to every restriction and continued to do creative work compatible with PCAP methods and values. He finally just eliminated them, saying the prison had no time for our workshops. They were so disillusioned that they left PCAP, vowing to do prison reform work and organizing on the outside. Two of them are PCAP associates; one worked for a while in New York with women in prison. See chapter 4, note 3 for his requirement of word-by-word scripts at another prison.

28. While I have become an expert troubleshooter and in the most difficult moments can sometimes enjoy the excitement of figuring it out, working together with corrections staff and saving our workshops or the exhibition, there are times I can't handle it. In the twenty years of PCAP I have twice hung up on assistant deputy wardens for programs, both times because they were lying in order to prevent workshops from existing or advancing. I remember an assistant special activities director perched on a table during a poetry reading, glowering, hostile, judgmental, dampening the spirit of the occasion, watching for what he imagined would be violations. He had already come down on one of the two very professional young women he was trying to eliminate. I might have been able to greet him and be friendly, had he shown any propensity to acknowledge me, but I'm not sure. I risked a long letter to the warden (who was one of our advocates), documenting and identifying this man's behavior toward our female members and in the end had no success. The warden backed his staff, while offering the two women a chance to reapply to work there. Neither wished to do so, because the treatment they had experienced had been so painful.

29. Eric in 2007 was in his fourth year teaching high school in St. Louis. He reported the following in the May 2007 *PCAP Associates Newsletter* (vol. 5, no. 1): "This past winter, Eric successfully organized the North St. Louis City community to fight his school district's decision to cut music programs from its middle schools. After three long months, the district administration reversed that decision, and is now preparing to hire 11 new music teachers to fill previous vacancies. The superintendent, however, has reportedly taken to referring to music as 'the M word.' Meanwhile, Eric is happy to report that he is back in prison, volunteering with St. Louis Prison Arts and facilitating three music workshops at the Hogan Regional Youth Center in St. Louis. May 21 will mark the culmination of a year's work, and workshop participants will present original group compositions ranging from drum pieces to songs and semi-comprehensible avant-garde sound . . . things." In 2008–9 he was studying urban education at Teachers College, Columbia University, and was in 2009 directing Columbia University's Global Initiative for Social Change Through the Arts.

Chapter Six

1. This section is excerpted (and slightly revised) from an article by Janie Paul and myself: "This is our bridge . . . and we built it ourselves," *Michigan Independent,* March 19, 2007, 8–9.

2. In 2007 we visited forty-two prisons. At that time there were around fifty prisons and camps and the prison population was near its peak of over 51,000 prisoners.

3. In his letter supporting our proposal for an NEA Access Grant, Danny wrote, "The annual exhibit has literally brought families closer together. . . . I had not seen, or heard, from my mother for fifteen years. And while watching the video from the Fifth Annual Exhibition of Art by Michigan Prisoners, I had seen my mother and my sister (who I had [also] not been in contact with for fifteen years) there in the crowd of other prisoners; family members who had attended the exhibit. I don't think that words can begin to explain how elated I was—and still am." Letter to the National Endowment for the Arts, May 31, 2000.

4. I don't have Tony's original letter, but I refer to it and what I said in a letter to him in an undated early March letter, 1996.

5. Actually, the work from Mid-Michigan Correctional Facility in St. Louis was brought over to us at Ionia Maximum Facility. Now, with the addition of two more prisons in St. Louis, we regularly go through St. Louis as part of a three-day swing through the middle of the state.

6. Currently Herschell is teaching fine arts at the West Michigan Center for Art and Technology in Grand Rapids. The Center is a nonprofit after-school program that works directly with inner-city schools. Two of his students have won scholar-

ships to Kendall College of Art and Design. He says he is doing the same work he was doing at Ionia Maximum Facility.

7. We notified them by phone if the work had been sold. When the exhibition came down, I drove the art that had not been picked up all over Michigan, into remote rural areas and into the hardest heart of our cities. I did this for several years, but others now drive the work—and we mail a lot of it (there is so much work now)—and it is an aspect of the work that I miss greatly. I learned a lot about my home state, and I was welcomed into homes, told stories, brought positive news that helped with family relations and visits, and had my picture of the effects of massive incarceration rounded out and filled in. It is worth noting here that we do not mail or deliver art unless the contact has responded to our original letter, telling us they wish to have the art.

8. Our flier: "This work is a small version of Adeline Kent Award winning installation artist Richard Kamler's October 1996 installation on Alcatraz Island." "A provocative, complex, visceral . . . call to action," the Alcatraz version will consist of a long narrow table of lead and gold leaf bisected by a vertical sheet of glass, "much like in a non-contact prison visiting room." "Ten seats are on both sides of the table. In front of each seat is a phone. Pick up a phone on one side of the table and hear the voice of a parent of a murdered child telling her story. Pick up the phone on the other side and hear the voice of the perpetrator telling his story. These voices seek a common ground; a context for communication and healing to occur." Richard gave a talk about the installation and his Search Light Project on February 21.

9. It has not always been easy to get an art workshop into the Scott Correctional Facility, but Janie Paul was able to facilitate one for a year. Before the Western Wayne Correctional Facility closed in 2004, we often had an art workshop there. Before Camp Brighton closed in 2007, we had a workshop there for one semester. We presently have one at Women's Huron Valley Correctional Facility. There is much more participation by women now.

10. In 2009 the typed single-spaced responses reached twenty-three pages.

11. The video we send each year is now much more elaborate—the opening reception is much more of an event with more celebration, the technology for recording the images has improved, and the art is accompanied with voice-over identification. Beginning with the Fourth Annual Exhibition in 1999, Matthew Schmitt, a PCAP associate who worked in juvenile facilities and prisons during his time at the University, has provided his improvised jazz piano music for the video. Twice a personal message from him to the artists has appeared at the end of the video.

12. *Doing Time, Making Space: 10 Years of the Annual Exhibition of Art by Michigan Prisoners* (catalog has no page numbers).

13. This grant goes to organizations that provide access to the arts to people normally denied such access. The University nominated PCAP for the grant and provided matching funds. In 2005, the University also successfully nominated me

for a Carnegie Foundation for the Advancement of Teaching and Council for the Advancement and Support of Education Professor of the Year Award. Any money I make from awards or speaking engagements goes to PCAP.

14. Subsequent speakers have included Bill Ayers, Jimmy Santiago Baca, Ellen Barry, Bell Chevigny, Bernardine Dohrn, Liz Fink, Lenny Foster, Stephen Hartnett, Michael Keck, Lateef Islam, Phyllis Kornfeld, Terry Kupers, Dorsey Nunn, Tony Papa, Christian Parenti, Sister Helen Prejean, Beth Richie, Raul Salinas, and Edmond Taylor. Every year formerly incarcerated artists talk about prisoner art, and family members of incarcerated people talk about the experience of having loved ones in prison. We have panels, with formerly incarcerated people, on prisoner-reentry and parole, and panels on the death penalty, mandatory minimums, prisoner health and mental health, the Michigan Battered Women's Clemency Project, restorative justice, and much more. Most years we have a YouthSpeak, where Detroit high school and Michigan incarcerated youth speak with each other about issues affecting them.

15. During the Fourteenth Annual Exhibition of Art by Michigan Prisoners, we held a special reception for Lionel, who had recently come home, and in June 2009 he joined our Advisory Board. The year before we held a similar reception for Billy Brown, who had been in every exhibition.

16. The artist later wrote to us that he was called to the Control Center and asked to destroy his work, but he refused to do so.

17. The letter from Norma Killough is no longer in the PCAP Archives, though the quotation from it is exact. Letter from Dan Bolden, June 13, 2002.

18. In fact, I learned later that when Patricia Caruso, then a regional prison administrator, received a copy of the letter, she put it in her briefcase to take with her to Lansing, intending to "find out what this was all about."

19. The other fallout was that when the Department reviewed the exhibition after it was "reinstated," they chose to end our practice of giving monetary awards to first-place winners chosen by judges. We are not sure why: perhaps the accounting became too complex. We have continued to give ribbons.

20. In 2007 there was one such comment out of 338 comments, none in 2009. I always eliminate the comment from the packet—the artists already know about public dislike for them and often address it in their evaluations. For example, an artist in 2007, answering a question about the usefulness of the critiques individual artists get from Art and Design faculty and students, wrote: "The critiques are wonderful. It still amazes me to read them, they are so positive. Prison is a very negative place and we expect that, your critiques show us that the world is not against us, that you believe in our abilities—for that we are grateful." For several years we asked whether the artists thought the exhibition broke stereotypes; they rated us high on that, but it was our lowest rating—the responses were skeptical.

21. Letter from Julie M. Southwick on behalf of Bolden, March 31, 2000 (she

enclosed pages 18 and 19 of *DOCS/TODAY*, March 2000; letter replying to Southwick, May 1, 2000.

22. The pseudo-artist priced the work much too high and it hadn't sold. The artist concerned notified us, and I can't remember the steps we took; I believe the artist decided to let it go.

23. This hasn't totally solved the problem. A couple of years later the artist in question continued to submit his work under other names. We asked for an investigation and were proven correct: he and his collaborators were told officially to never submit again.

24. Letter to the Michigan Council for Arts and Cultural Affairs, supporting our application for a grant, April 21, 1997.

25. Evaluation statement, Twelfth Annual Exhibition of Art by Michigan Prisoners, 2007.

26. Letter to the author, April 14, 2007. Beth Tuckerman, special activities director at Parr Highway Correctional Facility, in a long letter to the National Endowment for the Arts supporting our application for an Access Grant, in a section about the plays, writes: "One particular participant who was viewed by others as introverted and shy has now participated in four productions. He is currently a trained facilitator for our Smoking Cessation program and assists me in teaching classes of inmates how to 'kick the habit.' Three years ago I would never have envisioned that he would volunteer to stand up in front of a group, let alone, be a leader. I can only attribute the positive development of this individual to the theater workshops." June 5, 2001.

27. Letter to author, May 27, 2008. His mother is Heidi Crisi.

28. Letter to the National Endowment for the Arts, May 31, 2000.

29. Letter to the author, June 2007 (he did not give the letter a specific date).

30. Letter to Mumford, July 7, 2007. See my "Summer 1998: Blue Pattern in a Paper Bowl," *EPOCH* 51, no. 1 (2002): 116–27.

31. I have a particular case in mind here.

32. *Doing Time, Making Space*, n.p.

33. *Doing Time, Making Space*, n.p.

34. A great example of this is Jimmy Santiago Baca's autobiography, *A Place to Stand*, especially pp. 222–27, 236–45.

Chapter Seven

1. E-mail message from Gillian Eaton to author, November 28, 2007.

2. The student was African American, herself victim of a crime.

3. June 14, 2007.

4. See my essay, "A Piece of the Reply: Eighteen Years of the Prison Creative Arts Project," in Hartnett, *Empowerment or Incarceration?*

5. Gillian Eaton used process drama method to direct this play, drawing on inter-

views we did with each other and on stories and poems we wrote. We performed in Ann Arbor, Birmingham, Detroit, Flint, and Plymouth. The performance ended with the four formerly incarcerated actors stepping forward and saying to the audience, "Can we talk now?"

6. He never repaid, although when he baked Janie's and my wedding cake in 2007, he contributed the labor as his gift. He has taken a few jobs with benefits along the way, most recently with a car dealership, but he always leaves to pursue his goal full time.

7. Wendell Berry, *The Hidden Wound* (New York: North Point Press, 1989), 19.

8. Much of Michael's material for this play came from his early visits to Ann Arbor, where we arranged for him to visit prison and youth workshops and talk with the participants. Michael toured the country with *Voices in the Rain,* which is a powerful multimedia performance composed of monologues and original music and usually followed by a community conversation. He performs individual monologues in various settings, including prisons.

9. We have had a few, great portfolio projects at Cooley High School and Catherine Ferguson Academy and one portfolio project in a prison. We would love to have the resources to expand in the direction of the prisons.

10. *PCAP Associates Newsletter* 5, no. 2 (December 2007). In the past Maxey had not allowed boys to come off campus, but this was the second year in which the boys were actually permitted to come to the exhibition of art by incarcerated youth and speak and perform. We are not certain how the photo was taken; it would not have been with the collusion of Kate or the Maxey staff who accompanied the boys. They were all aware of the confidentiality stipulations. Whoever took the photo gave Kate the copy. Kate entered Northeastern School of Law in the fall of 2009.

11. Portfolio more than provided the challenge. "The work of recruiting, troubleshooting, setting up and facilitating orientations, responding to substantial journals, meetings, arranging and attending performances, facilitating transportation, and doing a lot of the technical errands necessary for a program that was, for the first time, an academic one (including setting credit up with the university, evaluating and—unfortunately—grading portfolio participants)—it demanded a lot of time, heart, and patience." Working closely with the university students, she learned that "there is nothing more powerful than to be witness to another person's transformation, and for most of the Portfolio interns, I saw nothing less." From an e-mail message from Anna to me, December 2, 2007.

12. This is not the girl's real name.

13. From an e-mail message from Anna to me, December 2, 2007. She echoes at the end Chris Lussier's revelation, that all of us, whatever our background, are missing something and we enter these creative spaces to find it. See the first epigraph to chapter 4 and subsequent discussion in that chapter.

14. This is not the girl's real name.

15. From Sari's term paper, written for Janie Paul. Sari in 2009 is PCAP's coordinator of membership and special projects.

16. The amount for the mentee rose to $500 in 2007.

17. In the January 2004 meeting, mentees defined the role of mentor: listening, alert, interested, active, honest, understanding, empathetic, and caring. They asked for linkage improvements: clear expectations at the outset, assistance navigating the local art world, more opportunities for exhibitions and readings, forthright, honest communication with the mentor, personal boundary setting by the mentor, and quarterly informal area meetings. From PCAP they asked for more regular communication, a linkage website and e-mail chat room (although so few mentees had Internet access), and for assistance finding updated transitional services. It was a lot and asked a lot, but the meeting was rich, energetic, and forward-looking. The outside experts were very encouraging, and Linkage and Portfolio were stimulated.

18. James Ben, Lessie Brown, Mary Heinen, Jerry Moore, Tracy Neal, Lionel Stewart, and India Sullivan. Anthony James, one of our first two former artists on the Advisory Board (Tracy was the other), was never a mentee.

19. In 2005, Leo Lalonde, spokesman for the Michigan Department of Corrections, said "we needed to get out of Western Wayne because it was on a landfill" (Joseph Kirschke, "Hard Time; Hundreds of Complaints Filed by Huron Valley's Women Prisoners," *Detroit Metro Times*, March 3, 2005). A 1994 Rouge River Remedial Action Plan Update rated the Western Wayne site at 33 out of a possible 48 (the highest) on its clean-up priority list and noted that "the cleanup plan was not approved by the MDNR and interim response activity has been, or is being, provided by state funds." http://www.epa.gov/grtlakes/aoc/rougeriv/1994_Rouge-River-RAP-Update.pdf. Some of what I report is word-of-mouth from prisoners at Western Wayne.

20. E-mail message, December 9, 2007. It shouldn't pass notice that not only were men and women incarcerated in these prisons (men at Western Wayne until 2000), but that other men and women came there to work forty hours a week and more.

21. According to a September 2006 Justice Department report, "56 percent of jail inmates in state prisons and 64 percent of inmates across the country reported mental health problems within the past year" (Bernard E. Harcourt," "The Mentally Ill, Behind Bars," *New York Times*, January 15, 2007, A19). Since returning citizens need to hold jobs, reintegrate with families, control tendencies to addiction and previous patterns of behavior, this is the most challenging and primary issue to address, according to Mary King, of the Washtenaw County Michigan Prisoner Re-entry Initiative.

22. See Terry Kupers's remarkable *Prison Madness*.

23. Bernstein, *All Alone*, 182–83. See also Craig Haney, "The Psychological Impact of Incarceration: Implications for Post-Prison Adjustment," paper commissioned by U.S. Department of Health and Human Services, for project titled "From Prison to Home: The Effect of Incarceration on Children, Families and Communities," 2001.

24. Letter to author, November 9, 2007.

25. Bernstein, *All Alone,* 182–83. The citation is from Judith Herman, *Trauma and Recovery* (New York: Basic Books, 1992), 74. See also Jimmy Santiago Baca's description of his prison years in *A Place to Stand.*

26. Devah Pager, *Marked: Race, Crime, and Finding Work in an Era of Mass Incarceration* (Chicago: University of Chicago Press, 2007).

27. See Western, *Punishment and Equality,* chapter 1. See my discussion of this in chapter 2.

28. Bernstein, *All Alone,* 148–49, 152–53, 155–56.

29. See chapter 2.

30. According to William J. Sabol, Todd D. Minton, and Paige M. Harrison in their U.S. Department of Justice Office of Justice Programs' publication "Prison and Jail Inmates at Midyear 2006," "the number of parole violators who were revoked and returned to prison increased by 14.1%. During 2005, the number of new court commitments increased at a lower rate (2.5%) than the number of returned parole violators (6.0%)" In Michigan, "the proportion of parolees returned to prison for technical parole violations doubles from 9.2% in 1984 to 18.3% in 1989, then drops back to 13.3%," and "in 2000, 40.6% of the entire parolee population has either been returned to prison for a technical violation or sent to a Technical Rule Violator Center." In 2001 the proportion of prisoners "serving beyond their parole eligibility date is 44%, or 20,784 prisoners." Citizens Alliance on Prisons & Public Spending, "Prison Expansion in Michigan—a brief history," http://www.capps-mi.org/history.htm.

31. In late 2007 a formerly incarcerated woman came to a clinic in Santa Fe, New Mexico, needing a $60 test in order to receive proper treatment. She could not afford it. The doctor haggled with the front desk and got permission to charge only $30. The woman still could not afford the test and went without it. (Told to me by Dr. Raya Chyorny.)

32. See Chapter 2, section titled "The Members of Congress did not state . . ."

33. Canadian documentary, *Sentencing Circle—Traditional Justice Reborn* (46 minutes), produced, written, and directed by Doug Cuthard and Vicki Hunter Covington, 1995. Filmwest Associates distributes the film in VHS and DVD.

34. This was a wonderfully appropriate collaboration for PCAP, given the number of incarcerated returning to Detroit and the number of neighborhoods affected by United States and Michigan incarceration policy. Founded in 1968 by Fr. William T. Cunningham and Eleanor M. Josaitis in response to the divisions and bitterness the 1967 Detroit riots brought to light, Focus: HOPE's "programs include a food program for eligible mothers, children and senior citizens; education and training in information technology, manufacturing and engineering; community arts programs; community and economic development initiatives; a manufacturing operation; children's day care and education; conference facilities; and volunteer and outreach

activities" (Focus: HOPE website). It was a privilege and honor to be welcomed into an institution that has fought for four decades for civil and human rights.

35. Because I was on sabbatical and not in town, I missed the opening, so much of this is from Mary Heinen's excellent report. I visited the gallery with Mary in early December.

36. Two potential mentees were invited to do spoken word, but both canceled. Katherine Weider's new documentary, *Acts of Art: The Prison Creative Arts Project,* received a special screening at the opening. One of the spoken word performers, phoenix Moore, joined PCAP, did a workshop at Vista Maria, and in 2008 became our coordinator of exhibitions and development.

37. The mentees were Thom Baxter, Lessie Brown, David Elliott, Marlon Lucas, and Anthony White. Coordinator Mary Heinen, a former mentee, displayed her macramé and hand-strung necklaces. Three mentors also exhibited: Tony Bacon, Donna Hiner, and Betty Price.

38. My report on this discussion comes from the minutes of the meeting and from the report of the meeting sent out to advisory board members.

39. Phil is one of a number of special activities directors—Christina Bates, Pete Kerr, Beth Tuckerman, Bobbie Waldron, and Kay Williams are among the others we have worked with most closely—who have understood and on occasion fought for PCAP and other programs in the prisons. It takes someone with special qualities to do this work.

40. E-mail message, June 9, 2008.

41. E-mail message, July 1, 2008.

Chapter Eight

1. The full story of this crisis is told in chapter 4 in the section titled "Crisis."

2. We didn't use the petitions (we would have added signatures from the community and university), because we were successful through Smith and Wilbanks.

3. I learned from the special activities director at the Huron Valley Men's Correctional Facility that she had told this to the warden there. I'm guessing that she called Dan Bolden with the same alarming message.

4. E-mail message from Janie Paul, "the meeting regulars," and me to pcapsummer@umich.edu, June 26, 1999. PCAP Archives.

5. PCAP Archives, which also have the original draft. The "revised draft" from which I quote is a remarkable document about the organization. I have included it in its entirety in the appendix, along with the single sheet we signed.

6. We had members sign that fall, but didn't continue the practice.

7. This workshop, facilitated by Katy Geary and a number of partners over the next years, was very successful: we maintained cordial relations and attended each other's readings.

8. August 30, 1999.

9. PCAP associates are former PCAP members. See chapter 10.

10. We had no clergy, which we have since remedied, and no one with a lot of money who could easily tap others with money, which we have not remedied! Since 1999 some members have retired from the board. Julie Ellison has been replaced by faculty members Pat Gurin and Patsy Yaeger; Luella Burke has been replaced by Millie Warren of the Thumb Correctional Facility; we have not replaced Marlys Shutjer with another juvenile facility director. We have also asked some inactive members to step down, while continuing to seek their advice. Chiara and Matt have remained, and we have added former PCAP administrators, now associates, Suzanne Gothard, Emily Harris, Rachael Hudak, and Jesse Jannetta. Chiara cofounded Maine Inside Out, which works in the arts with incarcerated and formerly incarcerated people; Matthew is city director for DOOR Hollywood, managing a group of yearlong missionaries living in an intentional community and serving both their neighbors and the community at-large by working for various homeless and poverty relief agencies; Suzanne is a graduate student at the Berkeley School of Public Welfare; Emily works for Free Battered Women in San Francisco; Rachael works with a progressive literacy nonprofit, Literature for All of Us; when Jesse left the job after two years, he went on to acquire a masters in public policy at Harvard's Kennedy School of Government, then worked as a research specialist for the newly established Center for Evidence-Based Corrections in California, working with Joan Petersilia and the California Department of Corrections and Rehabilitation, and is now with the Urban Institute in Washington, DC. Joe Summers of the Episcopal Church of the Incarnation and member of the Washtenaw County Michigan Prisoner Re-Entry Steering Committee is our second clergyperson. Our greatest retention difficulty is with former prisoners: two have either disappeared or become inactive (Lateef Islam and Edmond Taylor of the Fortune Society), we asked two inactive members to step down, and two returned to prison. We originally planned either to add *currently* incarcerated individuals or to have a number of them serve as a secondary Advisory Board. Bill Lovett advised us against these options: under Bolden the Michigan Department of Corrections might resent us giving them such positions. Later, when one Advisory Board member returned to prison, we kept him on and stayed in regular contact. Currently two former prisoners are on the advisory board: Jason Rios and Lionel Stewart.

11. Pilar also taught English 319 and 310 that year while I was on sabbatical. She is now a Ph.D. candidate in the University of Michigan School of Social Work.

12. For the current situation of Jesse, Suzanne, and Rachael see note 10 above.

13. For a brief description of PCAP's structure and policies, go to the appendix.

14. In the winter term 2008 we had a membership of sixty-one. Thirty-five members graduated or for other reasons did not return in the fall. In the winter term 2009, twenty of fifty-five graduated (the latter number includes myself and staff).

Chapter Nine

1. They had a very disruptive group. When a strict disciplinarian staff member who was suddenly assigned to them identified the boys' behavior as a security problem and called in security, Nan, Elise, and the boys were stunned. At the end of that session, our liaison told Nan and Elise the terrible things that had happened to the boys and the terrible things some of them had done. With the liaison's support and Nan and Elise scrambling, the boys had a play to perform at the end.

2. Becky planned to do a workshop in PCAP in the fall of 2009; she had already done two portfolio shows. Christopher planned to join PCAP in the fall, as did Hannah. Corey planned to take English 310 in the fall, then join PCAP in the winter. As it turned out, Hannah and Corey's commitments led them elsewhere.

3. The Detroit drop-out rate: "Cities in Crisis; A Special Analytic Report on High School Graduation," EPE Research Center, April 1, 2008. The report was issued by America's Promise Alliance, http://lists.isber.ucsb.edu/pipermail/lmresearch/2008-April/000673.html.

4. The workshop members and their prison audience were at Camp Valley, one step from going home into a tough world.

5. Not his real name.

6. See chapter 3, final section.

7. See Mike Davis's devastating study, *Planet of Slums* (New York: Verso, 2006).

8. *The Sorrow and the Pity* (1969) is situated in Clermont-Ferrand. The film is currently not distributed in the United States.

9. In 2007 Judge Marianne Battani of the Eastern District of Michigan ordered the parole board to review all parole-able life cases they had turned down since October 1, 1992, since they had applied "life means life" criteria to individuals who had been sentenced under different expectations. In July 2009, this is still being litigated and monitored, with new filings ahead. This gives Valeroso a shot at coming home—two wardens have notified the parole board that they want him out, and the University of Michigan School of Social Work has affirmed that their admission of him a number of years ago holds firm and that he may reapply. Mary came home in August 2002. Sharleen, after a brutal public hearing in which she did well, was left without a decision for over a year, then was denied commutation by the governor. It isn't over: she will be filing again for commutation and all who have worked with her will write strenuous letters.

10. Herman, *Trauma and Recovery*.

11. See my discussion of this incident in chapter 4, in the section titled "Crisis."

12. See opening section of chapter 7.

13. This and the following names are not the real names.

14. "Abraham Had Backers, So Where Are They?" *Detroit Free Press,* May 31, 2008,

13A. The other information for this paragraph comes from the report by John Wisely and Korie Wilkins, *Detroit Free Press,* May 31, 2008, 1A, 13A.

15. "Entering Prison," *Gargoyle* 50 (2005), 23–25.

Chapter Ten

1. Not all leave Ann Arbor. Some leave PCAP work and enter University of Michigan graduate schools (some who do so continue PCAP work and do not become associates) and others settle into careers in the area. They become Ann Arbor PCAP associates.

2. "Social Justice Careers: Alumni Making the Michigan Difference," a powerful day of discussion and panels: six of the twenty-six alums invited back to talk about their social justice work were PCAP associates (Sabrina Alli, Michael Burke, Mica Doctoroff, Vanesa Mayesky, Mary Paul, Alyssa Sorresso) and a seventh was a current PCAP member who had taken a year off to work in Arkansas (Andrea Bachman); two of the panels were moderated by PCAP members (Valerie Haddad and Julia Taylor).

3. *PCAP Associates Newsletter* 1, no. 1 (Fall 2002), n.p., PCAP Archives.

4. This material is from *Associates Newsletter* 2, no. 1 (Fall 2002); 3, no. 1 (Winter 2004–5); 3, no. 2 (Summer 2005); 4, no. 1 (July 2006); 4, no. 2 (October 2006); and 5, no. 1 (May 2007). Abbey Marshak, a new associate, has just taken a job with Human Rights Watch.

5. *Associates Newsletter* 1, no. 2 (Summer 2003); 2, no. 1 (Winter 2003); 2, no. 2 (Summer 2004); 3, no. 2 (Summer 2005) ("I am most proud of facilitating others to be able to provide for themselves and my ability to adapt in complex and difficult environments. Both skills I learned as a PCAP member"); 4, no. 1 (July 2006); 4, no. 2 (October 2006); 5, no. 2 (December 2007). Conversation, April 2008; e-mail message, June 30, 2009.

6. In *Associates Newsletter* 3, no. 2 (Summer 2005) she wrote, "because of my experience with PCAP, I have become interested in a career that explores the intersection between women's issues and criminal justice."

7. "The Brennan Center is trying to figure out how to attack the really big problem of incarcerated parents having their children taken away while they're inside because of unrealistic federal and state guidelines that say if a child is in foster care for 18 months, the parent's rights to the child should be completely terminated." *PCAP Associates Newsletter* 4, no. 1 (July 2006).

8. *Associates Newsletter* 1, no. 1 (Fall 2002); 2, no. 2 (Summer 2004); 3, no. 2 (Summer 2005); 4, no. 1 (July 2006); 6, no. 1 (July 2008); e-mail messages, June 22, 23, 2009.

9. E-mail message, June 5, 2009.

10. *Associates Newsletter* 5, no. 1 (May 2007); e-mail message, June 9, 2009.

11. *Associates Newsletter* 5, no. 1 (May 2007); e-mail message, June 12, 2009.

12. *Associates Newsletter* 5, no. 1 (May 2007); e-mail message, June 4, 2009.

13. E-mail message from Emi Kaneko, July 9, 2009.

14. *Associates Newsletter* 4, no. 1 (July 2006); 5, no. 2 (December 2007); 6, no. 1 (July 2008); e-mail message, June 5, 2009.

15. *Associates Newsletter* 5, no. 2 (December 2007); e-mail message, June 4, 2009.

16. *Associates Newsletter* 5, no. 2 (December 2007), e-mail message June 29, 2009.

17. *Associates Newsletter* 5, no. 2 (December 2007); 6, no. 2 (July 2008); e-mail message, June 4, 2009. See my discussion of Kate's portfolio experience in chapter 7.

18. *Associates Newsletter* 2, no. 2 (Summer 2004); 5, no. 2 (December 2007); e-mail message, June 8, 2009.

19. *Associates Newsletter* 3, no. 2 (Summer 2005); e-mail message, June 23, 2009. The quotation about the blog is from the blog itself.

20. *Associates Newsletter* 1, no. 2 (Summer 2003); 2, no. 2 (Summer 2004); 3, no. 2 (Summer 2005); 5, no. 2 (December 2007); e-mail message, June 5, 2009.

21. *Associates Newsletter* 1, no. 4 (July 2006); e-mail message, August 19, 2009.

22. *Associates Newsletter* 3, no. 2 (Summer 2005).

23. *Associates Newsletter* 3, no. 2 (Summer 2005).

24. The list needed some revision; a few people had been left off. The July 2009 *Newsletter* (plus three associates added in August) shows 39 members in the Detroit area, 1 in Asheville, NC, 1 in Atlanta, 2 in Austin, 3 in Baltimore, 3 in the Battle Creek area, 7 in the Boston Area, 1 in Boulder, 2 in the Chapel Hill/Durham area, 20 in Chicago, 3 in Cleveland/Columbus, 1 in Coral Gables, 2 in Denver, 1 in Gainesville, 1 in Greensboro, NC, 1 in Houston, 5 in the Los Angeles area, 1 in McAllen TX, 1 in Milwaukee, 1 in Mt. Pleasant, MI, 36 in the New York City area, 1 in Petersburg, Ohio, 2 in Philadelphia, 2 in Portland, ME, 2 in Portland, OR, 1 in San Diego, 14 in the San Francisco Bay area, 2 in Seattle, 1 in St. Louis, 1 in St. Paul, 1 in Tampa, 8 in the Washington, DC area, 1 in Whitesburg, KY, and 1 each in Berlin, Bogota, Bujumbura (Burundi), Kenya, Montreal, and Paris.

25. *Associates Newsletter* 2, no. 1 (Winter 2003). As of 2009 Sara was a social worker for the LifeWorks Street Outreach program in Austin, creating and facilitating groups intended to help homeless adults eighteen to twenty-three years old to access unemployment, leading an art group, yoga group, and acudetox group, and doing individual counseling.

26. *Associates Newsletter* 2, no. 2 (Summer 2004).

27. *Associates Newsletter* 4, no. 1 (March 2006).

28. *Associates Newsletter* 4, no. 1 (March 2006).

29. E-mail messages to the author: Jesse and Emily, September 23, 2009; Chiara, September 24.

30. E-mail message to author, September 23, 2009.

31. *Associates Newsletter* 5, no. 2 (December 2007). In 2009, Kate changed one of the sentences in this text without altering the content.

32. *Associates Newsletter* 5, no. 2 (December 2007). Chrissy in 2009 was about to start her third year at James F. Rhodes High School in Cleveland.

33. *Associates Newsletter* 5, no. 2 (December 2007).

34. *Associates Newsletter* 5, no. 2 (December 2007).

35. *Associates Newsletter* 2, no. 2 (Summer 2004).

36. *Associates Newsletter* 3, no. 1 (Winter 2004–5).

37. Kozol, *The Night Is Dark,* 91–93. For the discussion that follows this passage, see chapter 3.

38. On July 13, 2009, Kate wrote me in an e-mail message: "In the end, our school didn't get picked up by the state government, although we didn't pass Annual Yearly Progress, either. . . . Despite our struggles, I've decided I *do* want this school. . . . Working with PCAP taught me the merit of creating art in places where hope has often been lost, and prepared me to stick things out at our school. Last year, I proposed a partnership with historic Ford's Theatre in downtown Washington, DC, whereby our students worked with me, their teacher, and a professional actor who taught them the performance aspect of oratory. The course, 'Oratory in American Culture,' has been a rousing success, and culminated with a student performance of historic and original speeches onstage at Ford's. Students experienced learning by *doing,* and literally walking in the footsteps of great leaders at historic sites all over DC. Our students have won scholarships and awards for their oratory, they've been covered by the media, and the course has helped their learning in other areas as well. Former 'problem students' are now joining sports teams, student government, and drama club, and improving their grades and critical thinking skills. Many of these students now love history, and a colleague of mine recently told me: 'Your speech kids are show-offs in history class.' Fantastic. Due to the success of the program, we've secured funding for the upcoming school year. I've found that giving the students here agency in their education goes a long way. One young woman refused to speak in front of the class at the beginning of the year; her brother was murdered and her family was in shambles. After finally getting her to speak, she became one of our greatest class orators. She has even secured a position with the organization Learn Serve International, which will take her to Zambia next summer, where she will complete a service learning opportunity to work with people with HIV and AIDS. When she interviewed for the position, they asked her what her purpose in life was and she replied, 'to change the world with oratory.' I've never been so proud in my life."

39. *Associates Newsletter* 3, no. 1 (Winter 2004–5).

40. Kohl, *36 Children,* 224.

41. Dispatch, May 25, 2005.

Appendix

1. Between 2000 and 2004, the meetings were open the full two hours. However, in the fall of 2004 two members came every week and spoke at length, dominating the discussion, intimidating with their presence two new members, and making it impossible for us to work efficiently, intimately, and with trust, getting the business done that the members had been elected to do. In response, some committee members proposed the current meeting structure, opened it to membership discussion and alternative proposals, listened carefully, and then the five executive members voted unanimously for the change. It wasn't easy and some bitterness remains to this day.

2. Many members are competent to do a workshop alone, but we insist on two people so that they can compare notes and develop the workshop together, so that they can handle as a team difficult issues that come up in the workshop or prison, and so that they can support each other on every level.

3. After some discussion recently, we decided not to contribute writing or art to a forthcoming book studying the behavior of violent men.

4. And so on. We have smaller policies that are not necessarily written out. For example: we don't try to sneak in media people as nonmedia guests (the Michigan Department of Corrections generally forbids media); we don't pay outside artists to lead PCAP workshops.

BIBLIOGRAPHY

Works Cited

Note: The bibliography is organized into two main sections, Works Cited and Additional Resources. Works Cited is divided into three subsections: the first lists books, chapters in books, dissertations, magazines, newspapers, papers, and presentations; the second contains publications and reports by governmental and other organizations; and films appear in the third subsection. Additional Resources contains lists of recommended books and recommended films and a list of information resources.

Books, Chapters in Books, Dissertations, Magazines, Newspapers, Papers, and Presentations

Alexander, Buzz [William]. "Entering Prison." Poem. *Gargoyle* 50 (2005): 23–25.

Alexander, Buzz. "A Piece of the Reply: Eighteen Years of the Prison Creative Arts Project." In *Empowerment or Incarceration? Reclaiming Hope and Justice from the Prison-Industrial Complex,* ed. Stephen Hartnett. Champaign: University of Illinois Press, 2010.

Alexander, Buzz. "Summer 1998: Blue Pattern in a Paper Bowl." *EPOCH* 51, no. 1 (2002): 116–27.

Alexander, Buzz, and Janie Paul, eds. *Doing Time, Making Space: 10 Years of the Annual Exhibition of Art by Michigan Prisoners.* Ann Arbor: Prison Creative Arts Project, 2005.

Alexander, Buzz, and Janie Paul. "This Is Our Bridge . . . and We Built It Ourselves." *Michigan Independent,* March 19, 2007.

Alexander, William. "Clearing Space: AIDS Theatre in Atlanta." *Drama Review* 34, no. 3 (fall 1990): 109–28.

Alexander, William. "Creating Spaces: Two Examples of Community-Based Learning." In *Praxis I: A Faculty Casebook on Community Service Learning,* ed. Jeffrey Howard, 41–56. Ann Arbor: OCSL Press, 1994.

Alexander, William. "Creating Spaces." In *Praxis III*, ed. Joseph Galura, Jeffrey Howard, Dave Waterhouse, and Randy Ross, 161–73. Ann Arbor: OCSL Press, 1995.

Alexander, William. "Creating Spaces at Western Wayne Correctional Facility." Roundtable discussions by Western Wayne Correctional Facility staff and inmates and University of Michigan faculty and students. In *Praxis III*, ed. Joseph Galura, Jeffrey Howard, Dave Waterhouse, and Randy Ross, 297–321. Ann Arbor: OCSL Press, 1995.

Alexander, William. *Film on the Left: American Documentary Film from 1931 to 1942*. Princeton: Princeton University Press, 1981.

Alexander, William. "Inside Out: From Inside Prison Out to Youth." *Drama Review* 40, no. 4 (winter 1996): 85–93.

Alexander, William. "More Verses to Write; or, Lost and Presumed Dead." Manuscript, 2001.

Alexander, William. "Muerte al Polio!" *Tonantzin*, July 1988.

Alexander, William, and Tom Philion. "Students Support Fired Projectionists with Street Theater." *Labor Notes*, July 4, 1985.

Arax, Mark, and Mark Gladstone. "State Thwarted Brutality Probe at Corcoran Prison, Investigators Say." *Los Angeles Times*, July 5, 1998.

Arendt, Hannah. *Eichmann in Jerusalem: A Report on the Banality of Evil*. New York: Viking Press, 1963. Rev. ed., New York: Viking, 1965. New York: Penguin Books, 1994.

Baca, Jimmy Santiago. *A Place to Stand*. New York: Grove Press, 2001.

Bauman, Zygmunt. *Modernity and the Holocaust*. Ithaca: Cornell University Press, 2001.

Bernstein, Nell. *All Alone in the World: Children of the Incarcerated*. New York: New Press, 2005.

Berry, Wendell. *The Hidden Wound*. New York: North Point Press, 1989.

Bluestone, Barry, and Bennett Harrison. *The Great U-Turn: Corporate Restructuring and the Polarizing of America*. New York: Basic Books, 1990.

Boal, Augusto. *Games for Actors and Non-Actors*. New York: Routledge, 1992.

Boyte, Harry C. *Everyday Politics: Reconnecting Citizens and Public Life*. Philadelphia: University of Pennsylvania Press, 2004.

Bridger, Jeffrey C., and Theodore R. Alter. "The Engaged University, Community Development, and Public Scholarship." *Journal of Higher Education Outreach and Engagement* 11, no. 1 (2006): 163–78.

Brown, Michael. "The Bone Game: A Ritual of Transformation." *Journal of Experiential Education* 13, no. 1. (May 1990): 48–52.

Camus, Albert. *The Plague*. New York: Alfred A. Knopf, 1957. First published 1948.

Cervantes, Lorna Dee. *Emplumada*. Pittsburgh: University of Pittsburgh Press, 1981.

Chevigny, Bell, ed. *Doing Time: 25 Years of Prison Writing*. New York: Arcade Publishing, 1999.

Chomsky, Noam. *American Power and the New Mandarins*. New York: Pantheon Books, 1967.

Christie, Nils. *Crime Control as Industry: Towards Gulags Western Style?* 2nd ed. New York: Routledge, 1994.

Church, George J., and Richard Hornik. "Are You Better Off?" *Time,* October 10, 1988.

Coetzee, J. M. *Age of Iron.* New York: Penguin Books, 1990.

Croft, Howard. "Whether or Not We Want It, They All Get Out." Presentation at the George Mason University Conference "Behind Bars: Prisons and Communities in the United States," March 30, 1996.

Crozier, Michel J., Samuel P. Huntington, and Joji Watanuke. *The Crisis of Democracy: Report on the Governability of Democracies to the Trilateral Commission.* New York: New York University Press, 1975.

Davis, Mike. *Planet of Slums.* New York: Verso, 2006.

Detroit News. "Michigan Must Escape from Rising Prison Costs." Editorial, April 17, 2008.

Ellison, Julie. "The Humanities and the Public Soul." In "Practicing Public Scholarship: Experiences and Possibilities beyond the Academy," ed. Kathryn Mitchell, special issue of *Antipode: A Radical Journal of Geography* 40, no. 3 (May 2008): 463–71.

Ellison, Julie. Material from her original presentation on the humanities and the public soul. http://www.imaginingamerica.org/IApdfs/Ellison.HumanitiesPublicSoul.pdf (accessed February 3, 2010).

Fagan, Jeffrey, and Franklin Zimring. *The Changing Borders of Juvenile Justice: Transfer of Adolescents to the Criminal Court.* Chicago: University of Chicago Press, 2000.

Freire, Paulo. *Pedagogy of the Oppressed.* 30th anniversary ed. New York: Continuum International Publishing Group, 2007.

Garland, David, ed. *Mass Imprisonment: Social Causes and Consequences.* London: Sage Publications, 2001.

Goodman, Ken. *What's Whole in Whole Language.* Portsmouth, NH: Heinemann, 1986.

Gothard, Suzanne, and Megan Shuchman, eds. Untitled, unpublished booklet addressed to Buzz Alexander by his students and former students on the occasion of his receiving a 2005 Carnegie Foundation for the Advancement of Teaching and Center for the Advancement and Support of Education Professor of the Year Award. 2006.

Harcourt, Bernard E. "The Mentally Ill, behind Bars." *New York Times,* January 15, 2007, A19.

Hartnett, Stephen, ed. *Empowerment or Incarceration? Reclaiming Hope and Justice from the Prison-Industrial Complex.* Champaign: University of Illinois Press, 2010.

Hartnett, Stephen. *Incarceration Nation: Investigative Prison Poems of Hope and Terror.* Walnut Creek, CA: Altamira Press, 2003.

Heinlein, Gary, and Charlie Cain. "Prison Costs on Agenda." *Detroit News,* May 2, 2008.

Herivel, Tara, and Paul Wright, eds. *Prison Profiteers: Who Makes Money from Mass Incarceration.* New York: New Press, 2007.

Herman, Judith. *Trauma and Recovery.* New York: Basic Books, 1992.

Herter, Roberta. "Conflicting Interests: Critical Theory Inside Out." PhD diss., University of Michigan, 1998.

Horton, Myles, with Judith Kohl and Herbert Kohl. *The Long Haul: An Autobiography.* New York: Teachers College Press, 1998.

Huerta, Jorge A. *Chicano Theater: Themes and Forms.* Ypsilanti, MI: Bilingual Press, 1982.

Jose, Maria Cristina Y. "Women Doing Life Sentences: A Phenomenological Study." PhD diss., University of Michigan, 1985.

Kidd, Ross. "From Outside in to Inside Out: The Benue Workshop on Theatre for Development." *Theaterwork Magazine,* May/June 1982, 44–48, 50–53.

Kidd, Ross. "From Outside in to Inside Out (Part II): 'People's Theatre and Landless Organizing in Bangladesh.'" *Theaterwork Magazine,* January/February 1983, 29–39.

Kidd, Ross. "Popular Theatre and Popular Struggle in Kenya: The Story of the Kamariithu Community Cultural Centre." *Theaterwork Magazine,* September/October 1982, 47–59.

Kirschke, Joseph. "Hard Time: Hundreds of Complaints Filed by Huron Valley's Women Prisoners." *Detroit Metro Times,* March 3, 2005.

Kohl, Herbert. *36 Children.* First Plume printing, New York: Penguin, 1988.

Kozol, Jonathan. *The Night Is Dark and I Am Far from Home.* Touchstone edition, New York: Simon and Schuster, 1990.

Kozol, Jonathan. *Savage Inequalities: Children in America's Schools.* New York: Harper Collins, 1992.

Kozol, Jonathan. *The Shame of the Nation: The Restoration of Apartheid Schooling in America.* New York: Crown Publishers, 2005.

Kupers, Terry. *Prison Madness: The Mental Health Crisis behind Bars and What We Must Do about It.* San Francisco: Jossey-Bass Publishers, 1999.

Liptak, Adam. "To More Inmates, Life Term Means Dying behind Bars." *New York Times,* October 2, 2005.

Liptak, Adam. "U.S. Imprisons One in 100 Adults, Report Finds." *New York Times,* February 29, 2008.

Loury, Glen C., with Pamela S. Karian, Tommie Shelby, and Loïc Wacquant. *Race, Incarceration, and American Values.* Cambridge: MIT Press, 2008.

Matney, M. M. *First Year Student Survey 2006: Entering Student Profile.* Summary data from the Cooperative Institutional Research Program (CIRP). Ann Arbor: University of Michigan Division of Student Affairs, 2007.

Mauer, Marc. *Race to Incarcerate.* New York: New Press, 1999.

Mauer, Marc, and Meda Chesney-Lind, eds. *Invisible Punishment: The Collateral Consequences of Mass Imprisonment.* New York: New Press, 2002.

Melossi, Dario. "Gazette of Morality and Social Whip: Punishment, Hegemony, and the Case of the USA, 1970–92." *Social and Legal Studies* 2 (1993): 266.

Miller, Jerome G. *Search and Destroy: African-American Males in the Criminal Justice System.* Cambridge: Cambridge University Press, 1996.

Mitford, Jessica. *Kind and Usual Punishment: The Prison Business.* New York: Knopf, 1973.

Moore, Susanna. *The Big Girls.* New York: Knopf, 2007.

Oshinsky, David M. *"Worse than Slavery": Parchman Farm and the Ordeal of Jim Crow Justice.* New York: Free Press Paperbacks, 1997.

Pager, Devah. *Marked: Race, Crime, and Finding Work in an Era of Mass Incarceration.* Chicago: University of Chicago Press, 2007.

Parenti, Christian. *Lockdown America: Police and Prisons in the Age of Crisis.* London: Verso, 1999.

Paterson, Doug, Chris Brookes, Ken Fert, Arlene Goldbard, Ross Kidd, and Tom O'Reilly-Amandes. *We Are Strong: A Guide to the Work of Popular Theatres across the Americas.* Mankato, MN: Institute for Cultural Policy Studies, 1983.

Paulson, William. *Literary Culture in a World Transformed: A Future for the Humanities.* Ithaca: Cornell University Press, 2001.

Ramaley, Judith A. "Community-Engaged Scholarship in Higher Education: Have We Reached a Tipping Point?" Presentation at the Community-Engaged Scholarship for Health Collaborative Invitational Symposium, February 21–22, 2007. Available at http://web.uvic.ca/ocbr/assets/pdfs/community-engaged_scholarship.pdf (accessed February 2010).

Riley, Rochelle. "Abraham Had Backers, So Where Are They?" *Detroit Free Press,* May 31, 2008, 13A.

Sacks, Peter. *Standardized Minds: The High Price of America's Testing Culture and What We Can Do to Change It.* New York: Da Capo Press, 1999.

Sarat, Austin. *When the State Kills: Capital Punishment and the American Condition.* Princeton: Princeton University Press, 2001.

Shailor, Jonathan. "Humanizing Education behind Bars: The Theatre of Empowerment and the Shakespeare Project." In *Empowerment or Incarceration? Reclaiming Hope and Justice from the Prison-industrial Complex,* ed. Stephen Hartnett. Champaign: University of Illinois Press, 2010.

Shea, Christopher. "Life Sentence." *Boston Globe,* September 23, 2007. http://www.boston.com/news/globe/ideas/articles/2007/09/23/life_sentence/.

Silko, Leslie Marmon. *Ceremony.* New York: Viking, 1997.

Smith, Lillian E. *Killers of the Dream.* New York: W. W. Norton, 1949. Pbk. ed., New York: W. W. Norton, 1994.

Spritzer, Steven. "Toward a Marxist Theory of Deviance." *Social Problems,* no. 22 (1975): 638–51.

Steiner, George. *Language and Silence: Essays on Language, Literature, and the Inhuman.* New York: Atheneum, 1974.

Stone, Randolph N. "The Criminal Justice System: Unfair and Ineffective." Paper presented at the Chicago Assembly "Crime and Community Safety," November 19–20, 1992.

Taifa, Nkechi. "Laying down the Law, Race by Race." *Legal Times,* October 10, 1994.

Tannenbaum, Judith. *Disguised as a Poem: My Years Teaching Poetry at San Quentin.* Boston: Northeastern University Press, 2000.

Trounstine, Jean. *Shakespeare behind Bars: One Teacher's Story of the Power of Drama in a Women's Prison.* Ann Arbor: University of Michigan Press, 2004.

Western, Bruce. *Punishment and Equality in America.* New York: Russell Sage Foundation, 2006.

Whittell, Giles. "Welcome to Hell—Investigation—Corcoran State Prison in California." *The Times (London),* July 25, 1998.

Wiesel, Elie. *Legends of Our Time.* New York, Schocken Books, 1968.

Wiesenthal, Simon. *The Sunflower: On the Possibilities and Limits of Forgiveness.* 2nd ed. New York: Schocken Books, 1997.

Wisely, John, and Korie Wilkins. Untitled article. *Detroit Free Press,* May 31, 2008, 1A, 13A.

Publications and Reports

America's Promise Alliance. "Cities in Crisis: A Special Analytic Report on High School Graduation." EPE Research Center. April 1, 2008. http://lists.isber.ucsb.edu/pipermail/lmresearch/2008-April/000673.html.

Campaign for Youth Justice. "Youth in Adult Prisons Fact Sheet." February 2005. http://www.act4jj.org/media/factsheets/factsheet_26.pdf.

Citizens Alliance on Prisons and Public Spending. "Prison Expansion in Michigan—a Brief History." http://www.capps-mi.org/history.htm (accessed August 15, 2009).

"Easy School Search." Michigan Department of Education. 2007. http://www.easyschoolsearch.com/.

Hagstrom, Julie A., Cedrick Heraux, Emily Meyer, Lori A. Post, and Kimiko Tanaka. "Measuring Disproportionate Minority Contact in the Juvenile Justice System: An Examination of the Michigan Relative Rate Index." University Outreach and Engagement, Michigan State University. March 17, 2005. http://www.Michigan.gov/documents/DHS-dmc-appx-h-06_142986_7.pdf (accessed August 11, 2009).

Haney, Craig. "The Psychological Impact of Incarceration: Implications for Post-Prison Adjustment." Paper commissioned by U.S. Department of Health and Human Services for project titled "From Prison to Home: The Effect of Incarceration and Reentry on Children, Families, and Communities." 2001.

Pew Center on the States Public Safety Performance Project. "One in 100 behind Bars in America 2008." February 2, 2008. http://www.pewcenteronthestates.org/uploadedfiles/PSPP_1in31_report_FINAL_WED_3-26-09.pdf.

Rouge River Remedial Action Plan Update. 1994. http://www.epa.gov/grtlakes/aoc/rougeriv/1994_Rouge-River-RAP-Update.pdf.

Sabol, William J., Todd D. Minton, and Paige M. Harrison. "Prison and Jail Inmates at Midyear 2006." U.S. Department of Justice, Office of Justice Programs, document NCJ217675. June 2007. http://www.ojp.usdoj.gov/bjs/pub/pdf/pji.

Sentencing Project. "Facts about Prisons and Prisoners." December 2007.

Films

California Prison Focus. *Maximum Security University.*

Cuthard, Doug, and Vicki Covington. *Sentencing Circles—Traditional Justice Reborn.* 1995. Canadian documentary film.

Ophuls, Marcel. *The Sorrow and the Pity.* 1969. Not available in the United States.

Tofteland, Kurt. *Shakespeare behind Bars.* Act Now Productions, 2006. DVD.

Weider, Katherine. *Acts of Art: The Prison Creative Arts Project.* 2008. Documentary film.

Additional Resources

Books

Note: This is a list of books that have moved and influenced me; there are many excellent books and articles in the field, and I have not read them all. In terms of practice, Judith Tannenbaum's *Disguised as a Poem,* a report on her poetry workshop at San Quentin, listed in the first section of this bibliography, remains the best work in the field.

Bathanti, Joseph. *Coventry.* Charlotte, NC: Novello Festival Press, 2006.

Boal, Augusto. *Theatre of the Oppressed.* New York: Theatre Communications Group, 1985.

Brune, Krista, ed. *Creating behind the Razor Wire: Perspectives from Arts in Corrections in the United States.* Saxapahaw, NC: CAN/API publication, 2007.

Cleveland, William. *Art and Upheaval: Artists on the World's Frontlines.* Oakland, CA: New Village Press, 2008.

Conover, Ted. *Newjack: Guarding Sing Sing.* New York: Vintage Books, 2000.

Cummins, Jeanine. *A Rip in Heaven: A Memoir of Murder and Its Aftermath.* New York: New American Library, 2004.

Davis, Angela. *Are Prisons Obsolete?* Open Media Series. New York: Seven Stories Press 2003.

Dow, Mark. *American Gulag: Inside U.S. Immigration Prisons.* Berkeley: University of California Press, 2004.

Franklin, H. Bruce, ed. *Prison Writing in 20th-Century America.* New York: Penguin Books, 1998.

Garland, David. *Punishment and Modern Society: A Study in Social Theory.* Chicago: University of Chicago Press, 1990.

Humes, Edward. *No Matter How Loud I Shout: A Year in the Life of Juvenile Court.* New York: Touchstone, 1997.

Jackson, Spoon, and Judith Tannenbaum. *By Heart: Poetry, Prison and Two Lives.* Oakland: New Village Press, 2010.

Kauffman, Kelsey. *Prison Officers and Their World.* Cambridge: Harvard University Press, 1988.

Lamb, Wally, ed. *Couldn't Keep It to Myself: Wally Lamb and the Women of York Correctional Institution.* New York: Harper Perennial, 2004.

Lamb, Wally, ed. *I'll Fly Away: Further Testimonies from the Women of York Prison.* New York: HarperCollins, 2007.

Martin, Dannie M., and Peter Y. Sussman. *Committing Journalism: The Prison Writings of Red Hog.* New York: W. W. Norton, 1993.

Prejean, Sister Helen. *Dead Man Walking: An Eyewitness Account of the Death Penalty in the United States.* New York: Vintage Books, 1994.

Prejean, Sister Helen. *The Death of Innocents: An Eyewitness Account of Wrongful Convictions.* London: Canterbury Press, 2005.

Sereny, Gitta. *Cries Unheard: Why Children Kill; The Story of Mary Bell.* New York: Metropolitan Books, 1998.

Shelton, Richard. *Crossing the Yard: Thirty Years as a Prison Volunteer.* Tucson: University of Arizona Press, 2007.

Yaeger, Patricia, ed. Roundtable ("Prisons, Activism, and the Academy—a Roundtable with Buzz Alexander, Bell Gale Chevigny, Stephen John Hartnett, Janie Paul, and Judith Tannenbaum") and essays by Jonathan Shailor, H. Bruce Franklin, Avery F. Gordon, Tanya Erzen, Megan Sweeney, Jean Trounstine, Robert P. Waxler, Ruby C. Tapia, Jody Lewen, Ronald B. Harzman, and Larry E. Sullivan. *PMLA* (Publications of the Modern Language Association of America) 123, no. 3 (May 2008).

Films

Garbos, Liz, Wilbert Rideau, and Jonathan Stack, directors. *The Farm: Angola, USA.* Gabriel Films, 1998.

Khadvi, Laleh, director. *900 Women.* Gabriel Films, 2000.

Lichtenstein, Brad, director. *Ghosts of Attica.* Icarus Films, 2001.

Rosenblum, Nina, director. *Through the Wire.* 1990.

INDEX

Note: Page numbers in italic indicate figures.